DATE DUE

Bloom's Modern Critical Views

African American
    Poets: Wheatley–
    Tolson
African American
    Poets: Hayden–
    Dove
Edward Albee
Dante Alighieri
American and
    Canadian Women
    Poets, 1930–
    present
American Women
    Poets, 1650–1950
Hans Christian
    Andersen
Maya Angelou
Asian-American
    Writers
Margaret Atwood
Jane Austen
Paul Auster
James Baldwin
Honoré de Balzac
Samuel Beckett
Saul Bellow
The Bible
William Blake
Jorge Luis Borges
Ray Bradbury
The Brontës
Gwendolyn Brooks
Elizabeth Barrett
    Browning
Robert Browning
Italo Calvino
Albert Camus
Truman Capote
Lewis Carroll
Willa Cather
Cervantes
Geoffrey Chaucer
Anton Chekhov

Kate Chopin
Agatha Christie
Samuel Taylor
    Coleridge
Joseph Conrad
Contemporary Poets
Julio Cortázar
Stephen Crane
Daniel Defoe
Don DeLillo
Charles Dickens
Emily Dickinson
John Donne and the
    17th-Century Poets
Fyodor Dostoevsky
W.E.B. DuBois
George Eliot
T.S. Eliot
Ralph Ellison
Ralph Waldo Emerson
William Faulkner
F. Scott Fitzgerald
Sigmund Freud
Robert Frost
William Gaddis
Johann Wolfgang von
    Goethe
George Gordon, Lord
    Byron
Graham Greene
Thomas Hardy
Nathaniel Hawthorne
Robert Hayden
Ernest Hemingway
Hermann Hesse
Hispanic-American
    Writers
Homer
Langston Hughes
Zora Neale Hurston
Aldous Huxley
Henrik Ibsen
John Irving

Henry James
James Joyce
Franz Kafka
John Keats
Jamaica Kincaid
Stephen King
Rudyard Kipling
Milan Kundera
Tony Kushner
D.H. Lawrence
Doris Lessing
Ursula K. Le Guin
Sinclair Lewis
Norman Mailer
Bernard Malamud
David Mamet
Christopher Marlowe
Gabriel García
    Márquez
Cormac McCarthy
Carson McCullers
Herman Melville
Arthur Miller
John Milton
Molière
Toni Morrison
Native-American
    Writers
Joyce Carol Oates
Flannery O'Connor
Eugene O'Neill
George Orwell
Octavio Paz
Sylvia Plath
Edgar Allan Poe
Katherine Anne
    Porter
Marcel Proust
Thomas Pynchon
Philip Roth
Salman Rushdie
J.D. Salinger
José Sarramago

Bloom's Modern Critical Views

Jean-Paul Sartre
William Shakespeare
George Bernard Shaw
Mary Wollstonecraft
  Shelley
Percy Bysshe Shelley
Alexander
  Solzhenitsyn
Sophocles
John Steinbeck
Robert Louis
  Stevenson
Tom Stoppard
Jonathan Swift

Amy Tan
Alfred, Lord Tennyson
Henry David Thoreau
J.R.R. Tolkien
Leo Tolstoy
Ivan Turgenev
Mark Twain
John Updike
Kurt Vonnegut
Derek Walcott
Alice Walker
Robert Penn Warren
H.G. Wells

Eudora Welty
Edith Wharton
Walt Whitman
Oscar Wilde
Tennessee Williams
Thomas Wolfe
Tom Wolfe
Virginia Woolf
William Wordsworth
Jay Wright
Richard Wright
William Butler Yeats
Emile Zola

Bloom's Modern Critical Views

HANS CHRISTIAN ANDERSEN

Edited and with an introduction by
Harold Bloom
Sterling Professor of the Humanities
Yale University

CHELSEA HOUSE
P U B L I S H E R S
A Haights Cross Communications ◆ Company
Philadelphia

Library of Congress Cataloging-in-Publication Data applied for.
Hans Christian Andersen / [edited and with an introduction by] Harold Bloom.
    p. cm. — (Bloom's modern critical views)
  Includes bibliographical references and index.
  ISBN 0-7910-8129-X (alk. paper)
  1. Andersen, H. C. (Hans Christian), 1805-1875—Criticism and interpretation. I. Bloom,
Harold. II. Modern critical views.
  PT8120.H26 2004
  839.8'136—dc22
                              2004015306

Contributing Editor: Janyce Marson
Cover designed by Keith Trego
Cover photo: © Hulton-Deutsch Collection/CORBIS
Layout by EJB Publishing Services

Contents

Editor's Note

My Introduction seeks to define what it is in Hans Christian Andersen's strongest stories that has achieved permanence for them, with particular emphasis upon aspects of "The Little Mermaid", "The Wild Swans", "The Snow Queen", "The Red Shoes", "The Shadow" and "Auntie Toothache".

Elias Bredsdorff dwells on Andersen's universalism, while Wolfgang Lerderer considers both the writer in the work and the work in the writer.

Andersen's protagonists are seen by Celia Catlett Anderson as blending folklore and Christian spirituality, after which Jon Cech examines the storyteller's dark humors and personal vulnerability.

Sexual ambiguity, pervasive in the stories, is related by Karin Sanders to problems of representation in Andersen, who then appears as self-dramatist in an essay written by a namesake.

Denmark is the storyteller's context is studied by Alison Prince, a prelude here to this volume's most substantial essay, Niels Kofoed's placement of Andersen in European literary tradition.

Aage Jørgensen reads Andersen as a dialectic of *recognition* purchased at the high cost of emotional waning, while the biographer Jackie Wullschlager finds something of the same pattern in the writer's homoerotic romances, and Jørgen Dines Johansen analyzes the evasions of adult sexuality so characteristic of Andersen's art.

HAROLD BLOOM

Introduction

Andersen's prime precursors were Shakespeare and Sir Walter Scott, and his best work can be thought of as an amalgam of *A Midsummer Night's Dream* and the almost as magnificent "Wandering Willie's Tale" from Scott's *Redgauntlet*, with a certain admixture of Goethe and of the "Universal Romanticism" of Novalis and E.T.A. Hoffman. Goethean "renunciation" was central to Andersen's art, which truly worships only one god, who can be called Fate. Though Andersen was a grand original in his fairy tales, he eagerly accepted from folklore its stoic acceptance of fate. Nietzsche argued that, for the sake of life, origin and aim had to be kept apart. In Andersen, there was no desire to separate origin and aim. It cost his life much fulfillment: he never had a home of his own or a lasting love, but he achieved an extraordinary literary art.

Like Walt Whitman's, Andersen's authentic sexual orientation was homoerotic. Pragmatically, both great writers were autoerotic, though Andersen's longings for women were more poignant than Whitman's largely literary gestures towards heterosexuality. But Whitman was a poet-prophet, who offered salvation, hardly Christian. Andersen professed a rather sentimental devotion to the Christ child, but his art is pagan in nature. His Danish contemporary, Kierkegaard, shrewdly sensed this early on. From the perspective of the twenty-first century, Andersen and Kierkegaard strangely divide between them the aesthetic eminence of Danish literature. In this introduction to a volume of Andersen-criticism, I want to define precisely the qualities of Andersen's stories that go on making them imperishable, as we approach the bicentennial of his birth in 2005. Kierkegaard himself rightly analyzed his own project as the illumination of how impossible it is to become a Christian in an ostensibly Christian society. Andersen covertly had a rather different project: how to remain a child in an ostensibly adult world.

I myself see no distinction between children's literature and good or great writing for extremely intelligent children of all ages. J.K. Rowling and Stephen King are equally bad writers, appropriate titans of our new Dark Age of the Screens: computer, motion pictures, television. One goes on urging children of all ages to read and reread Andersen and Dickens, Lewis Carroll and James Joyce, rather than Rowling and King. Sometimes when I say that in public I am asked afterwards: it is not better to read Rowling and King, and then go on to Andersen, Dickens, Carroll and Joyce? The answer is pragmatic: our time here is limited. You necessarily read and reread at the expense of other books. If we lived for several centuries, there might be world enough and time, but the reality principle forces us to choose.

I have just read through the twenty-two *Stories of Hans Christian Andersen*, a new translation from the Danish by Diana Crone Frank and Jeffrey Frank. Andersen called his memoir, *The Fairy Tale of My Life*, and it makes clear how painful was his emergence from the working class of Denmark in the early nineteenth century. The driving purpose of his career was to win fame and honor while not forgetting how hard the way up had been. His memories of being read to by his father from *The Arabian Nights* seem stronger than those of the actual circumstances of his up-bringing. Absorbing the biographies of Andersen is a curious process: when I stand back from what I have learned I have the impression of a remarkable directness in the teenage Andersen, who marched into Copenhagen and collapsed himself upon the kindness of strangers. This peculiar directness lasted all his life: he went throughout Europe introducing himself to Heine, Victor Hugo, Lamartine, Vigny, Mendelsohn, Schumann, Dickens, the Brownings, and many others. A hunter of big names, he hungered above all to become one himself, and won through by the invention of his fairy tales.

Andersen was an outrageously prolific author in every genre: novels, travelogues, poetry, stage plays, but he mattered and always will entirely because of his unique fairy tales, which he transmuted into a creation of his own, fusing the supernatural and the common life in ways that continue to surprise me, more even than do the tales of Hoffmann, Gogol, and Kleist, setting aside the sublimely dreadful but inescapable Poe.

Sexual frustration is Andersen's pervasive though hidden obsession, embodied in his witches and icy temptresses, and in his androgynous princes. The progress of his fairy stories marches through more than forty years of visions and revisions, and even now has not been fully studied. Here I will give brief critical impressions and appreciations of six tales: "The Little Mermaid" (1837), "The Wild Swans (1838), "The Snow Queen" (1845), "The Red Shoes" (1845), "The Shadow" (1847), and "Auntie Toothache" (1872).

On its vivid surfaces "The Little Mermaid" suggests a parable of renunciation, and yet in my own literary sense of the tale, it is a horror story, centering upon the very scary figure of the sea witch:

She came to a large slimy clearing in the forest, where big fat water snakes gamboled and showed off their disgusting yellow-white undersides. In the middle of the clearing was a house built out of the white skeletons of shipwrecked humans; that was where the sea witch sat with a toad that she let eat out of her mouth the same way that people let a little canary eat sugar. She called the fat ugly water snakes her little chickens, and let them frolic on her huge spongy chest.

"I think I know what you want," the sea witch said. "You are being very unwise. You can have it your way, but it's going to bring you grief, my lovely princess. You want to get rid of your fish tail and replace it with two stumps to walk on, like a human, so the young prince will fall in love with you, and you will have him and an immortal soul."

At that, the sea witch laughed so loudly and nastily that the toad and snakes fell to the ground and rolled around. "You came just in time," the witch said. "After sunrise tomorrow I wouldn't have been able to help you for another year. I'll make you a drink, but before the sun comes up, you must swim to land, sit on the shore, and drink it. Then your tail will split in two and shrink into what humans call 'pretty legs.' But it hurts—it's like a sharp sword going through you. Everyone who sees you will say that you're the loveliest girl that they have ever seen. You will keep your gliding walk; no dancer will soar like you. But every step you take will feel like you are stepping on a sharp knife that makes you bleed. If you're willing to suffer all this, I'll help you."

"Yes!" the little mermaid said in a quivering voice, and she thought about the prince and about winning an immortal soul.

"But remember," the sea witch continued, as soon as you get a

human form, you can't ever be a mermaid again. You can never
swim down through the water to your sisters and your father's
castle. And unless you win the prince's love so that he forgets his
father and mother for your sake and thinks only about you and
lets the pastor put your hands together so that you become man
and wife, you won't get an immortal soul. The first morning after
he has married someone else, your heart will break, and you'll
turn into foam on the sea."

"I still want to do it," the little mermaid said. She was pale as
a corpse.

"But you have to pay me too," the Sea Witch went on, "and I
ask for quite a bit. You have the prettiest voice of anyone on the
bottom of the sea, and I'm sure you imagine that you'll charm
him. But you have to give me that voice. I want the most precious
thing you own for my precious drink. As you know, I have to add
my own blood to make the drink as sharp as a double-edged
sword."

"But if you take my voice," the little mermaid said, "what will
I have left?"

"Your beautiful figure," the witch said, "your soaring walk, and
your eloquent eyes—with all that you can certainly enchant a
human heart. Well, well—have you lost heart? Stick out your
little tongue. Then I'll cut it off as payment, and you'll get my
powerful drink."

There is a peculiar ghastliness about this, virtually unmatched in
literary fantasy. It has the aesthetic dignity of great art, yet a shudder goes
with it. Andersen's imagination is as cruel as it is powerful, and "The Little
Mermaid" is least persuasive (to me) in its benign conclusion. The story
should end when the mermaid leaps from ship to sea and feels her body
dissolve into foam. Something in Andersen could not abide in this nihilistic
sacrifice, and so he allows an Ascension in which his heroine joins the
daughters of the air, thus recovering her voice. The aesthetic difficulty is not
sentimentality but sublimation, a defense against the erotic drive that may
work for the rare saint but almost never in imaginative literature.

There is no consistent allegory in "The Little Mermaid", and whoever
finds a moral in it should be shot, a remark I intend in the spirit of Mark
Twain rather than the mode of Flannery O'Connor. I prefer Andersen's
revision of a Danish folktale, "The Wild Swans", which culminates in utter
ambivalence when another mute maiden, the beautiful Elisa, undergoes a

second marriage with a king so doltish he nearly burns her alive as a witch, at the prompting of an evil archbishop. The weird remarriage is appropriate in a tale where Elisa's eleven brothers experience a radical daily metamorphosis into eleven wild swans:

> "We brothers," the oldest said, "are wild swans as long as the sun is up. When it sets, we get our human shape back. That's why we always have to make sure that we have solid ground underfoot when the sun sets. If we were flying among the clouds, we would, as human beings, plunge into the deep. We can't stay here, but there's a country as beautiful as this one on the other side of the ocean. It's a long distance. We have to cross the big ocean, and there are no islands on the way where we can stay for the night—only a solitary little rock juts up in the middle of the sea. It's just big enough for us to rest on side by side, and when the sea is rough, the water sprays high above us.

That vision has the strangeness of lasting myth. There are disturbing overtones here. Are we, in our youth, wild swans by day, and human again only at night, resting on a solitary spot in the midst of an abyss? Meditating upon the self of half-a-century ago, at seventy-four I am moved to a Shakespearean sense of wonder by Andersen's marvelous extended metaphor.

In two famous stories of 1845, as he reaches meridian, Andersen achieved a fresh power of imagination. "The Snow Queen" is called by Andersen a tale in seven stories, or an "ice puzzle of the mind", a marvelous phrase taken from and alluding to the unfinished visionary novel of Novalis, *Heinrich von Ofterdingen*. Its evil troll, the Devil himself, makes a mirror, eventually fragmented, that is the essence of reductiveness; that is, what any person or thing is *really* like is simply the worst way it can be viewed. At the center of Andersen's tale are two children who at first defy all reductiveness: Gerda and Kai. They are poor, but while not sister and brother, they share fraternal love. The beautiful but icy Snow Queen abducts Kai, and Gerda goes in quest of him. An old witch, benign but possessive, appropriates Gerda, who departs for the wide world to continue her search for Kai. But my summary is a hopeless parody of Andersen's blithe irony of a narrative, where even the most menacing entities pass by in a phantasmagoric rush: talking reindeer, a bandit girl who offers friendship even as she waves a knife, the Northern Lights, living snowflakes. When Gerda finds Kai in the Snow Queen's castle, she warms him with kisses until he unthaws. Redeemed, they journey home together to a perpetual summer of happiness, ambiguously sexual.

The fascination of "The Snow Queen" is Gerda's continuous resourcefulness and strength, which derives from her freedom or refusal of all reductiveness. She is an implicit defense of Andersen's power as a story teller, his endless self-reliance. Perhaps Gerda is Andersen's answer to Kierkegaard, hardly his admirer. Gerda can be set against Kierkegaard at his uncanniest: *The Concept of Dread*, *The Sickness Unto Death*, *Fear and Trembling*, *Repetition*. The titles themselves belong to the Snow Queen's realm, and not to Gerda's and Andersen's.

The alarming and famous story, "The Red Shoes", always has frightened me. The beautiful red dancing shoes whirl Karen into a cursed existence of perpetual motion, that cannot be solved even when her feet (with her consent) are cut off. Only her sanctified death accomplishes liberation. Darkly enigmatic, Andersen's tale hints at what Freud called over-determination, and renders Karen into the antithesis of Gerda.

"The Shadow", composed during a hot Naples summer of 1847, may be Andersen's most evasive masterpiece. The author and his shadow disengage from one another, in the tradition of tales by Chamisso and Hoffmann, and Andersen's shadow is malign and Iago-like. He comes back to Andersen, and persuades him to be a travel-companion, but as the shadow of his own shadow, as it were. The reader begins to suffer a metaphysical bewilderment, augmented by the involvement of a princess who sees too clearly, yet takes the original shadow as her consort. Andersen threatens exposure of identity, and is imprisoned by his former shadow, and soon enough is executed. This crazy and embittered parable prophesies Kafka, Borges, and Calvino, but more interestingly it returns us to everything problematic and ambivalent about Andersen's relation both to himself and to his art.

My ultimate favorite story by Andersen is his chillingly hilarious "Auntie Toothache", composed less than three years before his death. He may have intended it as his *logos* or defining Word, and it is spoken by Andersen himself in the first person. As an inventor of a laughter that hurts, Andersen follows Shakespeare and prophesies Philip Roth. There is no figure in Andersen more menacing than Auntie Toothache:

> A figure sat on the floor; it was thin and long, like those that a child draws with a pencil on a slate. It was supposed to look like a person: Its body was a single thin line; another two lines made the arms, the legs were single lines too, and the head was all angles.
>
> The figure soon became clearer. It wore a kind of dress—very

thin, very fine—that showed that the figure belonged to the female sex.

I heard a humming. Was it her or was it the wind that buzzed like a horsefly in the crack of the windowpane?

No, it was Madame Toothache herself—Her Frightfulness, *Satania infernalis*, God save us from her visit.

"This is a nice place to live," she hummed. "It's a good neighborhood—swampy, boggy ground. Mosquitoes used to buzz by here with poison in their sting. Now I'm the one with the stinger. It has to be sharpened on human teeth, and that fellow on the bed has such shiny white ones. They've held their own against sweet and sour, hot and cold, nutshells and plum pits. But I'm going to wiggle them, jiggle them, feed them with a draft, and chill them at their roots."

As Her Frightfulness says: "Great poets must have great toothaches; small poets, small toothaches". There is a vertigo in the story: we cannot know whether Auntie Toothache and the amiable Aunt Millie (who encourages Andersen's poetry) are one person or two. The penultimate sentence is: "Everything goes into the trash".

The accent is of Koheleth (Ecclesiastes): all is vanity. Andersen was a visionary tale-teller, but his fairy-realm was malign. Of his aesthetic eminence, I entertain no doubts, but I believe that we still have not learned how to read him.

ELIAS BREDSDORFF

"*Introduction*" to
Hans Christian Andersen:
Eighty Fairy Tales

Hans Christian Andersen's fairy tales and stories have had their important place in world literature since the middle of the nineteenth century and have been translated into well over a hundred languages. The first four tales were published in Denmark in 1835, and the first English translations appeared in 1846. Within a short time, Andersen had become a household word both in Britain and in the United States. In 1875, on the occasion of his seventieth birthday, the London *Daily News*, a paper founded by Dickens, paid homage to Andersen:

> It has been given to *Hans Andersen* to fashion beings, it may almost be said, of a new kind, to breathe life into the toys of childhood, and the forms of antique superstition. The tin soldier, the ugly duckling, the mermaid, the little match girl, are no less real and living in their way than *Othello*, or *Mr. Pickwick*, or *Helen of Troy*. It seems a very humble field in which to work, this of nursery legend and childish fancy. Yet the Danish poet alone, of all who have laboured in it, has succeeded in recovering, and reproducing, the kind of imagination which constructed the old fairy tales.

Hans Christian Andersen was more a creative writer than a collector of folk tales. It is somewhat misleading to bracket him, as is often done, with

From *Hans Christian Andersen: Eighty Fairy Tales* (1982). © 1982 by Elias Bredsdorff.

1

the German brothers Jakob and Wilhelm Grimm, or with Asbjørnsen and
Moe, the two Norwegian collectors of traditional folk tales. Nevertheless, a
few of Andersen's tales, especially among the early ones, were based on
traditional Danish folk tales he had heard as a child. Two months before the
publication of his first four tales Andersen wrote to a friend: "I have set down
a few of the fairy tales I myself used to enjoy as a child and which I believe
aren't well known. I have written them exactly as I would have told them to
a child."

This group includes "The Tinderbox," "Little Claus and Big Claus,"
"The Travelling Companion," "The Wild Swans," "The Swineherd" (all of
them published in 1835–1838), and two later ones, "Simple Simon" (1855),
with the subtitle "A Nursery Tale Retold," and "Dad's Always Right" (1861)
(which begins: "Now listen! I'm going to tell you a story I heard when I was
a boy ..."). There are also elements of folk tales in "The Princess and the
Pea" and in "The Garden of Eden." Three of the tales have literary sources:
"The Naughty Boy" (based on a poem by Anacreon), "The Emperor's New
Clothes" (based on a fourteenth-century Spanish story), and the narrative
frame of "The Flying Trunk" (taken, with a few modifications and a
complete change of style, from a French eighteenth-century work). As for
the rest, the remaining 144 tales (out of a total of 156) are entirely Andersen's
own invention, though this does not mean, of course, that he did not use
themes or features from other sources.

Andersen entitled his tales *Eventyr og Historier*, thus making a
deliberate distinction between *Eventyr*, fairy tales containing a supernatural
element, and *Historier*, stories which lack that element. Thus "The Little
Mermaid" is a fairy tale, "The Emperor's New Clothes," a story. But the
dividing line is not always so clear, nor is Andersen always consistent. For
instance, in spite of its title, "The Story of a Mother" is not so much a story
as a fairy tale. Andersen first used the term *Historier* in 1852; until then he
had consistently used the term *Eventyr*. In his autobiography, he explains that
he had gradually come to regard the word *Historier* as a truer description of
his tales in their full range and nature: "Popular language puts the simple tale
and the most daring imaginative description together under this common
designation; the nursery tale, the fable and the narrative are referred to by
the child as well as by the peasant, among all common or garden people, by
the short term: stories."

Throughout, Andersen's style was unique, and far removed from that
of the traditional folk or fairy tale.

Since Andersen was writing primarily for children, he took great pains
not to use words they might have difficulty in understanding, and he showed

great ingenuity in paraphrasing complicated words and ideas. In "The High Jumpers" he speaks of "the man who writes the almanac," meaning a professor of astronomy. He writes "a student who was studying to become a parson" instead of a "student of theology." If he does use a word children may not know, he takes care to explain it: thus, he says about one of his characters that "he went in for conjuring and learnt to talk with his stomach, which is called being a ventriloquist."

Few writers employed truisms to such deliberately humorous effect as Andersen. Witness the opening lines of "The Nightingale": "You know of course that in China the emperor is a Chinese and his subjects are Chinese too."

Another of Andersen's special talents was that of conveying abstract ideas through a tangible reality. In "The Tinder Box," after the soldier has lifted the third dog down on to the floor and seen the chest full of gold coins, the amount of money is explained in terms which are fully comprehensible to a child. "There was enough for him to buy the whole of Copenhagen, all the sugar-pigs that the cake-women sell, and all the tin soldiers and rocking-horses in the world."

Expressions like "everybody" and "the whole world" seemed too abstract to Andersen, so that he often added something more tangible to them. For their jumping competition the three high jumpers "invited the whole world, and anyone else who like, to come and watch the sport." What could convey a better impression of open admittance? Perhaps the best example is the reward the Snow Queen promises Kay if he is able to combine the letters correctly: not only does she promise him his freedom but also "the whole world and a pair of new skates." The genius of Andersen's conception is clear, for that expression is imbued with both humour and a deep understanding of children's minds.

Some of Andersen's best tales are understood at two levels, by the child and by the grown-up person. Andersen himself once explained that his tales "were told for children, but the grown-up person should be allowed to listen as well." This is certainly true of such masterpieces as "The Little Mermaid," "The Emperor's New Clothes," "The Nightingale" and "The Snow Queen." But there are other tales which might actually appeal more to adults than to children. "The Story of a Mother," "The Bell," and "The Shadow" are all examples of this sort of story, for the true philosophy of these tales is beyond the comprehension of most children. In particular, "The Shadow" is an extremely sophisticated story open to many different interpretations; it could have been written by Kafka.

Andersen himself was a man of deep and apparently irreconcilable contrasts, and the same contrasts are to be found in his fairy tales and stories. "The Bell" and "The Shadow," for instance, have themes which, at first glance, seem quite similar, and yet they express two very different philosophies. "The Bell" is an optimistic story about the triumph of goodness and the victory of genius. In contrast, "The Shadow" tells a pessimistic story in which the learned man, a dedicated scholar and lover of truth and beauty, is beheaded, while his Shadow, the parasite, steals his fame and is rewarded by marrying the princess.

In a much-quoted comment concerning his tales, Andersen said: "They lay in my thoughts like a seed-corn, for them to spring forth and burst into bloom." The autobiographical element is obvious in many of the tales. It is not difficult to see Andersen as the ugly duckling, or as Mr. Larsen in "The Gardener and the Squire," yet he frequently appears in other tales in may different disguises. He is the soldier in "The Tinder Box"; he is the little mermaid, the outsider who came from the depths and was never really accepted in the new world into which he moved; he is the little boy in "The Emperor's New Clothes" who could see the emperor had nothing on; he is the poet in "The Naughty Boy"; and I could cite many more examples. As a Danish critic once said, Andersen wrote more self-portraits than Rembrandt ever painted.

Andersen put not only himself but also his friends and enemies into his tales, and scholars can point to many personal elements in them. But for the large majority of readers all over the world, children as well as adults, who read his tales with little or no knowledge of the author's life and background, most of this information is irrelevant. One can enjoy his fairy tales and stories without any background knowledge whatsoever. If this were not so, Andersen would never have been translated into most living languages, and even in Denmark he would have been largely forgotten by now.

Some of Andersen's tales were written in a matter of hours, or in the course of a few evenings; others took much longer. In 1844, writing to a friend about "The Snow Queen," he noted that "it came out dancing over the paper." He began writing this tale, one of his longest fairy tales, on December 5, 1844, and it was published in book form (together with "The First Tree") on December 21. The whole process of writing, setting up type, printing, binding, and publishing was done in the course of sixteen days.

On the other hand, "The Marsh King's Daughter," another long fairy tale, was rewritten six or seven ties before Andersen was certain that he could not improve upon it.

In 1949 I treated some of these translations, which were then still being reprinted, in an English journal under the heading, "How a Genius is

Murdered." As a result of the publicity surrounding that article, I was approached by a Danish publishing firm in Andersen's native town of Odense which wanted to commission a new translation of some eighty of Andersen's tales. They asked me if I knew of a qualified translator who might be willing to undertake such a task. I immediately asked my old friend R.P. Keigwin if he would be willing to do it. Keigwin possessed both an extensive knowledge of Danish and a very fine sense of style. In 1935, he had been responsible for an excellent translation of the first four tales by Andersen, published in the centenary of their first publication in Denmark. Keigwin understood the difficulty of the task: Andersen's language is full of colloquialisms, special Danish idioms, untranslatable puns and an intimacy between writer and reader which is strengthened by the frequent use of certain Danish adverbs that defy translation. In his preface to the 1935 volume, Keigwin wrote of Andersen:

> He sprinkled his narrative with every kind of conversational touch-crisp, lively openings, to catch the listeners attention at a swoop; frequent asides or parentheses; little bits of Copenhagen slang; much grammatical license; and, above all, a free use of particles—those nods and nudges of speech with which Danish (like Greek) is so richly endowed. So completely did Andersen maintain the conversational tone in his *Tales* that you are quite shocked when you occasionally come across some really literary turn.

Not all of Andersen's 156 fairy tales and stories are masterpieces, and R.P. Keigwin's translation includes a little over half their total number. Personally, I think that it is the best available version of Andersen's tales, taking into consideration both the quality of the translation and the choice of tales and stories.

"The True Wizard of the North" was a term that E.V. Lucas, the English critic, said he would rather apply to Hans Christian Andersen than to Walter Scott, "because whereas Scott took men and women as he found them, [Andersen], with a touch of his wand, rendered inhuman things— furniture, toys, flowers, poultry—instinct with humanity." Robert Lynd, another British literary critic, wrote about Andersen: "He can make the inhabitants of one's mantelpiece capable of epic adventures and has a greater sense of possibilities in a pair of tongs or a door-knocker than most of us have in men and women."

There has been a tendency in both Britain and the United States to regarding Andersen as being only a writer for the nursery, with the implication that he cannot be taken seriously as a literary figure. Or, as the Austrian writer Egon Firedell once put it: "The great public had adopted the same attitude to Andersen as a certain Prussian lieutenant of the guard did to Julius Caesar when he said that he could not possibly have been a great man since he had only written for the lower Latin forms. Similarly, since Andersen is so great an author that even children can understand him, the grown-ups have concluded that he cannot possibly have anything to offer them.

Let me conclude by quoting Andersen's own definition of the literary genre in which he was, and still is, the unsurpassed master:

In the whole realm of poetry no domain is so boundless as that of the fairy tale. It reaches from the blood-drenched graves of antiquity to the pious legends of a child's picture book; it takes in the poetry of the people and the poetry of the artist. To me it represents all poetry, and he who masters it must be able to put into it tragedy, comedy, naïve simplicity, and humour; at his service are the lyrical note, the childlike narrative and the language of describing nature.... In the folk tale it is always Simple Simon who is victorious in the end.... Thus also the innocence of poetry, overlooked and jeered at by the other brothers, will reach farthest in the end.

WOLFGANG LEDERER

The Fairy Tale of Andersen's Life

He arrived in Copenhagen "on Monday morning, September 5th, 1819."
It sounds like a birthday and, to him, it was.[1] Here, finally, he was setting foot
in the world for which he was born, and he lost no time about it. Having
rented a room in a small public house, he immediately sought the theater. A
ticket-seller offered him a ticket, and he "accepted his offer with
thankfulness" in the childlike and devoutly matter-of-course expectation that
he was being given a present. When the scalper angrily disillusioned him, he
fled in confusion.

But he rallied quickly. The next day he dressed in his confirmation suit
("nor were the boots forgotten, although this time, they were worn,
naturally, under my trousers") and further adorned with a hat that was too
big for him he presented himself at the house of a famous dancer, Madame
Schall. "Before I rung at the bell, I fell on my knees before the door and
prayed God that I here might find help and support. A maid-servant came
down the steps ... she smiled kindly at me, gave me a skilling (Danish) and
tripped on. Astonished, I looked at her and the money. I had on my
confirmation suit and thought I must look very smart. How then could she
think I wanted to beg?" (FT, 25–26). He managed to gain admittance anyway
and offered by way of introduction a letter from the old printer Iversen in
Odense. The only connection Iversen ever had had with the dancer was the

From *The Kiss of the Snow Queen: Hans Christian Andersen and Man's Redemption by Woman.* ©
1986 by The Regents of the University of California.

printing of handbills for her performances, but Hans Christian had cajoled the letter out of him in the firm belief that it would serve as a proper introduction. It accomplished just that—even though the dancer "had not the slightest knowledge of him from whom the letter came, and my whole appearance and behavior seemed very strange to her." He explained his yearning for the theater. She wondered what he could do. He asked permission to take off his boots and, using his broad hat for a tambourine, began to dance and sing passages from a musical play, *Cinderella*. "My strong gestures and my great activity caused the lady to think me out of my mind, and she lost no time in getting rid of me" (*TS*, 38–39).

An attempt to find some employment at the theater resulted in another snub and a moment of despair. But "with all the undoubting confidence of a child in his father" he prayed to God and, having regained his courage, bought a gallery ticket for the opera *Paul and Virginia*. It affected him so deeply that he wept, and this in turn attracted the kind attentions of some women who sat nearby. He explained himself to them, and they fed him "bread and butter, with fruit and cakes," as well as a sausage sandwich.

Even so, the next day found him penniless, and in his extremity he looked for work. He answered the advertisement of a cabinetmaker and was tentatively accepted as an apprentice. The following morning

> I went to the workshop: several journeymen were there, and two or three apprentices; but the master was not come. They fell into merry and idle discourse. I was as bashful as a girl, and as they soon perceived this, I was unmercifully rallied upon it. Later in the day, the rude jests of the young fellows went so far that, in remembrance of the scene at the manufactory, I took the resolute determination not to remain a single day longer in the workshop.
>
> (*TS*, 41)

The master tried to reassure him, but he was "too much affected" and hastened away.

Again he knew despair,[2] and again he rallied. This time he crashed the dinner party of an opera singer he had once read about, Giuseppe Siboni, who was at that moment entertaining a number of artists and writers. Hans Christian opened his heart to the housekeeper; the good woman was moved and induced the party to see him. He sang and recited poetry for them; at the end, overcome by "the sense of my unhappy condition," he burst into tears.

He was applauded. Siboni promised to give him singing lessons, and a Professor Weyse raised a small sum of money for him by subscription. To study with Siboni he needed to learn German, and a woman of Copenhagen with whom he had traveled from Odense arranged for him to receive free lessons from a language-master. Things were finally going his way, and he wrote a triumphant letter home. But within half a year, when he must have been about fifteen, his voice broke—or was injured, "in consequence of my being compelled to wear bad shoes through the winter, and having besides no warm underclothing" (*FT*, 31). This finished his singing, and Siboni counseled him to return to Odense and learn a trade.

We cannot help but raise an eyebrow. The tall, skinny boy with his long blond hair, pretty face, and soprano voice had repeatedly suffered from ribbing (and worse) on account of his girlish appearance. We would think he would have wished for an early change toward a more masculine demeanor. We would think he would know about and anticipate with some impatience the voice changes associated with puberty, and in his case already overdue. Instead, when the change does come, he considers it so unnatural that he ascribes it to a cold "in consequence of being compelled to wear bad shoes"—quite as if, had he only had proper shoes, he could have remained a soprano forever! This is passing odd. We also do not fail to notice that shoes, or boots, once again play some sort of symbolic, or magical, role. We shall have more to say about this later on.

Meanwhile, in spite or because of his new voice, Hans Christian was once again in despair. This time he bethought himself of a poet Guldberg, the brother of a colonel who had befriended him in Odense, and to this man he appealed for help. The poet received him kindly, gave him a substantial sum of money, and offered him lessons in Danish, it being apparent that Hans Christian both spoke and wrote his mother tongue rather poorly.

Needing a cheaper place to live, he took lodgings in "nothing but an empty store room, without window and light" but with permission to sit in the parlor. The landlady was a woman whom only years later he properly identified as a madam: "I found myself in the midst of the mysteries of Copenhagen, but I did not understand how to interpret them." Like the sun-god Phoebus, whose holy eye never sees the shadow, Hans Christian never spotted sin: "I never suspected what kind of world, it was which moved around me" (*TS*, 46–47).

He lived in a different world. The "stern but active dame" wanted twenty rix dollars monthly for the wretched room, and he could afford but sixteen:

> This troubled me very much; when she was gone out of the
> room, I seated myself on the sofa, and contemplated the portrait

of her deceased husband. I was so wholly a child, that as the tears
rolled down my own cheeks I wetted the eyes of the portrait with
my tears, in order that the dead man might feel how troubled I
was, and influence the heart of his wife. She must have seen that
nothing more was to be drained out of me, for when she returned
to the room she said she would receive me into her house for the
sixteen rix dollars. I thanked God and the dead man.[3]

He continued to play with his puppet theater and his dolls and to make
doll clothes from colored fragments of material he begged from various
stores—even though his voice had changed and even though he was now
receiving free lessons in Latin, acting, and dancing. He was told he would
never make either an actor or a dancer, but he was permitted to watch
performances from the wings. Occasionally he got on stage as an extra, and
finally, through the kindness of his dancing instructor, he was even assigned
a little part in a ballet: "That was a moment in my life, when my name was
printed! ... I carried the programme of the ballet with me at night to bed, lay
and read my name by candle-light—in short, I was happy!"[4]

Meanwhile, he was starving, and the imminent necessity of returning
to Odense with his tail between his legs suggested suicide to him as a
preferable alternative. But an extraordinary procession of benefactors—
widows and their daughters, retired admirals, assorted officials—not only fed
him in turn but listened to his first poetry and read his first dramatic
efforts—largely plagiarized pieces conveying such ignorance of grammar,
history, and the world that it was increasingly felt that he should be given a
proper education.

One of his would-be educators was the poet Frederik Høegh-
Guldberg, who went to many troubles and pains on Andersen's behalf, and
among other things arranged for him to have Latin lessons. When Andersen
proved anything but diligent, Guldberg lost his patience and lectured him
severely. Hans Christian's reaction was characteristic:

I realized that it was wrong of me to have neglected the Latin
lessons ... I walked homeward full of despair. He had told me that
I was "a bad person," and that affected me terribly. I stood for a
long time by the Pebblinge Lake ... and the horrible thought
struck me: "Nothing good can become of you ... God is angry,
you must die!" I looked into the water, and then thought of my
old grandmother, who would certainly not have thought that my
life would end in this way. This made me cry bitterly, but it

relieved my mind, and in my heart I begged God to forgive me for ... my sinful thought of jumping into the water.[5]

He had lost one protector, but about this time Jonas Collin, "one of the most distinguished men of Denmark" and currently director of the Royal Theatre, entered his life and began to shape it decisively. Collin was a man of grave demeanor and few words, and Hans Christian, so pitifully anxious to elicit a warm and sympathetic response from all he met, at first feared him and considered him an enemy. But Collin, sensing a spark of genius in the peculiar boy, obtained for him from King Frederick VI an annual stipend to run for several years and arranged for him to receive free instruction in the grammar school at Slagelse, a small town twelve Danish miles from Copenhagen.

In the eyes of a less astute observer than Collin, Hans Christian would, at that point, have appeared a dismal failure:

He had been rejected as a singer, as a dancer, as an actor, and as a playwright. He was clumsy and "different," and his appearance was unfortunate in every way, and to make things worse he had grown out of his suit without being able to afford to buy a new one. His coat was too short, so he tried to pull down his sleeves all the time, his trousers too short and too narrow, and his heels trodden down. He moved awkwardly in a vain attempt to cover up the many defects in his clothing. His whole behavior was often ridiculous.[6]

When he declaimed his poetry or his plays, his listeners had difficulty not to burst out laughing. A young physician who attended one of young Andersen's performances at the elegant house of a Mrs. Belfour wrote of it later:

In my opinion the whole performance (a reciting of plays, poems etc.) was just mediocre. But on the other hand, the great interest he took in it, the lack of restraint in his performance and his enthusiasm had such great appeal that I became somewhat indignant that they used him as a buffoon and a joker. The audience laughed at his tall, ungainly figure and his strikingly awkward appearance, which was especially noticeable in his movements and his walk. When we were going to eat he stumbled over the doorstep, tripped over his long legs, grasped the sandwich as if in a coma, lost his knife and fork, but talked

incessantly.... But that the seeds of greatness were in him was
quite clear.[7]

Andersen seems to have managed to overlook, or to reinterpret as
encouragement, all the laughter; and as to the "seeds of greatness" in himself
he was never in doubt. At any rate, things now were looking up. He had, in
a manner, been adopted by a good father—Jonas Collin—to whom he would
be able to turn with his problems and who would watch over him. And he
was now, at long last, really and truly to be a student—as his poor dead father
had always hoped—and so he wrote his mother a letter full of joy.

As it turned out, the next years of his life were anything but joyful. If
his memory can be trusted, the year was 1822. He would have been
seventeen years old when he joined a class of children aged perhaps ten to
twelve. With his beanpole figure he must have been twice the height of some
of them. Nevertheless, that is not what pained him; feeling so much a child
he may have fitted in uncommonly well. But he suffered bitterly from the
treatment accorded him by the rector, Dr. Meisling, a well-meaning
pedagogue with a sarcastic, bullying manner who never praised but criticized
constantly.[8] There was nothing Hans Christian could tolerate less than
criticism, and over and over again he dissolved in despair and wrote letters to
his various benefactors proclaiming his unworthiness and failure. In
response, he received much kindness and reassurance and so, his spirits
briefly buoyed, managed to carry on. But he remained terribly vulnerable:
"In my character-book I always received, as regarded my conduct,
'remarkably good.' On one occasion, however, I only obtained the testimony
of 'very good': and so anxious and childlike was I, that I wrote a letter to
Collin on that account, and assured him in grave earnestness, that I was
perfectly innocent, although I had only obtained a character of 'very good'"
(*TS*, 73).

Things got worse when the rector moved to a school in Helsingoer and
invited Hans Christian to come along and live in the rector's house. The
place was, to Andersen's perception, run like a jail: "When the school hours
were over, the house door was commonly locked ... I never went out to visit
anybody ... my prayer to God every evening was, that He would remove the
cup from me and let me die. I possessed not an atom of confidence in myself"
(*TS*, 75). He wrote one single poem during that time. It was called *The Dying
Child* (!).

In the end, thanks to a sympathetic teacher's intervention with Collin,
Hans Christian was removed from the school and permitted to return to
Copenhagen. As a parting shot the rector predicted for him that he "would

end his days in a madhouse." In view of his background, such a prognosis could not be taken lightly, and the boy understandably "trembled in his innermost being."

Released from "jail," he took a new lease on life. An intelligent young teacher tutored him in Latin and Greek and argued religion—Hans Christian could accept God as love, but would never consent to hellfire[9]— and, bubbling like a newly opened bottle of champagne, he produced some humorous and satirical poetry that was actually published. In September 1828, now twenty-three years old, he officially became "a student" (of the University). "Thousand ideas and thoughts by which I was pursued ... flew like a swarm of bees out into the world and indeed into my ... work." A humorous and fantastic travel piece, self-published, had some success, and a satirical play won the acclaim of his fellow students.[10] "I was now a happy human being; I possessed the soul of a poet, and the heart of youth; all houses began to open to me; I flew from circle to circle." His first collection of poems appeared the next year. "Life lay bright with sunshine before me."

A dark cloud soon appeared—one that was to darken the remainder of his life.

In the summer of 1830, when he was twenty-five, he visited, on one of the Danish islands, the home of a fellow student, Christian Voigt. And there

> A pair of dark eyes fixed my sight,
> They were my world, my home, my delight,
> The soul beamed in them, and childlike peace,
> And never on earth will their memory cease.
>
> (*TS*, 90)

The pair of dark eyes belonged to Riborg Voigt, Christian's sister, a pretty girl of twenty who served him tea, went for walks with him, and generally showed herself attentive and interested.[11] He realized, with some dismay, that he was falling in love: "I remained in that house but three days, and when I felt what I had never felt before, and heard that she is already engaged, I departed immediately."

They met again in Copenhagen, late in the year, and he handed her a little love poem; but far from pressing his suit, he apparently took it completely for granted, and bitterly bewailed in his letters, that she would have to marry the other: "I see that I will never be happy! All my soul and all my thoughts cling to this one creature, a clever, *childlike* creature such as I have never met before ... but she is engaged, and to be married next month.... I will never see her again. Next month she becomes a *wife*, then she will, then she must forget me. Oh, it is a deadly thought! ... If only I were dead, dead, even if death were total annihilation" (Andersen's italics).[12] So he writes in January 1831. In March he still protests and, one cannot help feeling, too much: "I will never be happy in this world, I cannot; with my whole being I cling to a creature who can never become mine!—Insuperable obstacles separate us forever. Oh, God has tried me hard, almost too hard. She is the most *childlike*, the most magnificent creature I know, but engaged, the bride of another!" (Andersen's italics).[13]

He wrote Riborg a highly emotional, but typically Andersenian, love letter:

> I think you have already sensed my feelings, I am not enough of a man of the world to conceal my heart, and I dream of a hope, without which my life is lost. DO YOU REALLY LOVE THE OTHER MAN? ... If [so], then forgive me ... if you have been insulted by this letter, then give me permission to see you once more ... for three months my heart and my thoughts have been obsessed ... now I can live in this uncertainty no longer, I must know your decision. But forgive me, please forgive me! I was unable to act otherwise. Good-bye!

In the very act of declaring his love, his letter already contains resignation and farewell.[14]

By April he is, or at least appears to be, all over this infatuation.[15] His head, and his letters, are full of plans for a trip through Germany, and by May he writes travelogues about it. It was not Riborg Voigt who was to become his dark cloud; but rather it was the awkward, mysteriously abortive nature of the encounter, a failure of nerve in romantic situations, that was to remain characteristic of him, and of which we shall have more to say.

The journey itself was no doubt to serve as a distraction, but not only from the pains of love. His heart was much more vulnerable, and far more often injured, by the arrows of criticism. His happiness depended on a smile, and a frown could precipitate him into despair. "I am a peculiar creature," he writes, "so easily distrustful of humanity, I find the world cold and dark; but a single friendly word, and I am reconciled with all of you."[16] He hid his hurt feelings behind an arrogance that was considered "the most unbearable vanity ... it was more than I could bear to hear [something] said sternly and jeeringly, by others; and if I then uttered a proud, an inconsiderate word, it was addressed to the scourge with which I was smitten; and when those who smite are those we love, then do the scourges become scorpions" (*FT*, 71).

In other words, he had become so hypersensitive and disagreeable that Collin sent him away for his own good and that of his friends. On the journey he was to rebuild his damaged pride in a manner that, again, became characteristic of him: he collected, and basked in, the attentions of famous men and women.

In the beginning these were mainly writers and artists to whom he managed to gain entry. On his first trip, in 1831 in Dresden, he met Tieck, the famous translator of Shakespeare, who "on taking leave of me, embraced and kissed me; which made the deepest impression on me" (*FT*, 72). And in Berlin he had an introduction to Chamisso (*FT*, 73), the author of *Peter Schlemiehl* and a good poet, who eventually translated some of Andersen's poems into German.[17] Upon returning to Copenhagen he promptly published his travel impressions, *Shadow Pictures*, as he eventually was to do after almost all of his journeys.

Two years later he journeyed to Paris, where one day "A man of Jewish cast came toward me. 'I hear you are a Dane,' said he. 'I am a German: Danes and Germans are brothers, therefore I offer you my hand!' I asked for his name and he said: 'Heinrich Heine'!" Together with Sir Walter Scott and E. T.A. Hoffmann, Heine had exerted the most formative influence on Andersen's youth. "There was no man I could have wished more to see and meet with" (*FT*, 88).

This is, at least in the early years of Andersen's travels, the only instance of someone introducing himself to Andersen, rather than vice versa; and, considering Heine's feelings about "being a German," the episode is somewhat questionable. Doubt seems even more justified in the light of what happened between them ten years later. Andersen reports in his diary on 26 March 1843 that he visited Heine, and he raves, "He received me graciously. He wanted me to believe that he had forgotten his German, that now all his joys and sufferings were French (his wife is a Frenchwoman); that for him Scandinavia is the only place where the treasures of poetry can still be found; and that, were he not so old, he would study Danish. He is interested in elves and goblins."[18] But Heine raved decidedly less. He wrote later, "Andersen called on me ... I thought he looked like a tailor. He is a lean man with a hollow lantern-jaw face, and in his outward appearance he betrays a servile lack of self-confidence which is appreciated by dukes and princes. He fulfilled exactly a prince's idea of a poet. When he visited me he had decked himself out with a big tie-pin. I asked him what it was he had put there. He replied very unctuously: 'It is a present which the Electress of Hessen has been gracious enough to bestow on me.' Otherwise he is a man of some spirit."[19]

In 1833 Andersen was not yet collecting dukes and princes, but he was rapidly heading that way. He did manage to meet Victor Hugo in Paris, the philosopher Schelling in Munich, the sculptor Thorwaldsen in Rome, and the dramatist Grillparzer in Vienna.

There followed a hiatus until, in 1838, the Danish Prime Minister, Count Rantzau-Breitenburg, had obtained for him from King Frederick VI an adequate travel stipend. But in 1840 Andersen set out on an extended journey. Having visited the Count in his ancestral castle in Holstein, he traveled—for the first time by railway—to Leipzig. There he engaged in a little game he was to play many times later on. He had heard that Mendelssohn-Bartoldi had enjoyed one of his novels, and had issued a vague invitation for Andersen to visit him if ever he came through Leipzig. Being told that Mendelssohn was rehearsing at the Gewandthaus, Andersen sent in a note to the effect that "a traveller was very anxious to call on him." The composer emerged, sorely vexed: "'I have but very little time, and I really cannot talk here with strangers!' he said. 'You have invited me yourself,' answered I, 'you have told me that I must not pass through the city without seeing you!'—'Andersen!' cried he now, 'is it you?' and his whole countenance beamed" (*FT*, 157). In this manner Andersen, over and over again—approaching strangers at first anonymously and then "revealing" himself—tested and heightened the favorable reception he could receive, the confirmation of his fame he could enjoy.

He continued his journey to Rome, Naples, Malta, and Athens—where he was a dinner guest of the King of Greece—and on to Constantinople, where he "found a cordial reception with the Austrian internuncius, Baron Stuermer," and crossed the Bosporus to Asia Minor to see the dancing dervishes in Scutari and Pera.[20] From Constantinople he meant to continue his journey to the mouth of the Danube and thence upstream to Vienna.

It should be pointed out that travel in those days was far from simple, far from safe, and mostly incredibly wearisome. Steamships and railways were just beginning to be built, and were sooty and most uncomfortable. Post chaises were much worse. A journey from Denmark to Italy could take weeks; the roads, especially over the mountains, were hazardous and dusty. The few existing inns were bad, their beds crawling with vermin. In the winter months heating was inadequate, and in the summer there was no defense against mosquitoes. Highwaymen were not uncommon and public conveyances often had to be accompanied by an armed guard. It was not exactly the sort of experience one would have expected someone of Andersen's finicky sensibilities to venture—much less to enjoy. In addition, his own quirks greatly aggravated the stresses of reality. He was afraid of dogs; he had such agoraphobia that he needed an escort to traverse a large square. He was so afraid of fire that he always carried a rope in his trunk so that, if necessary, he could escape through an upstairs hotel window. During the night he had to get up several times to assure himself that the candle had been properly extinguished; this in spite of the fact that he had himself, before he went to bed, carefully pinched the wick between his damp fingers.[21] He worried obsessively whether his passport was in order and had the required visas, whether he had locked the door to his room, whether he had paid the right amount in the right currency, whether someone was out to rob or murder him, and so on. "Oh, how good I am at tormenting myself!" he wrote.[22] But there was a stubborn streak in him whenever he had set his mind on something.

In this instance he was told that the proposed journey was not to be advised. The country was in revolt; it was said there had been several thousand Christians murdered. He was urged to give up the Danube route, and to return via Greece and Italy.

I do not belong to the courageous; I feel fear, especially in little dangers; but in great ones, and when an advantage is to be won, then I have a will, and it has grown firmer with years. I may tremble, I may fear, but I still do that which I consider the most proper to be done. I am not ashamed to confess my weakness; I hold that when out of our own true conviction we run counter to our inborn fear, we have done our duty. I had a strong desire to ... traverse the Danube ... I battled with myself; my imagination painted to me the most horrible circumstances; it was an anxious night. In the morning ... I determined upon it. From the moment that I had taken my determination I had the most immovable reliance on Providence, and flung myself calmly on my fate.

(*FT*, 167)

There were some exciting moments, some shooting, and the discomfort and boredom of ten days' quarantine at the Austrian border, in a building "only arranged to receive Wallachian peasants," with paved rooms, horrid provisions, and worse wine. The trip from Constantinople to Vienna took three weeks. Upon his return to Copenhagen he published his travel book, *A Poet's Bazaar*.

In 1843 he again went to Paris and this time, in addition to Victor Hugo, visited Lamartine, Alexandre Dumas, Alfred de Vigny, Balzac, Scribe, Gautier, and, as mentioned, once again Heine. On the return trip he managed to take in the poet Freiligrath in the Rhine town of St. Goar and the writers Moritz Arndt and Emanuel Geibel in Bonn. 1844 took him to Berlin to meet the composer Meyerbeer, and later to Weimar: "The reigning Grand Duke and Duchess gave me so gracious and kind a reception." But it was when he met the hereditary Grand Duke and his lady—a newly married princely pair—that his heart was deeply moved. More about this later.

From Weimar he traveled to Leipzig for a "truly poetical evening" with Robert and Clara Schumann. Andersen was delighted by the reception, and by the fact that Robert had set four of his poems to music.[23] Clara said of him later, "Andersen is the ugliest man imaginable, but he looks very interesting and has a poetically childlike mind."[24] Apparently the King (Christian VIII) and Queen of Denmark thought so too, for that summer they invited him to stay with them at a spa on the North Frisian Island of Foehr: "It was just now five-and-twenty years since I, a poor lad, travelled alone and helpless to Copenhagen. Exactly the five-and-twentieth anniversary would be celebrated by my being with my king and queen, to whom I was faithfully attached, and whom I at that very time learned to love with my whole soul.... The reality frequently surpasses the most beautiful dream" (FT, 220).

This should have been the pinnacle of his success and he should have been content. But, alas, his autobiography goes on, and it degenerates into a tedious recital of royalties visited and honors, medals, and decorations received. He visited Prince Radziwill in Berlin; received the Order of the Dannebrog from the King of Denmark; visited King Friedrich August II of Saxony; was introduced to the Grand Duchess Sophie of Austria, to Archduke Stephan, and to the future Emperor Franz Joseph; and so on and so on. There was no shortage of little countries, or of big ones—and they all had royalty to be visited and to be made much of.

He is aware of the effect he is creating: "It may appear perhaps, as if I desired to bring names of great people prominently forward, and to make a parade of them; or as if I wished in this way to offer a kind of thanks to my benefactors. They need it not, and I should be obliged to mention many other names still" (TS, 169). And he does mention other names, such as during his visit, in 1847, to England. From there he wrote to Jonas Collin's son Edvard: "Here is a paper which says that I am 'one of the most remarkable and interesting men of this day.' Last night I made my first appearance, and that in the most select society. I was at Lord Palmerston's. I talked to the Duke of Cambric [sic], the Duchess of Sutherland ... everyone knew my writing; in the end I was surrounded by fine ladies who talked of my tales ... I grew quite giddy, but not with pride."[25]

He was lionized as never before: invitations poured in from Lord Stanley, Lord Castlereagh, the Rothschilds, and so on. He even received an invitation from Prince Albert to visit him and Queen Victoria in Scotland, but there his nerve, and his purse—he would have had to hire a valet—failed him and, under many and bitter tears, he declined.[26]

When he had chronicled all this assiduously in his autobiography, there was one friend, who knew him well, who protested. He had sent the manuscript to Henriette Wulff, an old and wise friend. A hunchbacked spinster of great intelligence and warmth, she truly cared for him. She wrote:

> To me it is a total denial of oneself, of one's own person, of the gifts God has graciously given us, such an incomprehensible self-humiliation that I am surprised when somebody like YOU, Andersen—if you do recognize that God has given you special spiritual gifts—that YOU can consider yourself HAPPY and HONOURED to be placed—well, that is what it says—at the table of the King of Prussia or of some other high-ranking person—or to receive a decoration, of the kind worn by the greatest scoundrels, not to mention a swarm of extremely insignificant people. Do you really place a title, money, aristocratic blood, success in what is nothing but outward matters, ABOVE genius—spirit—the gifts of the soul?[27]

Andersen had no answer.[28]

Why indeed the parade of stars? What for? Why did he strive so mightily to be accepted and flattered by the great? And why does he—with all professed "humility"—make such a show of it?

To some extent, no doubt, the description of his spectacular ascent up the artistic and social register serves the legitimate and well-deserved end of illustrating the laborious metamorphosis of the poor cobbler's son into a world-renowned man of letters—the metamorphosis of the ugly duckling into a swan. Nor shall we begrudge him a word of his triumph. However, it is hard, in spite of his disclaimer, not to see in the recital of famous personalities and in his attachment to them, a certain sycophantic quality: a wish and need to derive from their company and approval a sense of security he basically lacked.[29] In this regard he failed completely. He continued to play, with regard to the great, as in his far more sustaining attachments to more faithful but less famous people (the Collin family above all) the role of a child. The quality he was lacking, and the lack of which he wished to conceal or to compensate for, was manhood.[30] In this regard he had failed,

at the age of twenty-five, with Riborg Voigt. He was to try seriously only
once more—and fail finally—at the age of thirty-five, with the famous
operatic singer Jenny Lind.[31]

He was thirty-five, and she twenty, when they first met. She was already
a well-known singer in Stockholm, and he a writer of rising fame. When he
learned that she, in company with her father, was visiting Copenhagen, he
felt it proper and appropriate to call on her. She received him "very
courteously, but yet distantly, almost coldly"; recoiling in his sensitive
manner, he gained "the impression of a very ordinary character which soon
passed from my mind."

She was back three years later, and as friends assured him she now knew
of him and had read his works, he permitted himself to visit her again. This
time, indeed, he received a cordial welcome. He encouraged her to perform
in Copenhagen. When she did, she was an instant success and won
enthusiastic acclaim. His own view of her changed in resonance to her
cordiality: she was not only the best singer and actress of her time, but "at
home, in her own chamber, a sensitive young girl with all the humility and
piety of a child" (TS, 209). We cannot help but notice the emphasis, and he
repeats, so that we should not forget: "An intelligent and child-like
disposition exercises here its astonishing power" (TS, 213). Must he indeed,
and at all cost, see her as a child? There is, apparently, only one alternative:
"Her appearance in Copenhagen made an epoch in the history of our opera;
it showed me art in its sanctity—I had beheld one of its vestals ... she is a pure
vessel, from which a holy draught will be presented to us." If she is not to be
a child, then she must be and remain "pure," a holy virgin, untouchable.

So, at least, reads the autobiography. But his diary, in the fall of 1843,
when he was thirty-eight, reads: "In love," and "I love her."[32] They were
meeting daily at that time, and when she left for home, he gave her a letter
of which his diary records: "She must understand." She no doubt
understood, but she made her position clear: she loved him like a brother. He
was bitterly hurt—as he many years later expressed in some of his stories
(such as Under the Willow Tree)—but he soon settled into resignation.

They met, off and on, in the years to follow. At Christmas 1845, they
were both in Berlin. He spent a lonely Christmas Eve in his hotel. Was it, as
he claims, because "every one of the many families in which I ... was received
as a relation had fancied ... that I must be invited out [elsewhere]"? (TS,
2.63–64). Or was he hoping for an invitation by Jenny? At any rate, when she
heard of his solitary Christmas, "there was (on the last evening of the year)
planted for me alone a little tree with its lights, and its beautiful presents—
and that was by Jenny Lind. The whole company consisted of herself, her

attendant, and me; we three children from the North were together on Sylvester [New Year's] eve, and I was the child for which the Christmas-tree was lighted." This "child" was now forty years old, and apparently quite resigned to remaining a lonely bachelor for the rest of his life.

Not that he was ever really alone.

He never owned a house of its own. By preference he stayed on as a houseguest in the homes of hospitable families—as he once stayed on, for five weeks and much beyond his welcome, at the house of Charles Dickens.[33] The description of him, written years later by Dickens's son, Sir Henry Dickens, paints a vivid picture:

> He turned out to be a lovable and yet a somewhat uncommon and strange personality. His manner was delightfully simple, such as one rather expected from the delicacy of his work. He was necessarily very interesting, but he was certainly somewhat of an "oddity." In person, tall, gaunt, rather ungainly; in manner, thoughtful and agreeable. He had one beautiful accomplishment, which was the cutting out in paper, with an ordinary pair of scissors, of little figures of sprites and elves, gnomes, fairies and animals of all kinds which might have stepped out of the pages of his books.... Much as there was in him to like and admire, he was, on the other hand, most decidedly disconcerting in his general manner, for he used constantly to be doing things, quite unconsciously, which might almost be called "gauche," so much so that I am afraid the small boys in the family rather laughed at him behind his back; but, so far as the members of the family are concerned, he was treated with the utmost consideration and courtesy.[34]

Dickens himself poked fun at him: "We are suffering a good deal from Andersen," he wrote (in a letter). "The other day we lost him when he came up to London Bridge Terminus, and he took a cab by himself. The cabman driving him through the new unfinished streets at Clerkenwell, he thought was driving him into remote fastnesses, to rob and murder him. He consequently arrived here with all his money, his watch, his pocketbook, and documents, in his boots—and it was a tremendous business to unpack him and get them off." When Andersen departed, Dickens put up a card over the dressing-table mirror: "Hans Andersen slept in this room for five weeks—which seemed to the family ages!"[35]

Not mentioned in Dickens' description is the usual manner in which

Andersen "sang for his supper" in his later years. Typically he would recite tales in the family circle after dinner or in the nursery. As his skill in that genre became renowned, he grew to resemble exactly the storyteller surrounded by children that we fancy him to have been.

When he did not stay at someone else's house or country mansion—and he appears to have stayed at more than thirty—he lived in rented rooms, or at a hotel. His popularity was such, and he knew so many ladies who were to him as mothers or grandmothers, that one or the other or several of them would invariably come to his quarters to look after him and to furnish his rooms with flowers.[36]

Through much of his life the house of Jonas Collin was his "home of homes," a place where he always felt welcome and always found understanding and loyal support. Jonas himself had directed his youth, and his son Edvard, whom Andersen regarded as a brother, became, though three years younger than Hans Christian, his business manager and practical adviser in all matters regarding publications and finances. It is characteristic of Andersen that he submitted—no doubt profitably—to this management, even though Edvard, as stern as father Jonas, grated on him: "No matter how much affection ties me to Edvard, I still feel that he cannot be a real friend to me! It may be that the very qualities which give him character become cutting edges which injure my sensibilities."[37]

When, after the death of Jonas Collin in 1861, that "home of homes" broke up, two highly respected Jewish families from Copenhagen, the Henriques and the Melchiors, became increasingly important to him and more or less "took over." Mrs. Dorothea Melchior, in particular, saw in motherly fashion after his physical and emotional wellbeing and in the end became his nurse. He died at her summer villa, just outside of Copenhagen, on 4 August 1875, shortly after his seventieth birthday.

NOTES

1. All his life Andersen considered this his "fateful date," though he later changed it to 6 September to conform with a printing error in his autobiography. It was also on that day that he was recommended for a study grant by the Royal Theatre. He memorialized the date every year until his death, though eventually in an increasingly despondent mood (Niels Birger Wamberg, "H.C. Andersen og hans skæbnedato," *Anderseniana*, 1970–73, pp. 188–204).

2. "He thought of going all the way back to Funen by boat in the hope that the ship would sink and he would be drowned" (Bredsdorff, *Hans Christian Andersen*, 31). His predicament was in truth quite serious, and later on he formulated it like this: "When the sculptor commences modelling the clay, we do not yet understand the work of art which he will create.... How much more difficult is it then to discover in the child the worth and

fate of the man! We here see the poor boy ... the instinct within him, and the influence without, show, like the magnetic needle, only two opposite directions. He must either become a distinguished artist or a miserable, confused being." And he feared both alternatives: "A rare artist must he become, or a miserable bungler—a sparrow-hawk with yellow wings, which for his superiority is pecked to death by its companions" (*Only a Fiddler*, 40, 41).

3. *TS*, 47. With reference to this episode, Helge Topsøe-Jensen and Paul V. Rubow, "Hans Christian Andersen the Writer," *American-Scandinavian Review* 18 (1930): 205–12, comment that, despite Andersen's constant appeals to God he was "in his religious action and reaction like a savage ... what he actually did was to use *magic* ... whether he had learned it of the witches or invented it himself" (210–11).

4. Andersen was so absorbed in his theatrical activities that he found no time to study or even to make little excursions out of town. But he did learn somewhat how to conduct himself with poise and a certain elegance, and acquired a sense of language and music that later stood him in good stead (Povl Ingerslev-Jensen, "Statist Andersen," *Anderseniana*, 1970–73, pp. 137–87). The roles he was permitted to play have been reconstructed through a survey of the costumes of the time, preserved at the Royal Theatre (Frederick J. Marker, "H.C. Andersen as a Royal Theatre Actor," *Anderseniana*, 1966–69, pp. 278–84).

5. Bredsdorff, *Hans Christian Andersen*, 39–40.

6. Ibid., 44.

7. Julius Clausen, "Young Hans Christian Andersen," *American-Scandinavian Review* 43 (1955): 47–52, 51.

8. Meisling had grounds for criticism. Andersen, while adept at mathematics, was surprisingly poor in Latin and spelling, and these shortcomings he feared would eventually keep him out of the University. A recent study suggests that the problem was not cultural or characterological but neurological. Andersen, it is claimed, must have been constitutionally dyslexic, with auditory and visual defects—a complicated word-blindness and dysgrammaticism with clumsy sentence construction. If this diagnosis is correct, it could offer an additional reason for Andersen's "oral" style of writing (Axel Rosendal, "Årsagerne til H.C. Andersen stavevanskeligheder," *Anderseniana*, 1974–77, pp. 160–84). Regardless of the validity of this contention, it is certainly true that Meisling traumatized Andersen deeply. Nightmares about him troubled the writer all his life, and only close to his death did he have a dream in which something like a reconciliation with Meisling takes place (Bredsdorff, *Hans Christian Andersen*, 67–68).

9. Bredsdorff, *Hans Christian Andersen*, 70.

10. *Journey on Foot to Amager; Love on Saint Nicolas' Tower*.

11. Spink, *Hans Christian Andersen and His World*, 33–34.

12. Andersen, *Der Dichter and die Welt*, 44–45.

13. Ibid., 47.

14. Bredsdorff, *Hans Christian Andersen*, 76–77.

15. Otto, the hero of *O.T.*, writes: "Was I not once convinced that I loved Sophie, and that I never could bear it if she were lost to me? and yet it needed only the conviction 'She loves thee not,' and my strong feeling was dead. Sophie even seems to me less beautiful; I see faults where I formerly could only discover amiabilities! Now, she is to me almost wholly a stranger" (253).

16. He never overcame his distrust, but knew himself well enough to see it and to

deplore it. Thus he writes in his diary in 1850: "I felt I was bound to him. His friendship was a greening palm against which I rested my head. Then along came a certain woman and I said to her: 'My faith is in him!' 'Your faith!' she repeated, smiling. Oh, in that smile there was devouring death. It breathed over my tree, which seemed to bend; I grew dizzy. Oh, what a deadly poison filled the air in that instant,—I grieve that he could change toward me, could be the first of us to feel less warmly! And yet in that instant I too felt the same change. I distrust him. I can be shaken in my faith merely by a mocking smile" (Carl Lorain Withers, "The Private Notebook of H.C. Andersen," *The Forum* 78 [1927]: 417–29, 421).

    17. Heinrich Harries, "H.C. Andersen and Heinrich Zeise," *Anderseniana*, 1962–65, pp. 233–95, 236. Oddly enough, one of these poems, "Der Soldat," beginning with "Es geht mit gedämpfter Trommeln Klang" (Adalbert von Chamisso, *Chamissos Werke* [Leipzig und Wien: Meyers Klassiker Ausgaben, 1907], vol. 1, 134), became a typically death-loving marching song of the German army (Lederer, *The Fear of Women*, 262–65). The popular tune is not by Schumann—who also set this same poem to music—but by a man named Friedrich Silcher, who composed it in 1837 (Gerhard Pallman and Ernst Lothar von Knorr, *Soldaten Kameraden* [Hamburg: Hanseatische Verlagsanstalt, 1942]). It is also odd in other ways. Among the poems translated by Chamisso, it is the only military one. The others deal in more typically Andersenian fashion with a little girl expecting a brother to be born out of a fountain ("Die kleine Liese am Brunnen"); a young man watching smiling blue eyes through ice-flowers on a windowpane ("Märzveilchen"—the last line reading "God help him when the ice-flowers melt!"); a mother daydreaming happily about the future of her baby boy who, according to the ravens, is some day to be hanged as a robber ("Muttertraum"); a fiddler who has to play at his beloved's wedding ("Der Spielmann"); and a rejected lover who, having to live in the same house with his now-married beloved, longs for death ("Der Müllergesell"). "Der Soldat" ("The Soldier") is, for all I know, the only poem Andersen wrote in that vein, the only time he ever wrote anything about a real soldier—and one could well wonder: whatever got into him? He claims in his autobiography (*FT*, 5) that the poem was inspired by his witnessing the execution of the Spanish soldier in 1808. But was it? Is the execution the main thing, or is it a love poem? I am offering a rough translation, so that the reader may judge:

> The muffled drums mark our pace
> How long yet the road, how far the place
> Oh, were it but over and he were at rest
> My heart is breaking in my chest.

> I've loved just him as long as I live
> Him alone, who now his life must give.
> To martial music we reach the square
> I too, I too am commanded there.

> Now for the last time does he sight
> God's world bathed in joyful light
> Now they are binding tight his eyes
> God take you up into paradise!

The nine of us took aim at last
Eight bullets simply whistled past
Their aim by grief and pain was marr'd
But I, I shot him through the heart.

18. F. J. Billeskov Jansen, "Quelques extraits du Journal Parisien," *Adam International Review* 22, nos. 248–49 (1955) 38.

19. Grindea, "The Triumphant Ugly Duckling," 3.

20. Bredsdorff, *Hans Christian Andersen*, 149.

21. Julius Clausen, "H.C. Andersen Abroad and At Home," *American-Scandinavian Review* 18 (1930): 228–34, 229.

22. Bredsdorff, *Hans Christian Andersen*, 150, 286–88.

23. *FT*, 215, and Peter Ostwald, *Schumann* (Boston: Northeastern University Press, 1985), 163–64.

24. Miron Grindea, Editorial Comment, *Adam International Review* 22, no. 248–49 (1955) 2.

25. Bredsdorff, "H.C. Andersen in Britain," 22.

26. Bredsdorff, *Hans Christian Andersen*, 194–95.

27. Ibid., 234.

28. He did give an answer, of sorts, toward the end of his, life when, at sixty-five, he published the long story—or short novel—*Lucky Peer*, a deeply cynical and pessimistic work. There a wise mentor, an Edvard Collin figure, whom Andersen, perhaps in acknowledgment of the loving care he was then receiving from the Melchior family, makes a Jew, tells the spectacularly successful singer and composer Peer: "How young you are, dear friend, that it can please you to be with these people! In a way they are good enough, but they look down on us plain citizens. For some of them it is only a matter of vanity, an amusement, and for others a sort of sign of exclusive culture, when they receive into their circles artists and the lions of the day. These belong in the salon much as the flowers in a vase; they decorate and then they are thrown away" (*The Complete Andersen*, Longer Stories, 373). Lucky Peer, incidentally, is "lucky" not just in his career, but above all because he drops dead at the height of it, being thus spared the many years of decline that Andersen suffered—and from having to ask for the hand of the now willing aristocratic young lady he loved. "Lucky Peer! More fortunate than millions!" (384).

29. In 1837 he wrote to Henriette Hanck: "My name is gradually beginning to shine, and that is the only thing for which I live. I covet honour and glory in the same way the miser covets gold; both are probably empty, but one has to have something to strive for in this world, otherwise one would collapse and rot" (Bredsdorff, *Hans Christian Andersen*, 134). The famous Danish critic, Georg Brandes, wrote in 1869—and Andersen, then sixty-four, must have been smarting when he read it—that "the criticism that can with justice be made of Andersen's 'Story of my Life' is not so much that the author is throughout occupied with his own private affairs (for that is quite natural in such a work); it is that his personality is scarcely ever occupied with anything greater than itself, is never absorbed in an idea, is never entirely free from the ego. The revolution of 1848 in this book affects us as though we heard someone sneeze; we are astonished to be reminded by the sound that there is a world outside of the author" (*Creative Spirits of the Nineteenth Century* [New York: Thomas Y. Crowell, 1923], 40).

30. Brandes, who knew Andersen personally, wrote of him:

> A great man he did become. A man never. It never occurred to him for one
> second of his life that he might for once, in a good cause, attack the mighty
> ... only one fundamental trait, one untiring, all-consuming, all absorbing
> ambition never faltered nor failed for one moment of his long life ... to
> become famous, to be honored and considered, feted and paid homage to! ...
> He writes with amazing frankness: "Only in being admired by all can my soul
> find happiness; the most unimportant person who does not do so has power
> to make me feel despondent!" He trembled before every breath of wind that
> might rend a leaf from his laurel tree.
>
> ("Hans Christian Andersen,"
> *Contemporary Review* 87 [1905]: 640–56, 640–41)

31. There was another, "unserious"—meaning halfhearted—infatuation. Andersen
met the Countess Mathilde Barck, seventeen years of age, in Scania in 1839, and felt
himself "leaning towards" her. He alludes to her in his *Picture Book Without Pictures*: "A
poet whispered a name which he begged the wind not to betray—a count's coronet
sparkles above it, and therefore he did not say it aloud." A correspondence ensued, but by
25 January 1844, he wrote to a friend: "I think you have heard me mention Countess Barck
... one of the most beautiful girls I have seen. Some years ago she made a strong impression
on me. I almost think I could have fallen in love with her, but it did not happen, a poor
poet and a countess—I went away!" (Elias Bredsdorff, "H.C. Andersen og Mathilda
Barck," *Anderseniana*, 1974–77, pp. 137–57).

32. Spink, *Hans Christian Andersen and His World*, 74.

33. A detailed account of Andersen's relationship with Dickens ("A Friendship and its
Dissolution") is given by Elias Bredsdorff "Hares Andersen and Charles Dickens,"
Anglistica, vol. 7 (Copenhagen: Rosenkilde and Bagger, 1956).

34. Quoted from Spink, *Hans Christian Andersen and His World*, 92.

35. Ibid., 94. The italics are Dickens's; but we cannot fail to notice once again the
importance of *boots* (or shoes) in Andersen's scheme of things.

36. He was sixty-two years old before he could be persuaded to buy himself his first
bed. He wrote: "Now I am going to have a house, even a bed, my own *bed*; it terrifies me!
I am being weighed down by furniture, bed and rocking chair, not to mention books and
paintings.... I have had to invest one hundred rix dollars in a bed, and it is going to be my
death-bed, for if it does not last that long, then it isn't worth the money. I wish I were only
twenty, then I'd take my inkpot on my back, two shirts and a pair of socks, put a quill at
my side and go into the wide world" (Bredsdorff, *Hans Christian Andersen*, 251).

37. Andersen, *Der Dichter und die Welt*, 70.

WOLFGANG LEDERER

Andersen's Literary Work

The past chapter has, in barest outline, sketched Andersen's rise to fame; it has not even mentioned that on which his fame was based, nor shall we discuss it in any detail now. But since we are primarily concerned with *The Snow Queen*, it would behoove us to look briefly at Andersen's opus insofar as it comes before or after and thereby assign *The Snow Queen* its proper place in the whole picture.

A surprise immediately awaits us, for surely most American readers are unaware that Andersen wrote anything but fairy tales, or that this unique genre did not begin to occupy him—and tentatively at that—until relatively late in his career.

We are, of course, somewhat prepared for this: we know that his chief passion was the stage, ever since his father put on plays with him before he was eleven years old, and that the most illustrious title, to his mind, was that of a poet. So it is not surprising that his first efforts aimed along those lines.

We already know of several of these early efforts. A "national tragedy," *The Robbers of Wissenberg*, was written when he was barely sixteen. It contained so many errors that, as he says, "there was scarcely a word in it correctly written," and it was returned to him by the director of the Royal Theatre with the notation: "People do not frequently wish to retain works which betray, in so great a degree, a want of elementary knowledge" (*TS*, 59).

From *The Kiss of the Snow Queen: Hans Christian Andersen and Man's Redemption by Woman*. © 1986 by The Regents of the University of California.

27

His second effort, a tragedy entitled *Alfsol*, was again rejected, but it showed enough promise to gain him financial support and entrance to the grammar school already mentioned. His first poem, *The Dying Child*, written during the unhappy days of Slagelse when he was twenty-two, is touching and sad without sentimentality and stands up remarkably well:

> Mother, I am tired, I'll drowse away.
> By your heart I'll find my sleeping place.
> Promise me you'll weep no more today
> For your salt tears burn upon my face.
> Here it's cold, outside the wind is wild ...[1]

His first published work, it was well received.

He had two other minor successes when he was about twenty-four: a whimsical *Walking Tour from Holmen's Canal to the Eastern Point of Amager* (two locations within Copenhagen), and a parody on Schiller, a verse play called *Love on St. Nicholas Tower*. There followed travel pieces, opera libretti, and more poems. When he was twenty-eight, he produced a verse drama, *Agnete and the Merman*, which was such a flop that critics considered him "finished." His despair can be imagined, but he pulled himself together and two years later came out with a more or less autobiographical novel, *The Improvisatore*, which was an immediate success.

He wrote several more novels: two during the ensuing two years, both autobiographical (*O.T.* and *Only a Fiddler*), and three in his later years, finishing the last one when he was sixty-five. None of them, though not without some merit, would have assured him popularity in his lifetime, much less immortality. The last one, *Lucky Peer*, was eventually omitted from the first *Collected Edition* to be brought out in America—which in any case had omitted all his dramatic and lyrical efforts. The public, it appeared, was interested only in his fairy tales, not in his novels and travel books.[2] These are still read in Scandinavian countries,[3] though his operatic libretti, of which he wrote a number, have, to the best of my knowledge, vanished there also. Some of these works, though far from all, were well received in his day, but a good many met a highly critical and derogatory reception—particularly in his own country—and caused him much anguish and many a fit of deep depression.

What saved him from despair while he was alive, and from oblivion after his death, were, of course, the fairy tales. The first batch came out while he was riding high, a month after the successful *Improvisatore*. He called it *Tales Told for Children*, and included in it *The Tinder Box, Little Claus and Big*

Claus, The Princess on the Pea, and *Little Ida's Flowers*. With the exception of the last, they were Danish folktales, retold.[4] Even so, the critics declared them utterly unfit for children, full of violence and immorality, and in bad style at that.[5] The first published review of his first tales ran like this:

> Among Mr. Andersen's tales the first three, "The Tinder Box," "Little Claus and Big Claus," and "The Princess on the Pea," may well amuse children, but they will certainly not have any edifying effect, and your reviewer cannot answer for their being harmless reading. At any rate, no one can possibly contend that a child's sense of propriety is increased by reading about a princess who goes riding off in her sleep on a dog's back to visit a soldier who kisses her, after which she herself, wide awake, tells of this incident as "a curious dream"; or that a child's idea of modesty is increased by reading about a farmer's wife who, while her husband is away, sits down at a table alone with the parish clerk, "and she kept filling up his glass for him, and he kept helping himself to the fish—he was very fond of fish"; or that a child's respect for human life is increased by reading about episodes like that of Big Claus killing his grandmother and of Little Claus killing *him*, told as if it were just a bull being knocked on the head. The tale of the Princess on the Pea strikes the reviewer as being not only indelicate but quite unpardonable, in so far that a child may acquire the false impression that so august a lady must always be terribly sensitive.[6]

Andersen was admonished to stop wasting his time on such unworthy material and indeed he himself seems at first to have been in doubt as to the value of these stories. He was, after all, working almost without precedent. Up to the middle of the seventeenth century children listened to the same stories as the adults, and nothing was tailored especially for them. When the first texts for children appeared, they considered a child "a damned soul who must be saved from perdition by a rigorous pietism. Children were not born to live happily but to die holy and true. Education lay in preparing the soul to meet its maker. The result of this was a crop of seventeenth-century books zealously depicting for children the holy lives and joyous deaths of their little contemporaries."[7] The first book of fantasy especially for children was *Tales of Mother Goose* by Charles Perrault, published in France in 1697 and not in English translation until 1729. It was only the Romantics who began to appreciate folktales and who considered the possibility that children were, by nature, perhaps not all bad.[8] The Brothers Grimm were contemporaries of Andersen's (and he had his typical meeting with them, arranging first to be rejected and then admired), but they merely recorded, in anthropological fashion, orally transmitted folktales. So Andersen was indeed breaking new ground, and he had reason for apprehension.

But he persevered despite the critics and, almost, as if he could not help himself. These stories wanted to be written, wanted out.[9] In that same year of 1835 three more appeared, and from then on he published several stories each year—usually before Christmas—until he was sixty-eight years old. In 1843, when he was thirty-eight, and eight years after he had published the first tales, he wrote in a letter:

> I believe that I have now found out how to write fairy tales! The first ones I wrote were, as you know, mostly old ones I had heard as a child and that I retold and recreated in my own fashion; those that were my very own, such as "The Little Mermaid," "The Storks," "The Daisy," and so on, received, however, the greatest approval and that has given me inspiration! Now I tell stories of my own accord, seize an idea for the adults—and then tell it for children while still keeping in mind the fact that mother and father are often listening too, and they must have a little something for thought.[10]

From now on his little volumes no longer had the title *Fairy Tales Told for Children*, but simply *Fairy Tales*.

They are very uneven in quality, and if one were graphically inclined, one could construct a curve with a steep ascent on one side and a lengthy decline on the other, indicating the quality, or lack thereof, of his output. The steep ascent starts in his thirty-second year with *The Little Mermaid* and *The Emperor's New Clothes*. There follow, during the next eight or nine years, most of the stories we all know and that, all over the Western world and to this day, form an almost obligatory furnishing of any middle-class nursery: *The Steadfast Tin Soldier, The Ugly Duckling, The Fir Tree*, and *The Little Match Girl*. Two others, *The Red Shoes* and *The Snow Queen*, were written when he was forty and in love with Jenny Lind. Some twenty-five other stories written during those years may also be familiar to a good many readers: *The Galoshes of Fortune, The Wild Swans, The Nightingale*,[11] and *The Shepherdess and the Chimneysweep*—among them.

But there followed, after *The Little Match Girl*, some 120 more stories spread over the next twenty-seven years. Most of these would be unknown to

most readers, and many of them are repetitive, pedantic, and uninspired—
some emanating a cloying and not very convincing religiosity,[12] others
driven by a didactic zeal that blights what poetic or literary merit they may
have. However, sparks of beauty, humor, and sheer genius flash in many of
them, and during Andersen's lifetime—a time perhaps more sympathetic to
instructive efforts than ours—even these stories were eagerly welcomed and
read. Or was it that the masterpieces of his "golden years" had so enchanted
the world that he could do no wrong, or at least was easily forgiven?
However that may be, it was the stories that earned him his fame, his place
at the most illustrious dinner tables, his personal and close friendship with
the Danish royal family, and no end of honorary medals and titles and
esoteric memberships. There was even the night when, according to the
prophecy of the wise woman who predicted his great future when he wanted
to leave home, Odense was lit up in his honor: on 6 December 1867, the city
council declared him an honorary citizen of Odense, and at the culmination
of a special school holiday a banquet and a torchlight procession were held
in his honor. The ugly duckling had become a swan indeed!

But as to *The Snow Queen*: where in Andersen's life and work does it
have its place? At the pinnacle, no doubt: not the pinnacle of his honors,
which came late, as it should; but at the pinnacle of his creativity. Not only
is *The Snow Queen* one of his longest stories; it is his most inventive and
inspired.[13] It is also his most profound. The story is the best he could
produce at the height of his faculties and of his craft. It is the most
consummate expression of what he knew and of who he was.

Having reassured ourselves that we are, indeed, dealing with a crucial
work, we shall now proceed and ask: what is it that this masterpiece has to
tell us, not only about the man who wrote it but perhaps about man in
general, about mankind?

NOTES

1. Hans Christian Andersen, *Poems*, trans. Murray Brown (Berkeley, Calif.: Elsinore
Press, 1972), 86.

2. Waldemar Westergaard, ed., *The Andersen-Scudder Letters* (Berkeley: University of
California Press, 1949), xxiii.

3. *A Poet's Bazaar* (1842), about a journey to Turkey; *In Sweden* (1851); *In Spain*
(1863).

4. Paul V. Rubow, "Et vintereventyr," in *Reminiscenser* (Copenhagen: Ejnar
Munksgaard, 1940), points out to what degree all of Andersen's tales are permeated by
motifs common in folktales. But whenever it could be done without stunting the story he
eliminated from them the more cruel and violent features (Sara P. Rodes, "The Wild
Swans," *Anderseniana*, 1951–54, pp. 352–67, 353).

5. Spink, *Hans Christian Andersen and His World*, 53.

6. Bredsdorff, *Hans Christian Andersen*, 123–24.

7. Bettina Hürlimann, *Three Centuries of Children's Books in Europe* (London: Oxford University Press, 1967), xii.

8. Ureaka, "Adult Symbolism in the Literary Fairy Tales of the Late Nineteenth Century," 18–35.

9. Martin Lotz, "The Object World of Hans Christian Andersen," *Scandinavian Psychoanalytic Review* 6 (1983): 3–19, suggests what may have been driving Andersen to write his stories: "He found his own way of identifying with his father by telling fairy tales to children. This was an activity that would remind him of some of the few moments where he had seen his father happy" (13). He was, in other words, wearing his fathers shoes.

10. Grønbech, *Hans Christian Andersen*, 91–92.

11. For a Kleinian interpretation of this story, see Stephen Wilson, "Hans Andersen's *Nightingale*. A Paradigm for the Development of Transference Love," *International Review of Psychoanalysis* 7 (1980): 483–86.

12. W.H. Auden speaks of "the namby-pamby Christianity of some of his heroes" ("Some Notes on Andersen," *Adam International Review* 22, nos. 248–49 [1955]: 12).

13. Ordinarily Andersen rewrote and polished his stories a good deal, and the final product might be quite different from the first draft (Grønbech, *Hans Christian Andersen*, 133); but of *The Snow Queen* he wrote: "It has been sheer joy for me to put on paper my most recent fairy tale, 'The Snow Queen'; it permeated my mind in such a way that it came out dancing over the paper!" (Bredsdorff, *Hans Christian Andersen*, 177). Indeed he had begun writing *The Snow Queen* on 5 December 1844, and it was published in book form on 21 December! (ibid., 353–54)—a speed, not just of writing but of printing and publishing, unheard of in our electronic age.

CELIA CATLETT ANDERSON

Andersen's Heroes and Heroines: Relinquishing the Reward

Hans Christian Andersen's fairy tales have sometimes been described as too adult or too pessimistic for children. For example, May Hill Arbuthnot in her classic *Children and Books*, although praising Andersen as an allegorist, notes that "because of the double meaning, the adult themes, and the sadness of many of these stories, the whole collection is usually not popular with children."[1] P. L. Travers found a "devitalizing element" of nostalgia in the tales.[2] Bruno Bettelheim has commented that the conclusions of some of Andersen's stories are discouraging in that "they do not convey the feeling of consolation characteristic of fairy tales," and Jack Zipes accuses Andersen of teaching lessons in servility to the young.[3] Andersen's tales continue, however to be published, read, discussed, and used as a basis for children's theater, and the most popular of them have an undeniable appeal for children. Furthermore, the most popular tales, such as "The Ugly Duckling," "The Little Mermaid," "The Steadfast Tin Soldier," "The Little Fir Tree," and "The Nightingale," include for the most part, those stories that were original with Andersen. His view of the world, then, the problems he poses and the solutions he offers must touch some nerve in us; there must be something more to them than simple pessimism, more than a servile call to compromise.

Andersen does indeed often deliberately undercut the facile happy

From *Triumphs of the Spirit in Children's Literature*. Edited by Francelia Butler and Richard Rotert. © 1986 by Francelia Butler.

ending that is the trademark of fairy tales, but are his many characters who fail to win a reward defeated in spirit? I would argue that they are not. Take the one that may be, perhaps, saddest of all his protagonists, the little fir tree (or pine tree as Erik Haugaard translates it).[4] The tree fails to appreciate its youth in the forest, is bewildered and frightened during its one glorious evening as a baubled Christmas tree, is exiled to an attic, and there is unable to hold an audience of mice who want to hear stories of "bacon or candle stumps" (232), not of "How Humpty-dumpty Fell Down the Stairs but Won the Princess Anyway" (229). Hauled out into the spring sunlight, the pine tree is forced to recognize that it is a dead thing among the green renewal of the season and achieves its one brief moment of wisdom: "If I only could have been happy while I had a chance to be" (233). Finally the poor tree is burned, sighing its sap away in shots, and "Every time the tree sighed, it thought of a summer day in the forest, or a winter night when the stars are brightest, and it remembered Christmas Eve and Humpty-dumpty: the only fairy tale it had ever heard and knew how to tell. Then it became ashes" (233). The tree dies unfulfilled, yes, but in one sense undefeated. It never loses its vision of the possibility of beauty in the world. Like King Lear, the tree is ennobled by wisdom that comes too late.

When we read this tale to our son, then eight years old, he had tears in his eyes and commented that it was the saddest story he had ever heard. Initially, I judged this as a negative reaction, a rejection of the story, but I was wrong. He returned to the story again and again. Like the small boy who rips the golden star from the tree's branch and pins it to his chest, our son took something shining from the story and, for all I know, wears it to this day.

Of course not all of Andersen's tales end sadly. Even considering only those stories that are not simply retellings of old folktales (and therefore with conventional conclusions), we can find several types of endings. There are some which express religious optimism, and some which reward the hero or heroine with acceptance and love. Stories in the first group are rather self-consciously overlaid with Christianity and conclude optimistically. To mention only one of these, consider "The Old Oak Tree's Last Dream," a story quite different in tone and message from "The Pine Tree." The oak lives three hundred and sixty-five years, many of them as a landmark for sailors. It pities the mayflies and flowers for their short existences, but learns in a death dream of ascension into a joyous heaven that "Nothing has been forgotten, not the tiniest flower or the smallest bird" (548–49). The story concludes

The tree itself lay stretched out on the snow-covered beach. From the ship came the sound of sailors singing a carol about the joyful season, when Christ was born to save mankind and give us eternal life. The sailors were singing of the same dream, the beautiful dream that the old oak tree had dreamed Christmas Eve: the last night of its life. (549)

At least for the believer, this conclusion is more encouraging than that which gives the pine tree only ashes of regret.

Another class of stories in Andersen does include more tangible rewards. In these, the protagonists win acceptance by remaining true to their natures and persisting in some quest or duty. "The Ugly Duckling" comes immediately to mind, but perhaps "The Nightingale" is an even better example. In that tale, the small bird is as plain and dull in plumage at the end as at the beginning, but its ability to remain natural, to sing a spontaneous, honest song finally wins it the respect of the emperor who has been saved by the power of its singing and now realizes the false choice he made in earlier preferring the bejewelled, mechanical bird who can sing only one song. Of all Andersen's stories, this may be the one in which the triumph of spirit over matter is most simply and directly presented.

Love is the ultimate form of acceptance, and the tale "The Snow Queen" most fully elaborates this theme. Bettelheim concedes that this tale belongs among the tales that console.[5] An allegory of reason versus love, "The Snow Queen" is, like all allegories, explicitly symbolic, and this very explicitness makes the story a good choice for analysis.

The childhood paradise of Gerda and Kai is blighted by Kai's growing away from Gerda into a cynical stage of adolescence (symbolized by the splinters of the mirror of reason that have entered his eyes and heart and by the numbing kisses of the Snow Queen who kidnaps him). Gerda, like the sister in Andersen's retold folktale "The Wild Swans," endures much suffering before she is able to restore Kai to his natural state as a warm-hearted, loving person. The story is a classic example of what Marie-Louise von Franz describes as the projection of anima—the suffering, brave woman as a projection of the man's problem with his feminine side. In this case the identification is very appropriately used since Gerda, in bringing about the union of intellect and emotion, is indeed a Sophia-like figure.

The story is one of Andersen's most successful blendings of Christian and folk elements. It contains not only many magical creatures (the Snow Queen herself, a talking raven, and a Finnish white witch), but also a hymn in place of the usual incantation, angels formed from the breath of prayers, and a wise old grandmother who knows both the language of ravens and that of the Bible. After Gerda, through her persistence, reaches the ice castle and frees Kai with her warm tears, the two retrace her steps and finally arrive back at the old grandmother's apartment. Andersen tells us that "as they stepped through the doorway they realized that they had grown: they were no longer children" (261). But the grandmother is reading "Whosoever shall not receive the Kingdom of Heaven as a little child shall not enter therein" (261). Kai and Gerda understand the lesson and "There they sat, the two of them grownups; and yet in their hearts children; and it was summer: a warm glorious summer day!" (261). In choosing that particular text from the New Testament, Andersen voices a central theme shared by Christian theologians and writers for children. For the child, and for all of us, the test of spirit is to grow into intellectual wisdom without losing the capacity for emotion, for love.

Certainly this is a central theme with Andersen himself. Elizabeth Cook holds that "two of his strongest themes are the plight of the outsider, and the primacy of Love over Reason."[6] We see these ideas combined in two tales where the endings are unhappy and love must be its own reward. In both "The Little Mermaid" and "The Steadfast Tin Soldier" the main characters persist and suffer and do not win. These stories, along with "The Pine Tree," "The Little Match Girl," and that very complex Andersen tale "The Shadow," are probably most responsible for the author's reputation for pessimism. The mermaid is promised eternal life at the last minute, but in this story the Christian promise is not as successfully woven into the plot as it is in some others (the tale always seems to me to end with the mermaid's dissolution into foam). Are these stories, then, about the defeat of the spirit? As I said earlier, I think not. Neither the mermaid nor the tin soldier turn aside from their goal, nor do they become bitter or vengeful. Through many trials they continue to be humane and loving. Many of Andersen's heroes and heroines, though they suffer greatly, remain true to their ideals. If not rewarded, neither are they defeated. And the true triumph of the spirit, after all, consists not in winning the prince or princess, the kingdom or riches, or even immortality, but in being worthy of the winning.

Much that is written for and about children springs from the premise that the young need the hope and encouragement provided by the success of the heroin the stories presented to them, and that they cannot cope with models of failure. This may be true for certain ages and types, but it is in many cases a condescending and even dishonest attitude. Hope can help develop a child, but false hope can absolutely devastate. Hans Christian Andersen knew that when Humpty-dumpty fell, he didn't win the princess anyway and that a storyteller who claims he did is a liar and, further, that an innocent, like the foolish pine tree, who believes the lie will reap much unhappiness.

The child who comes to Andersen for spiritual sustenance will learn that we must both test our dreams and be tested by them and that in this world some bright dreams have gray awakenings. Will this harm or strengthen a child? I think it strengthened our own children, that our son drank courage, not despair, from the tears he shed over the story of the pine tree. In Andersen's tale "The Pixy and the Grocer" the pixy peeks through the keyhole and sees the turbulent visions that the poor student enjoys while sitting under the magic tree of poetry. Before such splendor, the pixy "experienced greatness.... He cried without knowing why he cried, but found that in those tears happiness was hidden" (426). So art redeems us; as Tolkien put it so well in his famous essay on children and fairy stories, "It is one of the lessons of fairy stories (if we can speak of the lessons of things that do not lecture) that on callow, lumpish, and selfish youth peril, sorrow, and the shadow of death can bestow dignity and even sometimes wisdom."[7] Hans Christian Andersen gives us in his stories "peril, sorrow, and the shadow of death" but also "dignity" and "wisdom."

NOTES

1. May Hill Arbuthnot and Zena Sutherland, *Children and Books*, 4th ed. (Glenview, Ill.: Scott, Foresman, 1972), 313.

2. P.L. Travers, "Only Connect," *Quarterly Journal of Acquisitions of the Library of Congress* (October 1967); repr. in *Only Connect: Readings on Children's Literature*, ed. Sheila Egoff, G. T. Stubbs, and L. F. Ashley (New York: Oxford University Press, 1969), p. 198.

3. Bruno Bettelheim, *The Uses of Enchantment: The Meaning and Importance of Fairy Tales* (New York: Knopf, 1976), 37; Jack Zipes, *Fairy Tales and the Art of Subversion: The Classical Genre for Children and the Process of Civilization* (New York: Wildman Press, 1983), 94.

4. Hans Christian Andersen, *The Complete Fairy Tales and Stories*, trans. Erik Haugaard (Garden City, N.Y.: Doubleday, 1983). Page numbers for quotes from this edition are given in the text.

5. Bettelheim, *Uses of Enchantment*, 37.

6. Elizabeth Cook, *The Ordinary and the Fabulous: An Introduction to Myths, Legends, and Fairy Tales for Teachers and Storytellers* (London: Cambridge University Press, 1971), 43.

7. J.R.R. Tolkien, "Children and Fairy Stories," from *Tree and Leaf*, in Sheila Egoff, G.T. Stubbs, and L.F. Ashley, *Only Connect*, New York: Oxford University Press, 1969, p. 120.

JON CECH

Hans Christian Andersen's Fairy Tales and Stories: Secrets, Swans and Shadows

Among the 156 "tales and stories" that Hans Christian Andersen wrote between 1835 and 1872, a dozen or so are among the best-known, most frequently anthologized and reprinted retellings of fairy tales or literary fairy tales of any canon. Indeed, such stories as "The Ugly Duckling," "The Princess and the Pea," and "The Emperor's New Clothes" have been retold so often, and in so many different forms, that they have become part of the public domain of our oral folk tradition. Bo Grønbech claims that Anderson's tales have been translated into over a hundred languages; only the Bible and Shakespeare have been translated into more. Not long after the appearance of the first of Andersen's tales, one of his friends had quipped that Andersen's novels and plays might make him famous in Denmark, but his fairy tales would make him immortal. The friend's intuitive pronouncement has not been far off the mark.

This enormous success could not have been more unlikely, more unexpected than it was for Andersen, the son of a poor washerwoman and a melancholy cobbler from the Danish coastal town of Odense. When the fourteen-year-old Andersen left for Copenhagen in 1819, with thirteen thalers in his pocket and without an education, a trade or prospects, only two people in the world believed he would ever amount to anything: the local fortune-teller and Andersen himself. In *The Fairy Tale of My Life*, Andersen

From *Touchstones: Reflections on the Best in Children's Literature, Volume Two: Fairy Tales, fables, Myths, Legends, and Poetry*. © 1985 by the Children's Literature Association.

tells how, in her anxiety, his mother had consulted this "wise old woman," who had, after reading her cards and Andersen's coffee grounds, reassured her with the now famous prediction: "Your son will become a great man, and in honor of him Odense will one day be illuminated" (22). Andersen begged his mother to let him go to Copenhagen to seek his fortune there; he had dreamed that something wonderful would happen to him. "First one has to endure terrible adversity," he told his mother. "Then one becomes famous" (Stirling 53).

And suffer he had and did. The facts are well-documented in the numerous biographies of Andersen and in his diaries and *The Fairy Tale of My Life*, the autobiography which he revised frequently during his life. The grinding poverty of his childhood and youth, the desperate, depressing struggle for this lad from the wrong social class to climb the ladder of literary success, the unhappiness in his romantic life, the restless travelling, the hysteric phobias (of rabies, hotel fires, or being accidentally thought dead while asleep and buried alive), the "black" moods that swept over him—all are revealed by his biographers and more often than not by Andersen himself. He was, he informs us, the ugly duckling, the lowest in the town's pecking order—awkward, painfully sensitive, vulnerable—the brunt of crude jokes and coarse criticism. Famous as he later became, he never quite got over those early traumas, or the later scars. But they became the fuel of his fantasies and the substance of his stories. Reginald Spink quotes Andersen's own words to support that idea: "Most of what I have written is a reflection of myself. Every character is from life. I know and have known them all" (70). Spink observes:

> Andersen never stopped telling his own story; that was the way he abreacted. Sometimes he tells it in an idealized form, sometimes with self-revelatory candour. In tale after tale—"The Tinder Box," "Little Claus and Big Claus," "The Steadfast Tin Soldier," "The Swineherd," "The Ugly Duckling"—he is the hero who triumphs over poverty, persecution, and plain stupidity, and who sometimes, in reversal of the facts, marries the princess ("Clodpoll") or scorns her ("The Swineherd"). (100)

For Andersen, the creative process was an act of remembering, of stating and then transforming biographical facts in order to somehow exorcise the demons that haunted him, those shadows that never quite stopped threatening to take over the poet and his identity.

But there are lives and there are lives. Not every *roman à clef* becomes a best-seller, let alone a classic; and not every reified life experience succeeds as a work of literature. In many of his fairy tales and stories, Andersen offered his readers a theme and its variations which was not only personal to him, but also had and continues to have a universal appeal: the rags-to-riches, duckling-to-swan theme. Every swineherd or common soldier is a potential prince, and every ugly duckling a swan, if they are true to their own good, decent nature. This idea, which appears with such frequency in Andersen's works, creates an immediate bond of identification and sympathy between Andersen and his readers, especially his younger readers who, like numerous heroes and heroines in Andersen, are struggling and are desperately in need of stories that frame the chaotic and conflicting emotions of this experience. In his tales Andersen is the champion of the underdogs, the downtrodden, the spurned, the impoverished—in short, those with every reason to hope for whatever transformations will lead to a better life.

Of course, this sense of hope, of a brighter and ultimately happy future (if one perseveres and remains good and kind in the process of enduring) is at the very core of the traditional fairy tale, as Bruno Bettelheim has pointed out in *The Uses of Enchantment*. Andersen had drawn his inspiration and the vehicle for expressing this theme from the traditional fairy tales that, he tells us in the notes he wrote to accompany his stories, he "had heard as a child, either in the spinning room or during the harvesting of the hops" (1071). Unlike other Romantic artists who also used the form and subject matter of the folk fairy tale, Andersen did not have to learn about his material second hand through study or from collecting trips in the countryside. He was steeped in its traditions; the world of the fairy tale "was his own world and had been so since birth" (Grønbech 95). This oral/aural sense of story, he felt, was important to capture, and he tried to do this, beginning with his first volume of stories which appeared in 1835. Of the four stories in this volume ("The Tinder Box," "Little Claus and Big Claus," "The Princess and the Pea," and "Little Ida's Flowers"), only the last was an original creation. The others were based on tales from the oral tradition, but elaborated upon in Andersen's inimitable style. His life-long friend, Edvard Collin, remembers how Andersen, during visits to his house, would tell the Collin children

> stories which he partly made up on the spur of the moment, partly borrowed from well-known fairy tales; but whether the tale was his own or a retelling, the manner of telling it was entirely his own, and so full of life that the children were delighted. He, too, took delight in letting his humor run free. He spoke continually with plenty of phrases that children used, and gestures to match.

Even the driest of sentences was given life. He didn't say, "The children got into the carriage and then drove away," but, "So they got into the carriage, good-bye Daddy, good-bye Mummy, the whip cracked, snick, snack, and away they went, giddy up!" People who later heard him reading aloud his tales would only be able to form a faint impression of the extraordinary vitality with which he told them to children.

(Grønbech 89)

We hear this surging verbal energy in the swaggering first paragraph of Andersen's first published fairy tale—"The Tinderbox":

A soldier came marching down the road: Left... right! Left... right! He had a pack on his back and a sword at his side. He had been in the war and he was on his way home. Along the road he met a witch. She was a disgusting sight, with a lower lip that hung all the way down her chest.

Andersen wrote to a friend as he was finishing this first collection, which he called *Fairy Tales for Children*, to explain what he was doing: "I want to win the next generations, you see!" (Grønbech 89). But by 1843, he had changed the title of those little volumes, containing three or four stories each, to *Fairy Tales*; and, within another ten years, they became, simply, *Stories*. But it had not taken Andersen twenty years before he "found out how to write fairy tales." Within a few years of beginning the stories, he wrote to a friend to say: "Now I tell stories of my own accord, seize an idea for the adults—and then tell it for the children while still keeping in mind the fact that mother and father are often listening too, and they must have a little something for thought" (Grønbech 91–2).

We see Andersen's concern with reaching the adult listening to (or reading the tale) throughout the fairy tales and stories. Andersen can't resist such an "adult" touch in "The Ugly Duckling," for example, when an old duck comes to call on the mother duck who has just hatched out her brood (except for the ugly duckling's egg). She brags to her guest that each of the new ducklings "looks exactly like their father." But then she quickly adds: "That scoundrel hasn't come to visit me once" (217). In "The Nightingale," after the bird has been summoned to the emperor's palace and has made the monarch weep with his music, Andersen, with his tongue in his cheek, describes the trickle-down effects of the concert:

"That was the most charming and elegant song we have ever heard," said all the ladies of the court. And from that time onward they filled their mouths with water, so they could make a clucking noise, whenever anyone spoke to them, because they thought that then they sounded like the nightingale. Even the chambermaids and the lackeys were satisfied; and that really meant something, for servants are the most difficult to please. Yes, the nightingale was a success. (207)

But there is more than just "a little something for thought" for the adults in many of the stories that Andersen began to include in these collections. Take, for instance, "The Sweethearts," a tale about a wooden top and the leather ball with which he is in love. She rejects his attentions, telling him that "mother and father were a pair of morocco slippers, and ... I have a cork inside me." The ball gets lost on her ninth bounce, but the top, still very much in love with her, stays on as a favored plaything in the house, eventually getting rewarded with a coat of gold paint. Years later when he, too, is lost one day, he winds up in the same trash can as the ball. Her years of exposure have left her unrecognizable, but she proudly announces herself as before. At that moment the maid finds the top and retrieves him from the trash, never noticing the ball. And Andersen leaves the reader with the biting (and male chauvinist) commentary about life and love: "You get over it when your beloved has lain in a gutter and oozed for five years. You never recognize her when you meet her in the garbage bin" (215).

Similarly, stories like "The Shadow," have pushed beyond the boundaries of the literary fairy tale to become psychological fantasies directed toward an older reader. This story, one of Andersen's darkest and most enigmatic, examines what happens when a young scholar, an intellectual, sends his shadow across the street to the house of a beautiful woman, who turns out to be Poetry, while he himself remains aloof and detached, engrossed in his philosophical treatises and reveries on the other side of the street. Years pass, the scholar travels and writes, and the shadow, meanwhile, takes on a human form and a life of its own, becoming richly successful because it can peep into mankind's deepest secrets and because "he knew how to tell about some of what he had seen and how to hint at the rest, which was even more impressive" (342). Through an ironic reversal of events befitting a writer like Kafka, the philosopher becomes the shadow's shadow; the shadow goes on to marry the princess, and the philosopher, in the closing lines of the story, is executed. As the shadow has told the philosopher when he objects to the absurdity of becoming the shadow's servant, "that's the way of the world, and it isn't going to change" (341).

Andersen was criticized for writing such pessimistic and unfamiliar tales—such "philosophical" stories. He responded to his critics in the notes to his collected stories by arguing that "through the years ... (he) tried to walk every radius, so to speak, in the circle of the fairy tale." The problem lay, Andersen felt, with some of those who had grown up with his earlier stories and thus expected a particular kind of tale from him. Somehow they had "lost the fresh spirit with which they once approached and absorbed literature (1087). To an extent, that is still true today. The popular notion of Andersen is that he is a writer or adapter of fairly traditional fairy tales; he has yet to receive the recognition he deserves as one of the pioneers and important innovators not only in the form of the literary fairy tale, but also in the forms of fantasy (what Andersen collectively referred to as the "wonder tale"). Tales like "The Millennium" (which begins: "They will home on wings of steam, the young citizens of America will fly through the air, across the great ocean, to visit old Europe.") are at the threshold of science fiction. "Auntie Toothache," the last story that Andersen wrote, is a grotesquely absurd visit to a nineteenth century Twilight Zone, where a young poet is visited in his dream by the archetypal spirit of tooth problems. Andersen serves up the malaise to us in the form of an aunt who, in the waking world, has over-indulged the poet with sweets and with encouragement to keep writing his sentimental verse. In the young man's nightmare, though, "Auntie Toothache" treats him to an "Ode to Pain" on his wisdom teeth and forces him to admit that her power is "greater than poetry, mathematics, philosophy, and all the rest of the music ... stronger and more penetrating than all other feeling that has been painted on canvas or carved in marble ... older than all the others ... born right outside the gates of paradise, where the wet winds blow and the toadstools grow" (1066). She leaves only when the poet, in a dental delirium, agrees to stop writing verse forever. Andersen wrote this sardonically witty story when he returned to Odense in December of 1867 to be made an honorary citizen of the town—the highest accolade that his neighbors could bestow on him—and to be feted at an evening banquet when, as the gypsy had predicted, the city would be illuminated to celebrate his accomplishments. On the day of the festivities, Andersen was suffering from an excruciating toothache, the victim of one of life's supreme poetic injustices. But as so often happened with Andersen, he transformed that bitter experience immediately into art.

Almost as often as Andersen allows his characters to triumph, it seems, he offers stories in which fortunes are frustrated (as above), love is unrequited, or at the farthest extreme, lives are lost. There are too many dead or dying children in Andersen to suit many modern tastes (see "The Mother," "The Little Match Girl," and "The Angel"), and too many lovers who don't attain their heart's desire and are left in a kind of emotional limbo. Perhaps the most famous of these impossible loves is that of "The Little Mermaid," whose sacrifices for the prince go unnoticed and unrewarded, and who is left, despite the objections of generations of readers and all the logical and emotional directions of the story, without the "love of a human being," "an immortal soul," and thus without a way to "God's kingdom"—at least not until she serves a three hundred year penance with the other "children of the air." But after condemning her, Andersen offers a kind of reprieve:

> "You may be able to go there before that," whispered one of the others to her. "Invisibly, we fly through the homes of human beings. They can't see us, so they don't know when we are there; but if we find a good child, who makes his parents happy and deserves their love, we smile and God takes a year away from the time of our trial. But if there is a naughty and mean child in the house we come to, we cry; and for every tear we shed, God adds a day to the three hundred years we already must serve. (76)

This was not one of Andersen's better endings, and readers have often objected to its heavy-handed manipulation.

A similarly dispiriting story is "The Little Fir Tree," often considered to be one of Andersen's most autobiographical fables. In this story Andersen creates a character (the little tree) who wants, in a sense, what every person— certainly every child wants—"to grow, to grow ... to become tall and old; there's nothing in the world so marvelous" (226). And when it hears from the sparrows in the forest about Christmas and the special place of the tree in the festivities, it can't wait to be carted away to be decorated, even though the wind and the sunshine advise it to set aside these desires and "be happy with us ... be glad you are young; enjoy your youth and your freedom, here in nature (227). Of course the tree is chosen the next year, plays its rather terrifying role in the celebration, and then is quickly removed to the attic, where it is stored for the winter. There it whiles away the days telling a story it heard on Christmas Eve to the mice who come to stay the winter in the house. But unlike the main character in the tree's story (ironically titled "How Humpty-dumpty Fell Down the Stairs but Won the Princess Anyway"), there is no ultimate triumph or happy ending for the little tree. As it is being consumed on a spring-cleaning bonfire, it thinks "of a summer day in the forest, or a winter night when stars are brightest, and it remembered Christmas Eve and Humpty-dumpty: the only fairy tale it had ever heard and knew how to tell. Then it became ashes" (233).

Andersen is commenting here on the vain, fleeting nature of fame, in contrast to the stability of an existence that is more accepting, modest, and rooted—a lesson he was having to deal with in his own rather itinerant, unsettled life, and in terms of the ups and downs of his literary fortunes, which often sent him into tantrums or depressions. He is clearly trying to tell another kind of "fairy tale"—one that expressed the other, dark side of his artistic vision. This pessimistic bleakness in Andersen, which sometimes seems so cruelly moralistic (as it does, say, in "The Red Shoes") seems out of keeping with the sympathy that Andersen is so intent on creating for many of the other protagonists in his tales.

There are other contradictions, problems, and ambiguities in Andersen's work. One doesn't always know, for instance, why Andersen ridicules the pomposity and pretentions of the aristocracy on one page and then forgives them on the next. In "The Nightingale," Andersen satirizes the ways of the Emperor of China's court and the Emperor's own shallow willingness to settle for the artificial nightingale's song. The nightingale, who is really the figure of the poet and the perceptive proletarian center of the story, tells the Emperor at the end: "I love your heart more than your crown." But then it adds: "... and yet I feel that the crown has a fragrance of something holy about it" (211). One explanation for this waffling is that Andersen himself was a son of the working class who aspired to be and ultimately became the darling of the salons and courts of Europe. In a sense, he was living the contradiction that he wrote about. These and other problematic contradictions arise throughout Andersen's stories to baffle or puzzle the reader because Andersen seems frequently less interested in maintaining a consistent point of view or tone than in letting loose mercurial impressions and almost free associations.

What, then, makes Andersen's tales "classics"? Why should they be considered "touchstones"? A very obvious reason is that many of Andersen's tales continue to be read, and to affect those who read them deeply. Regardless of how we might react to them individually, many of his stories are passed from generation to generation, through edition after edition, becoming household names and a part of our universal, literary vocabulary. Ursula Le Guin speaks for many when she writes that she "hated all the Andersen stories with unhappy endings. That didn't stop me from reading them, and rereading them. Or from remembering them" (104).

The secret to this success lies, perhaps, in the fact that Andersen was connecting with exactly that in his readers—secrets. On one level, Andersen was tapping the secret, emotional realms of his own troubled experience, often writing from his own despair out of what Keats might have called "negative capability." But Andersen succeeded in projecting these incidents onto a larger, more public screen, through forms and symbols ostensibly reserved for children but which Andersen was keenly aware would usually be introduced to children by adults. Ultimately, Andersen meant his stories to be for everyone, and to deal with the secrets that all of us keep in common but are unable or unwilling to tell. Etymologically speaking, the words for "secret" and "sacred" share the same Germanic roots: what is secret is also personally sacred to us, from those deepest yearnings to the most petty jealousies and vanities.

On the one hand, there is Andersen's composite hero, the duckling/swan, swineherd/prince, nightingale/poet, soldier/king. He frequently must undergo great suffering and trials but nevertheless remains steadfast and true to his principles and, thus, to his own inner nature and its humanity. This is the duckling's way, and the tin soldier's, and little Gerda's in "The Snow Queen." Andersen is able to touch those chords of sympathy within his readers because, on some fundamental level, they, too, have shared these feelings and have hoped for the same optimistic resolution. Often this character is flawed, wounded, incomplete, but through his perseverance, kindness, and love he compensates for these inadequacies and becomes whole, metaphorically if not literally. At times this character is a poet, like the nightingale, whose songs "sing not only of those who are happy but also of those who suffer ... of the good and of the evil that happen around you, and yet are hidden from you" (211). Sometimes she is disguised as a little child, whose stalwart love can melt the icy heart of her friend, a captive in the Snow Queen's palace. But whoever he or she is, this persona with dozens of faces expresses those profoundly human desires to love and be loved, and to seek a way to fulfill those feelings.

On the other hand, Andersen also explores those other, darker reaches of the psyche that we do not like to admit exist within ourselves. These shadowy realms appear in many of the tales, and they are Andersen's way of dealing with the dark side of his own soul. At its grimmest, in such tales as "The Shadow," Andersen is wrestling with the need for the artist to be aware of the nether reaches of the psyche, even if these shadows may contain evil. To repress, to deny, to not confront these forces, as Ursula Le Guin argues, is to be ultimately ruled by them, to become their victim as an artist and as a human being.

> "For the shadow," Le Guin insists, is not simply evil. It is inferior, primitive, awkward, animal-like, childlike; powerful, vital, spontaneous. It's not weak and decent, like the learned young

man from the north (in "The Shadow"); it's dark and hairy and unseemly; but, without it, the person is nothing. What is a body that casts no shadow? Nothing, a formlessness, two-dimensional, a comic-strip character. The person who denies his own profound relationship with evil denies his own reality. He cannot do, or make; he can only undo, unmake. (107)

Yet there is another dimension to Andersen's exploration of the shadow: humor. A finely tuned sense of humor gives many of Andersen's stories a vitality that holds them from the abyss of bitter gloom, despair or unrelieved seriousness. Andersen's humor can be very dark indeed, as in "A Drop of Water," where he has his main characters, who are looking through a magnifying glass at a miniature but surprisingly vicious city they have discovered there, try to decide whether or not they are observing a microcosm of "Copenhagen or some other big city" or just plain "ditch water." In "Big Claus and Little Claus" the humor is deliciously macabre, when Big Claus ironically ties himself up in what will become his own shroud and violently demands that Little Claus push him into the river. In "The Tinder Box" Andersen's humor is suggestively risqué: when the soldier has the magic dog fetch the sleeping princess for him, he cannot resist kissing her, for "he was a soldier all over."

Finally, in "The Emperor's New Clothes," Andersen provides us with the kind of humor that manages to touch everyone's pet vanities. No one knew better than Andersen about the serious side of this kind of public embarrassment; he had felt it keenly since he was an awkward child walking down the center aisle of the church in the squeaky new boots of which he was so proud. This particular story—one of Andersen's most famous—was also rooted in the facts of the writer's life. Haugaard retells the incident from Andersen's diaries:

> A foreign artist arrived in Copenhagen and announced in the newspapers that he had come to paint portraits of the most famous Danes, and he hoped that these great personages would come to the studio he had just rented. The very next morning who should appear at his door but Andersen and one of the actors from the Royal Theatre, a man known for his self-love and conceit. Andersen looked at the actor and could not help laughing, both at him and at himself. (74)

"To write the Emperor's New Clothes," Haugaard goes on, "one must be able to be as foolish as the emperor—although I admit that it is more important to be as wise as the child who saw that he was naked. But only the genius can be both at the same time and, therefore, be able to write the story."

P.M. Pickard writes that Andersen used "so much courage in displaying so much vulnerability" (78). This struggle of opposing elements within Andersen is at the paradoxical heart of his works—as it evidently was in his life. Throughout his works, Andersen tried to preserve a precarious balance between competing sides of his nature: the courtly and the colloquial, the exalted and the mundane, the realistic and the Romantic, the conservative and the iconoclast, the hopeful and the pessimistic. These and other dramatic oppositions give Andersen's stories their rich complexity and expressive range. Andersen took real emotional and artistic chances in his tales "for everyone." Because he did, Andersen was instrumental in creating a children's literature that could become a vehicle for carrying both traditional messages and values as well as an author's personal visions. Andersen wrote, as Keats puts it, "on the pulses," casting light on the shadows, telling his own, and our own, secrets, giving them a song and wings.

REFERENCES

Andersen, Hans Christian. *The Complete Fairy Tales and Stories.* Trans. Erik Christian Haugaard. New York: Doubleday, 1974

———. *The Fairy Tale of My Life.* 1868; rpr. New York: Paddington Press, 1975.

Grønbech, Bo. *Hans Christian Andersen.* Boston: Twayne, 1982.

Haugaard, Erik Christian. "Portrait of a Poet: Hans Christian Andersen." *The Open-Hearted Audience: Ten Writers Talk about Writing for Children.* Ed. Virginia Haviland. Washington: Library of Congress, 1980.

Le Guin, Ursula. "The Child and the Shadow." *The Open-Hearted Audience.*

Pickard, P.M. *I Could a Tale Unfold: Violence, Horror and Sensationalism in Stories for Children.* New York: The Humanities Press, 1961.

Spink, Reginald. *Hans Christian Andersen and His World.* New York: G.P. Putnam's, 1972.

Stirling, Monica. *The Wild Swan: The Life and Times of Hans Christian Andersen.* New York: Harcourt, Brace and World, 1965.

KARIN SANDERS

Nemesis of Mimesis:
The Problem of Representation in
H.C. Andersen's Psychen[1]

"Pip! Det er det Skønne!"[2]

During his impressionable first visit to Rome in 1833–1834, Hans Christian Andersen observed the digging of a grave for a young nun who had just died. In the grave a statue of *Bacchus* was unearthed. Nearly thirty years later, in 1861, this memory was transformed or "translated" to *Psychen*. The "translation" of *Bacchus* to *Psyche* seems to have caused the author considerable problems but manages nonetheless to raise some significant questions concerning the nature of art and immortality, of mimesis and (gender) identity. The conspicuous disparity between Psyche, Greek Goddess of the spirit, and Bacchus, Roman God of wine, invites the reader to look behind the obvious representations in order to examine other meanings hidden in the written image.

Sculpture as metaphor here grants a possibility to analyze how a figural image, as a textual device *different* from that of a written text, plays a significant role in the understanding of a written narrative.[3] How does this "alien object" infuse qualities into the writing, enhancing the intentions of the text as well as eventually puncturing it. I hope to demonstrate how this "textual conflict" may subvert any easy understanding of gender markings.

Psychen takes place in Rome at a time when "konsten var erkjendt,

From *Scandinavian Studies*, vol. 64, no. 1 (Winter 1992). © 1992 by the Society for the Advancement of Scandinavian Study.

hædret og lønnet" (art was acknowledged, honored, and rewarded)[4] during the reign of the Renaissance masters Raphael and Michelangelo. A young, poor, and idealistic artist lives in an old temple pursuing his art in a desperate attempt for perfection. He avoids the temptations of the sensual night life of Rome and isolates himself from his fellow artist friends. One day the sight of a young woman empowers and inspires him to create a masterpiece of sculpture called *Psyche*. Rumor of the splendid statue eventually reaches the young woman and her father. They come to the artist's studio, and the father, a nobleman, immediately recognizes his daughter's image in the artist's creation and places an order for the statue to be done in marble. When the statue is finished, the artist goes to the man's palace, meets the young woman, forgets himself, and passionately declares his love for her. She violently rejects him, and in despair he joins his friends for a sinful night. Unable to face the statue after his "defilement," he lowers it into the ground, burying it in a dried-up well. Eventually, the artist joins a monastery and dies—still full of torment, religion having offered no solution. Following the customs of the monastery, his skeleton is put on display, decaying until only his skull remains. The skull is eventually disintegrated by a lizard who runs in and out of the empty eye sockets. Centuries later a young nun is buried outside a nunnery built on top of the artist's temple. While the grave is being dug, the statue of Psyche is exhumed, then admired as an anonymous masterpiece from the past.

II

At one level, the statue may be seen as a representation of the young noble woman—as a transformation, in the text, of the woman's body into an artistic form, of person into *objet d'art*. This is an obvious aspect of the text. However, a closer look at the story challenges the obvious and offers a possibility of investigating the problem of *re*-presentation itself. In order to understand this challenge, we need to take a look at other representational figures suggested implicitly by the text and then move on to the question: how is representation represented?

Although Psyche is the only explicit mythological figure in the story, the text is saturated with implicit mythological references that overlap and often are entangled in each other. Perhaps the most obvious is that of the young artist as a Pygmalion figure. Like Pygmalion, the young artist shuns the real women around him. Like Pygmalion, he creates his "dream woman." And even more important, like Pygmalion who creates his statue from an already-engraved image depicting Aphrodite, the artist creates his statue from an already-existing painting by Raphael named "Psyche." Although it was the sight of the young noble woman that inspired the artist's creation, he immediately recognized her as an image *already* represented:

> [...] *saaledes havde han ingen Qvinde seet, jo! malet af Raphael, malet som Psyche, i et af Roms Paladser. Ja, der var hun malet, hergik hun levende.* (106)

> (He had never seen such a woman before. Yes—painted by Raphael, painted as Psyche, in one of the palaces of Rome. Yes—there she was painted, here she walked alive.)

Psyche is literally described as a phantasmagoric picture that has stepped out of the frame, and now is wandering free. When the artist makes his representation of her and names it after the painting of Raphael, he then—like Pygmalion—creates an image of an image.[5] He implants her in a transhistoric tradition of Psyche representations—thus putting her back in the "frame," *his* frame, or rather his embracing framing. The young woman is, in other words, perceived through a filter of multiple previous images. The lens through which she is seen is adjusted towards a particular system of perception; she is seen through the veil of Psyche. His "inner eye," to paraphrase Wordsworth, "had seen such sights before."[6] It is this veil, this presumed obstacle to seeing clearly, that becomes a vital part of the constructs and problems of visuality in the story.

Not unlike Pygmalion, the young artist wishes to merge the representation of Psyche, his "dream woman," with the young woman he saw, hereby symbolically giving it life. In this case the attempted "life-giving" process takes place through an apparent symbolic exchange, in which the statue serves as an exchangeable object between the father and the artist. The sublimity of the representation of his daughter causes the father (who "owns" the girl) not only to provide the money to form her in marble but also to grant the artist access to the "real thing." Our artist does not succeed in taking advantage of this unique possibility, however. A closer reading of the text gives us a clue as to why. When the father and daughter come to see the statue it is the father, not the daughter, who recognizes the woman in the statue.

> *Den unge Pige selv stod her i Stuen og med hvilket Smiil, da hendes Fader, sagde de Ord: "Det er jo Dig lyslevende." Det Smiil kan ikke*

formes, det Blik kan ikke gjengives, det forunderlige Blik, hvormed hun saa paa den unge Kunstner. (106)

(The young girl herself stood there in the room, and what a smile when her father said these words: "But it is you completely." That smile can not be molded, that gaze can not be reproduced, that peculiar gaze, with which she looked at the young artist.)

As this passage clearly shows, her smile evades molding and her gaze cannot be copied. It is precisely not she herself, who is copied. It is an image of an image, not a direct image of the girl. In fact, when the artist confronts the girl in the palace, she is not Psyche-like at all. Quite the contrary.

"Afsindige," sagde hun, "Bort, ned" og hun vendte ham Ryggen. Skjanhedsansigtet havde et udtryk af hiint forsten ende Ansigt med Slangehå René. (109)

("Madman," she said. "Begone, down" and she turned her back to him. The face of beauty had a resemblance of that petrifying face with serpent hair.)

Thus the artist has made a terrible blunder which leaves a significant fissure in his project. When he, with his "blinded" vision, thought he saw a young Psyche, he now—still "blinded"—thinks he sees another vision: a Medusa. His "blinded" vision never allows him to see her as anything but his own projection. The perilous metamorphosis of the young Psyche into a Medusa prompts an outburst of repressed sexuality in our virtuous protagonist, described in a characteristically Andersenian manner as an orgasmic eruption of a volcanic crater overflowing with burning lava. This desire ultimately throws him into the sinful night and eventually destroys him, as he cannot rid himself of his secret, this "Slange" (serpent). In the passionate night he "sins" with women from the Campagna, who, as the artist's friend claims, are equal to the beloved marble-woman since "Begge ere Evadøttre" (Both are daughters of Eve). These alluring women too are re-presented in art. Not in erect, white marble, but in flat, colorful paintings ("glødende, yppige Billeder"; glowing, voluptuous pictures). These paintings are spread upon the floor of the artist's friend's studio—they can be "stepped on."[7]

The virtue of the artist is intact as long as he believes in the power of his beautiful creation. It is the aesthetic experience of beauty that seems to support his morale and distinguishes him from the sybaritic others. When the gaze of the woman-as-Medusa takes away this innocence in the artist, it is not only his purity that is violated, but his entire belief in pure art. The "unveiling" of the imaginary Psyche woman reveals an evil "truth" (the cruel Medusa face) that immediately must be "reveiled" (the cloth-veil and the well-as-veil) to sustain (although seemingly in vain) the illusion of ideality. When his passionate words confront the woman and provoke her fury: "Væk, ned" (Begone, down), it is evident that his project is doomed. "Der fløj Ord fra hans Tunge, han vidste det ikke selv; ved Krateret at det kaster glødende Lava" [109] (Words flow from his tongue, he did not know it, does the crater know that it expels glowing lava). It is at this point in the narrative we understand that the artist is not only seeking the imaginary, he is reaching for the real: the impossible. The self-absorbed artist does not understand that in order to preserve the potency of the spectacle of the young woman, it must remain a spectacle—that it is strictly limited to his gaze.

Like the gaze of Medusa, the gaze of the young woman is petrifying, and we may assume that, as in the myth of Medusa, it is not only her gaze that petrifies but the mere *sight* of her.[8] The sight that inspired the artist to create his masterpiece is thus the same sight that ultimately destroys him. The seductive sight turns out to be a paralyzing demonic eye: a deadly eye, a mythological gorgonian gaze. His desiring gaze has been turned back at himself in a spiteful and vengeful manner. In fact it is precisely the petrifying gaze of the woman that marks the *difference* between her and her reflection in the marble stone. Hence, the act of petrifaction that indeed takes place in the statue now must take on a new signification. Her appropriation of his gaze "translates" the story of Psyche into a quite different story from the one he inscribed in the marble. If, as I have argued, we may assume that the artist made a blunder and did not make a representation of the young woman—she could not be "cited"—of whom, then, did he make a representation in marble? The text itself points towards a possible answer.

When the artist first catches sight of the woman she is immediately described as a reflection of his entire artistic yearning. Later when the statue is finished he is described as seeing it as a divine fulfillment—as his initiation into life itself and possibility for immortality—in other words a reflection of his ambitious longings. The implicit petrifaction of him by the woman-as-Medusa through the reversal of the gaze transforms the plot of the story and leaves us to assume that the statue is in fact: a re-presentation of himself. He is the one who is "petrified"; it is his name, his fate, that is echoed in the marble. The woman, as we saw, is not properly constrained into the field of vision as *one* image. She breaks the frame and speaks with a monstrous voice revealing the complete disparity between her resemblance to Psyche and her "true" face as Medusa.

According to tradition, Psyche was punished for transgressing the taboo of seeing her beloved Cupid.[9] Her punishment was torment in the underworld. Likewise the artist—not the woman—is punished; not only for having seen wrongly, but for seeing what he should not have seen. The text in fact gives him a warning that he overlooks. It specifically directs our attention towards the green juicy leaves springing out of the marble basin in the garden where the girl is first seen, suggesting a sensuous and dangerous quality. Like Psyche he goes through torment and repentance, but unlike Psyche he is not reunited with the loved object of his desire but remains symbolically in the underworld. Why then is his punishment so severe?

If the statue can be seen as a representation of the artist himself, then the worshiping of the statue initially performed by the artist, signifies an act of self-reflection, self-worship, thus repeating the ancient myth of Narcissus.[10] The real tragedy of Narcissus was not that he fell in love with his own reflection. It was rather that he did *not* recognize his own image in the water as his own. This ultimately led to Narcissus's destruction. The artist does not recognize the statue as his own reflection because he does not recognize himself in the shape of woman. This obviously does not mean that he becomes woman but rather that he, as a consequence of the problem with delimiting gender in the mimetic representation, comes to occupy the place of woman. In other words, the framing of the woman is transported to a framing of him(self). The subject of the story becomes his own object and self-destructs in the act of re-presenting himself.

What is at stake in *Psychen* is a reversibility of gender which ultimately results in a sense of feminization of the artist. It is this "destructive" feminization through the mimetic project—this duplication of himself through the sight of the woman—that brings him to despair, and that Andersen seems to fear. The artist literally goes mad, falls apart, after the collapse of his mimetic project. His body breaks away from the self-inflicted exile in which he has preserved his physical energy for the divinity of his art. But only to be exiled again in yet another "hysteric" punishment of his body in the dark abyss of the monastery. When his attempt to cancel the social difference between himself and the young noblewoman fails, it renders not only the "inscription" of the woman upon the stone meaningless but indeed his entire social, sexual, and artistic identity. The life-giving Pygmalion, who can turn stone into life, has been overpowered by the death-giving Medusa, who can turn life into stone. Thus the artist retains the self-afflicted position of the exiled other. The place of woman.

There is one aspect in which all of the mythical connotations in this story overlap. All, in one way or another, revolve around a problem of sight, gaze, reflections, and taboos; they are all centered around the pivotal point of the visual. The image of the lizard slipping in and out of the empty eye sockets of the dead artist's skull underlines the destructive desire of the gaze. His white-boned skeleton is a dysphoric, "castrated" echo of the white marble form. The artist's determination to find "truth" in the visual is rendered an illusion. The *vera ikona* (true image) turns out to be a catastrophic image. Disoriented perception causes the protagonist to fuse person and *objet d'art* and results in a problem with delimiting the meaning inherent in the figural representation. Lack of distance between the real and the image, between the represented and representation thus creates a zone of confusion where the chaotic search for truth seems doomed. A struggle that in this case becomes the very suspense of the story.

III

The problem of visuality in *Psychen* is more than anything connected to the problem of mimesis, of representation. This is what the myth of Pygmalion initially referred to. The indirect representation of Pygmalion points toward the ultimate error that the artist commits: the transgression of the biblical taboo against creating "overtly mimetic" art. In Exodus it says:

> Thou shalt not make unto thee a graven image, nor any manner of likeness of any thing that is in Heaven above or that is in the earth beneath or that is in the water under the earth. Thou shalt not bow down unto them, nor serve them. (Ex. 20:4–5)[11]

The two taboos in this excerpt from the Exodus—not to "commit" mimesis and not to worship the image—are both violated by the artist. But his creation of the sculpture, his transgressing of the commandment, points toward a contradiction. On one hand, it is the victory of mimesis—his perfect masterpiece—that grants him praise from everyone. He is seen as a superior artist, as a rival to nature. But this triumph—this overtly perfect mimesis—provokes at the same time the punishment for imitating God, taking on the role of the Creator, of God. It is within this conflicting view of mimesis that the artist is trapped. On one hand, a view "that privileges it," on the other hand, a view "that punishes it" (Meltzer 110). He is caught in a conflict that I will call Nemesis of Mimesis. Justice and vengeance of Nemesis mirrors itself onto Mimesis, literally letting the *Ne*(mesis) "slash" into *Mi*(mesis) as a retribution for "committing mimesis."

This is a mechanism similar to what René Girard calls the "double bind of imitation—which turns back against the imitator even though the model and the whole culture specifically encourage him to imitate" (Girard 290–91). It is the paradox of imitation that "the more perfect the imitation is, the less it is known as a work of imitation" (Drost 310). Our artist loses the mimetic pleasure—the gratification of his work—because he fails to acknowledge (literally fails to see) the difference (and hereby the similarity) between the real object and its imitation. The imitation is too perfect. By measuring one with the other, letting one be the other, the otherness of the art product disintegrates and moves away from being merely art. Thus the artist performs a unique and tragic fusion between the imitated and the imitation involving himself. His desire (for the woman and ultimately for eradication of difference between her and the statue) is the glue between the two. When this glue proves to have petrifying implications, he leaves his trade and echoing her words "Væk, ned" he buries, not only the statue, but eventually himself, in the catacombs of the monastery. The pleasure of the sublimatory act of creating a masterpiece only had meaning if it gave him *all*. His genius—this "gift from God"—is invested into a single moment. When he realizes that he never had what he lost, he is thrust into a limbo where all meaning is lost. His attempt at eradicating *difference* proves to be a virtual suicide.

When the sculpture becomes a problem for the artist as well as for the text it is because it is pointing towards a curious facet of mimesis. At the same time as it is built upon the idea of an illusion, it cannot be recognized as such by the artist. It becomes a kind of mimetic trap. But it cannot be understood as a trap, because its meaning is veiled—or, as Meltzer claims, "it is built upon the idea of the lie, and so cannot be recognized as a trap when it most forcibly is one" (191). The artist cannot *read* it and thus persists in regarding it as a creation of divine purity, unfit to be sullied by the undisguised desire of his gaze.

As we have seen, the representation of the sculpture *Psyche* almost immediately employed two *signatures*: that of the young artist and that of Raphael. In the textual economy of the story we saw how the young girl is wedged in between the painting by Raphael and the inner image (itself an imitation) of the artist. In a comparable manner, the artist is caught in a trap of an already existing name: the name of Raphael, or rather the names of Raphael. More precisely, he is caught between Raphael as libertine and Raphael as divine artist. The conflict between sin and purity, mortality and immortality, according to the artist's friends, is merged in the artist Raphael. And to become like Raphael, they urge the artist to unite "life and self." His blinded vision, however, his inability to see himself, deters him from realizing the integration of sexuality and transcendence that he is so desperately seeking. The hope that the sculpture provided is no longer able to mediate in this conflict because its meaning has shifted.

This conflict can be seen as an intricate part of *mimetic rivalry*. What the artist desires is the domain of the rival, the domain of Raphael. Raphael is his master-model and the artist desires what he, Raphael, presumably desires: immortality, artistic power, and women, thus creating "a triangle of relationships" between artist-master–desired object—a variation of the Lacanian doctrine that desire is the desire of the Other (Girard 323). A certain measure of identification between the desired object (Psyche) and the idol(s) (Raphael, Michelangelo) takes place so that only the appropriation of the desired object is seen as a way to *be like*, to seize (through imitation) the power of the masters, and ultimately of God. This is why the loss of the desired object is so catastrophic. It is not just a rejection of the artist as a socially unfit lover, but of his very existence and identity as an artist. Although his masterpiece is recognized as a competent rival to those of Raphael and Michelangelo, Andersen demonstrates that successful artistic rivalry does not always guarantee the genius a place on Olympus or a place, a name, in history. The author emphasizes this by literally letting the artist lose his signature. A signature that ironically enough never establishes itself in the text in the form of a *proper name*. Our artist has no proper name, he remains a generic *artist*, a stand-in for other artists—like the author himself. Although solidly planted on Olympus with Europe's other great writers, Andersen apparently never lost his fear and doubts concerning his own artistic identity and, as it is well documented in his diaries, constantly sought affirmation and approval from others to solidify his belief in *his own name*. The proper names of Raphael and Michelangelo emerge in Andersen's diary on the day between the initial inception of *Psychen* and the day he started the actual writing. On May 6, 1861, Andersen went to the Vatican to look at frescoes by the masters who were to be eulogized in the story. The viewing appears to have been a disappointment:

> ... *men baade Raphaels og Michael Angelos Fresco synes mig aldre og forrøgede fra jeg sidst saa dem, Farverne vare saa morke og udslidte.*

> ... but both Raphael's and Michelangelo's frescos seemed to me older and sootier than the last time I saw them; the colors were so dark and worn. (Andersen, *Diaries* 274)

The fact that the immortal and celebrated productions of Raphael and Michelangelo were fading might have induced him to place emphasis on what became a central theme of this story: the survival of art. Furthermore, the apprehension that he might have experienced in identifying with the great masters, whose works were now "old" and "worn," might have influenced him in stressing the significance of the survival of the name of the artist.

The mimetic exchange inherent in the significance of the name(s) of Raphael/Michelangelo in *Psychen* takes the form of a *violence* that ends in self-mutilation. The artist seems to set himself up for failure in a manner bordering on masochism.[12] The mechanism here has been described by Girard as a complex part of mimetic desire: by first "changing its models into obstacles, mimetic desire in effect changes obstacles into models" (327). Masochism is in this aspect, according to Girard, directly connected to the real or assumed violence of the rival. The obstacle placed by the rival—assumed or not—eventually may be perceived as the original object of desire. When our artist redirects his desire away from the woman-as-object or art-as-object towards self-sacrifice, suffering, masochism, it is the perceived *evil* inside himself that becomes the focus of his desire: "Han straffede sit Legeme, men indenfra kom det Onde" (He scourged his body, but from within came the evil yet again). Earlier this self-punishment was manifested in his sisyphean repetition and destruction of his art:

> *Det blode Leer bøjede sig i Skjønhedsformer for hans Fingre, men Dagen efter, som altid, brød han itu, hvad han havde skabt.* (106)

(The soft clay bent in shapes of beauty by his fingers, but the day after, he destroyed, as always, what he had created.)

IV

Perhaps the tragedy of the artist results from a confusion of two distinct modes of mimesis: Apollonian and Dionysian. In the text Dionysian desire seems to take over Apollonian mimetic desire, perhaps as *mnemic* traces of the carnal Bacchus (also known as Dionysos)—a reminder of the original spectacle, that inspired Andersen to write *Psychen*. The reappearance of the original material, of Bacchus, breaks as a *Nemesis* into the *Mimetic* representation thus prohibiting any comprehensible and clear-cut interpretation of its meaning. The Apollonian demand for self-knowledge and aesthetic distance is disrupted by Dionysian ecstasy and lack of distance.[13] While producing his Apollonian statue, the artist becomes virtually intoxicated with himself and his mark on the marble stone. He is so absorbed into his own imitation that he "becomes" this imitation. The Apollonian sculpture's impenetrable surface is supposed to maintain a distance from the fragmented sensual world surrounding it.[14] This sensual and seductive world engulfed the artist in a Dionysian night of sin or more precisely, a night of fluidity: wine and women. But as Medusa broke into Psyche, Dionysos breaks into Apollo, definitively refusing to let the sculpture assert itself as an ultimate signifier, as a phallic celebration of the male artist through the hard, smooth, glossy marble stone. The sculpture is "tainted" by Dionysian desire. Thus the story leaves the artist forever particularized and desperately searching for wholeness, truth and unity, only to find the disintegration of his body through the actual pulverization of his white bones.

The reversibility of gender that the sculpture refers to, the fact that the sculpture is marked by not one, but two genders, gives it a gliding, un-fixed meaning, an enigmatic quality. This is emphasised in the marble sculpture's tenacious and restless fluctuation between emerging from, and re-merging with, the earth. We first encounter the unfinished marble block, which the artist had inherited, as an archaic piece of purity covered with leaves and dirt. After its molding, it is thrust into a well in the ground by the artist in a sexually connotated symbolic act, that can be seen, not only as an aggressive penetration of Mother earth—but also as a repression of the painful conflict that the sculpture signified. The persistent importance of the sculpture in the text is finally underlined in its re-emerging from the "grave" in a sacrificial exchange for a young nun, a virgin, we may assume. The restless movements show that it does not belong to the underworld, nor does it belong to the world above. More than a symbol of "the spirit that survives psychical decay" (Friedman 9), it provides a multiple message that cannot be confined to any one realm.

Another important aspect is focused on the sculpture as a figural object with a particular *sensory* quality. The first "draft" of the sculpture is formed in clay. But the clay is too "fleshy and life-like," too close to the actual body of the woman. It is not able to transcend time like marble. Furthermore, the smooth white surface of the marble offers a unique possibility of providing the spectator with a reflection. The tradition of classicism that the sculpture refers to often erased the pupil from the eyes, hereby indirectly underlining the eyes as being blind or as mini-mirrors. There is no Medusa gaze here. The sculpture's three dimensionality accentuates this aspect. The sculpture has an inside as well as an outside (surface). It displays itself, as well as hides itself. It is a condensed form, as well as an open form. It alludes to something present, as well as something absent, something in the past. To a fulfillment and to a lack.

The text's obvious difficulties in providing the reader with an understandable and indisputable meaning of the sculpture can be seen as an intricate part of its radical *otherness* in relation to the written narrative.[15] The sculpture-as-such is visual and in a sense fundamentally non-verbal. Clearly, in the story we cannot see it with our eyes, nor can we walk around it to examine it as we can a statue in a museum. It is a static object—radical other to the on-going narrative of the written story. *Narrative time* is virtually clashing with *sculptural space*. When a narrative employs such a figural image, it is often used to reflect the "meaning" of the text. That is, it is used as an addendum to the figural meaning—as a mimesis "of the assumptions of the text."[16] But if we insist on looking at it as a radical other to the written story, it is obvious that the sculpture refuses to mimic any clear meaning. I would rather argue that it ruptures the progression of the narrative. First and foremost, as I have already pointed out, the sculpture becomes an increasing problem within the story, a problem for the artist. It did not want to represent what he wanted it to represent. Instead of becoming the vehicle for his immortality, his signature, it represented the inscription of his death. When the persistent statue re-emerged it was in the form of an anonymous work of art, without his signature on it. In other words, instead of bringing life to the statue, by symbolically attempting to merge it with the girl, the motionless, deadened statue points towards the death of the artist—and mimetic creation is once more problematized.[17] In this respect the sculpture inscribes death, not only for the artist, but also for the woman. Both can be seen as contained in the representation of the sculpture and both are survived and replaced by it.

Just as the sculpture refuses the intentions of the artist, it also ruptures any clear understanding of *Den skønne kunst* (*Beauty of Art*). The fragility of *Den Skønne Kunst* as anything but a garment is apparent and seems to have been perceived by Andersen as an existential problem. Is art more than a vain garment for the artist's pride? This problem of consolidating artist and product as a reflection of self-identity, is shown when the sculpture becomes an obstacle at all levels of the narrative, for writer, as well as reader. It is not content to speak with a mimetic voice. It is settled in the text persistent in its otherness.

The narration of the story echoes in an ingenious way the subject matter. When the story starts, it immediately employs a secondary narrator: the bright morning star.

I Dagningen, i den røde Luft, skinner en stor Stjerne, Morgenens klareste Stjerne, dens Straale sittrer mod den hvide Væg, som om den vilde der nedskrive, hvad den i Aartusinder saae her og der paa vor omdreiende Jord. Hør en af dens Historier! (105)

(At dawn, through the red air, shines a large star, morning's brightest star; its ray quivers upon the white wall, as if it would there inscribe what it had seen for thousands of years here and there on our revolving earth. Listen to one of its stories!)

This narrator-star "writes" down the first part of the story on a white wall, using its rays as an amorphous pen, as if inscribing an archaic scripture. It is important to note, however that the story inscribed by the star-narrator is the "happy" Pygmalion story. The serene "pen" is allowed to represent, on the page of the white wall, a successful mimesis, the first successful creation of the statue. Thus the story of the statue is *doubly* represented. It is inscribed on the white wall, as well as in the first life—like "draft"—the clay. At the critical point in the story, when the father and daughter arrive at the studio, the star-narrator is superseded by a we-narrator.

En Dag traf det sig saa, ja den klare Stjerne fortæller intet derom, den saa det ikke, *men vi vide det: et fornemt Romersk selskab kom....* (107; emphasis added)

(One day it happened, well, the bright star tells nothing about it, *it did not see it*, but we know it, that a party of noble Romans came....)

From this point on the narrator-star must content itself with the role of on-looker, its ray-pen has been extinguished. It is no longer allowed to inscribe, with its eternal power, the problematic story of a sculpture that evades a fixed meaning, eludes an obvious mimesis. Through the explicit use of the "star-pen" to inscribe the story, Andersen underscores two aspects of the narrative. First and foremost, the story is directly emphasized as *writing*. Thus, the text points back towards itself as representation. Secondly, the "star-pen" indirectly parallels the hands of the artist. The "hand-as-pen" inscribing his vision, his story—first on the "draft," echoing all the clay-drafts discarded earlier—then on the final version. The two "scriptures" in the story, the blank white page of the wall and the white marble of the sculpture, thus refer not only to the inscription on the wall as writing but also to the scripture on the marble as writing. The sculpture, however—because of its radical otherness—still tries to avoid being reduced to a blank page, like the white wall. The sculpture as figural image never really allows itself to be completely embraced by the text; it maintains it's otherness.

Although they tell the same story, there is a significant difference between the story inscribed on the wall and the story inscribed on the marble. While the first depicts the triumph of mimesis, the second depicts the problem of mimesis. Consequently the sculpture as a textual image can also be seen as an image of writing, or more precisely, as a representation of the act of re-presenting; a representation of the *power* of writing and the *problem* of writing. Seen from this perspective, the text can be said not only to represent the story of the artist for us; it also represents itself. This self-reflexivity of the text, its mirroring of itself in the sculpture, gives the sculpture the position of a textual *mise en abyme*.[18] The sculpture simultaneously mirrors the text (reflects the written narrative) *and* echoes the double motion of the sculpture/artist into the abyme/abyss: the descent (the falling, the vertigo) into the "underworld": well/monastery/graveyard.[19]

If we read the sculpture as "a metaphor for inscription," it can be seen as an "iconic encapsulation" of writing (Meltzer 54), a self-reflective but not a self-conscious apparatus. At the same time, as the text directs us towards the problem of writing, it seeks to control this radical other, the statue, to reduce it to its own terms hereby adding yet another commentary to the problem of mimesis. The taboo against mimesis did not, as we well know, include writing. "It is not accidental that the prohibition against a 'graven image, *nor any manner of likeness*' is given to Moses in *writing*" (Meltzer 75). Thus the problem of "committing mimesis" interestingly enough becomes a problem *in* the text but not a problem *for* the text.

Andersen sets up a complex tropological system of reflections (the reflection on the surface of the marble, on the wall, in the exchange of gazes, etc.) that cross each other in a way that intensifies the opacity of the story. In fact this system of reflections can be said to play Echo to the fate of Psyche and the artist: he becomes as shadow of his former self just as his skeleton becomes the virtual shadow (double) of the sculpture. The doubling of the artist-as-skeleton with the sculpture has, as the story itself, a fascinating connection to Andersen's first stay in Rome. Thus it might not only have been the exhumed sculpture that inspired Andersen to write *Psychen*. Rome was in 1833 the scene of Raphael's second burial.[20] Andersen notes in his diary:

> *Vi vare heldig nok komme til Raphaels Begravelse. Paa Academiet*
> *gjemtes et Dodninghoved der udgaves for hans, for nu at overtydes*

derom, aabnede man Graven og fandt ham heel og holdende; nu skulle da Liget igjen begraves og det skete denne Aften i Pantheon, vi fik Billiet, det var en herlig Hvælving, paa en sort Forhøining stod Mahonie Kisten bed ekket med etgyldent Klæde, Presterne sang et miserere, Kirken aabnedes og man nedlagte de oplæste Efterretninger om ham, blev derpaa forseglet, et usynligt Chor sang smukt imidlertid, jeg saae Thorvaldsen med et Voxlys i Haanden ligerom de andre første Mend. (216)

We were lucky enough to make it to Raphael's burial. There was a skull kept at the Accademia that people claimed to be his. In order to prove it, they opened the grave and found him all in one piece. Then the body had to be reburied, and this took place this very evening in the Pantheon. We got a ticket. It was a magnificent vault; on a black platform stood a mahogany casket covered with a golden drape; the priest sang the *Miserere*. The casket was opened, and within it were placed the findings concerning the artist, which had been read aloud; then it was sealed, while an invisible choir sang beautifully. (Andersen, *Diaries* 49)

The spectacular scene described here must have captivated Andersen's imagination with its theatricality and worshiping of the artist. But the exhumation and re-burial of the "eternal artist" proved to be just that: a theatrical performance. Only nine days later he states that "Raphaels Hovedet som jeg nu har seet ikke er hans" [224] ("Raphael's head, which I have just seen, is not Raphael's head" [Andersen, *Diaries* 57]).[21] The "loss" of the remains of the great artist, the fact that the resurrection of Raphael proved to be an empty gesture, is indirectly repeated in the dissemination of the fictional artist skeleton.

By letting the artist pine away without any genuine enlightenment of his psyche, his soul, Andersen might be said to challenge the platonic notion of an ideal world. Plato's axiom that "clarity of vision acquires metaphysical significance," that "the path that leads to truth moves progressively from a vision of shadows and specular images to the contemplation of ideas" (Perniola 238) is circumscribed and implicitly depreciated in *Psychen*. In fact, our artist fails on all accounts and the author does not give us any *idea* or *truth* to hold on to in the end. "The metaphor of the 'naked truth,'" says Perniola, comes from a conflation of the concept of truth as visual precision and the idea that eternal forms are the ultimate objects of intellectual vision. From this foundation, the entire process of knowledge becomes an unveiling of the object, a laying it entirely bare and an illumination of all its parts. The body itself then comes to be considered an obstacle, a tomb of the soul. (238–39)

The sculpture-body not only becomes a "tomb for the soul"—it kills it. Although the author appears to adhere to the platonic axiom that only when "the soul (is) stripped of the body ... does it acquire complete freedom," the pessimism of the story does not allow the reader to believe the last convulsive declamation of faith from the artist (Perniola 239):

> *"Psychen herinde aldrig døe!—Leve i Bevidsthed?—kan det Ufattelige skee? Ja! ja! ufattelig er mit Jeg. Ufattelig Du, o Herre! hele din Verden ufattelig;—et Underværk af Magt, Herlighed Kjærlighed!"—Hans Øine lyste, hans Øine brast.* (116)

> ("Psyche within me never die!—live in consciousness! Can the inconceivable be? Yes, yes! Inconceivable am I. Inconceivable you, o Lord! The whole of your world is inconceivable; a wonder of power, glory—Love!" His eyes shone, his eyes burst.)

The simultaneous lighting and bursting of the eyes—"Hans Øine lyste—hans Øine brast"—deflate any real *in-sight* in our protagonist. The instant he "sees" he goes "blind." The world, God and the I is as "ufattelig" (inconceivable) as the sculpture has proven to be. As metaphor it comes to signify this impenetrable and bewildering message. It carries no catharsis, no hope as an "eternal form" for man. Thus by blocking the mimetic promise of the sculpture Andersen implicitly questions the acme of western aesthetic tradition as we know it, here in the words of Winckelman: "The only way for us to become great, or if this be possible, inimitable, is to imitate the ancients." Andersen lets the artist imitate Raphael who, as we know, in turn imitated the relics of antiquity of Greece. Thus the author lets the imprint on the "eternal marble stone" echo the "masterpieces of Greek art." When the sculpture fails to carry any "eternal" value or hope, it implies—however subtly—a loss of faith in the traditional aesthetic maxim that certain ideal forms of beauty are "better" than others, that to be "inimitable" one must imitate the ancient Greeks. The burial of the sculpture in the narrative of *Psychen* is then also a burial of unconditional adoration for the Greek body.

Rising like Phoenix out of the human chaos, self-punishment and fragmentation, the sculpture nevertheless survives as a solid form that both inscribes and defies death. And as a solid *form* it is able to keep its contour unbroken while the human artist loses his to corrosion and decay. It manifests itself as an epitaph over the life that has been lived—and wasted— and resurrects itself as something more than just a sculpture. The replacement of the corpse mortem (artist/virgin-nun) by the steadfast stone becomes a cruel *reminder* of what *was* the *idea* behind the artistic *form* and thus becomes an ironic remembrance of the Greek Psyche myth: a butterfly, the symbol of the soul—the very belief that it seems to negate. Thus both the *idea* and *form* here become the location for an aesthetic battle that might be said to encompass a philosophical question of reflexivity. Implied in Andersen's story is a radical questioning of the Hegelian hypostasis of sculpture as the first art form fit to idealize the human body—a hypostasis echoed in the writings of the Danish Hegelian philosopher Johan Ludvig Heiberg, to whom Andersen had an ambivalent relationship. When our protagonist in *Psychen* is denied (in)sight, he is located away from a position, as a speculative subject. That is, he is denied, as a subject, the ability to conceptualize himself and thus denied the reward of becoming a "man" through seeing himself do it. By taking away the sculpture as a successful reflective device, Andersen appears to deconstruct the paradigm of *det gode, det sande og det skønne* (goodness, truth, and beauty) with which Heiberg ruled a major part of nineteenth-century Danish culture. The sculpture resists being reduced to a container for ideality. The insurgent, responding gaze of the woman fractures any smooth reflection.

V

The connection between mimesis and psychoanalysis is obvious. Mimesis concerns itself with the problem of identification, of producing something identifiable in which we can mirror ourselves. Psychoanalysis too, of course, concerns itself with the question of identification. In his theory on the mirror-stage, Lacan ties the problem of identification to the problem of the visual. The mirror-stage refers to the time in which the subject, through an actual or symbolic mirror, learns to see itself as an entity, as separate from others. Philippe Lacoue-Labarthe broaches an equation of a psychoanalytical (Lacan's "Mirror-stage") and a philosophical (Plato's *The Republic*) theorizing of mimesis. He says: "And let us not be surprised here if we begin to see Lacanian terminology coming progressively to double Plato's lexicon." Both are involved, he claims, with "a resentment against the original maternal domination and original feminine education, these being always the sign, for the subject, of its constituted incompleteness" (Lacoue-Labarthe 127). Seen through this bifocal Lacanian/Platonic lens, the mimetic problem for the text (and the artist) appear to be connected to a problem with "an original maternal domination." The artist as subject does not, as we have seen, come into being successfully, and his fragmented self ends up echoed in the splitting of gender in the statue. The uncanniness of the doubling process is, although in a very oblique way, connected to this gender shift implied in the statue. One might argue that the inscription (shaping) of fiction in the conformable material of the statue comes to echo the "original" molding of the infant child. In *The Republic* Plato writes:

> You know that the beginning of any process is most important, especially for anything young and tender. For it is at that time that it takes shape, and any mold one may want can be impressed upon it. (47)

If one can parallel the imprints on the un-finished infant with the imprints made on the conformable sculpture—and if these imprints can be associated with an "original" maternal/feminine discourse—then the feminization of the artist might be seen as part of an involuntary envelopment in a disconcerting (maternal/feminine) discourse that asserts itself through the instability of gender in the statue. It is this discourse, provided through the "splitting" gaze of the woman that tells the *other* story of Psyche. The imprint on the *tabula rasa* of the inherited marble is then an imprint itself inherited from the "natural submission to maternal or feminine discourse in general."[22] The anxiety over devouring Medusas, the fear of submission under a discourse other than the patriarchal, seems to have been unconsciously known to Andersen. Furthermore, he appears to have had an acute understanding for the subversive potential in this story. In his diary entry from October 1863 he expresses apprehension over the fact that the English version had been dedicated to the Princess of Wales without his consent: "Jeg synes ikke om at *en Historie som 'Psycken' dediceres til en ung Dame*" [5:421] ("I'm not at all pleased to have *a story like 'The Psyche'* dedicated to a *young woman*." [Andersen, *Diaries*, emphasis added]). Later (April 19, 1868) he seems to find it embarrassing to read *Psychen* aloud with a women present: "Besøgt Hultmann og vilde læse for ham 'Psycken' men da hans Frue blev i Stuen var jeg generet ved at læse den" [8:52] (Visited Hultmanm and wanted to read "The Psyche" for him but when his wife remained in the room I was embarrassed to read it). Why, one must ask, was Andersen so embarrassed? Was it because of the ironic fact that a "maternal, feminine discourse" seemed to subsume a male protagonist?

When pagan imagery appears to survive soul-searching Christianity, when the insurgent Medusa disrupts the sweet dream of Psyche, and when "hysteric" Dionysus taints the somber Apollo, it apparently leaves *Psychen* unfit for the ear of woman and decisively unfit to be dedicated to a young woman—to carry her name?

The use of sculpture as a written image was not new to H.C. Andersen, when he published *Psychen* in 1861. It appears again and again throughout his authorship. In his early novel *Improvisatoren*, from 1835, sculpture plays an important role as metaphor for the ideal woman, for the hope of transcendence through woman. The quality of sculpture is here transported directly to a young girl, even to the degree of giving her the blind eyes of the classical statues. In this early, optimistic rendition of sculpture Andersen lets sculpture as metaphor convey an unquestionable promise of *ideality* in *reality*. Thus he not only let the male protagonist go through an act of symbolic sexual cleansing in order to prepare him for the ideal sculpture-woman, he also transformed the sculpture-woman into a prosaic realistic figure by giving her sight and social status—a little red blood in her white marble veins.

With this background it is interesting to note that in *Psychen* H.C. Andersen chooses *not* to engage in any easy answers, any mediation. He leaves the story fragmented, unsettled, and unsettling. The apparent loss of belief in a blessed unity of man and woman seem to surface parallel with the questioning of the artistic project *per se* and sculpture in particular. Throughout H.C. Andersen's authorship we find representations of woman as object *and* as desiring subject. But he seldom articulates as clearly as in *Psychen*, just how woman escapes representation. Here woman remains enigmatic, avoiding being molded into any fixed term; she remains in the position of other. A position H.C. Andersen most certainly could identify with and a position that the artist in *Psychen* seems to appropriate. In the end is it not this distant and evasive woman who has been the focus of desire in the constructions of woman in patriarchy—precisely because she escapes any fixed meaning? Andersen answers this question through a simultaneously fearful exposure of the power of the reflective medusan gaze and a perceptive—even if involuntary—understanding of the complexity of art and gender.

The "mystery" of *woman* remains a mystery in *Psychen*. Art cannot confine her. In fact, the transformation of body to form in *Psychen* is full of implications that question art's ability to represent at all. The promise of fulfillment offered by the beauty of woman *and* by the beauty of art is shown to be illusionary by Andersen; it is a promise full of treason, an invalid promise. Both are seen as seductive, and both are guilty of instigating vanity.

> *Konsten var en Troldgvinde, der bar os ind i Forfængelighed, ind i jordiske Lyster. Falske vare vi mod os selv, falske mod vore Venner, falske mod Gud. Slangen talte altid i os: "smag, og Du skal blive som Gud!"* (113)

> (Art was a sorceress that carried us to vanity, to earthly lusts. We were false towards ourselves, false towards our friends, false towards God. The serpent always spoke within us, "taste, and you shall be as God.")

Art and woman have become one in the form of the serpent who does not talk "*til* os" (*to* us) but "*i* os" (*in* us). If art commits itself solely to capture the illusion of beauty and woman, it will fail and itself become an illusion. This pessimistic view is what sifts through the fissures of the text together with woman. Yet, it is precisely when she is able to slip through the cracks of that re-presentational form, that *her* story becomes *his* story. They follow each other into exile.

In the end *Psychen* simultaneously questions and insists upon the very notion of immortality through art, as the closing lines of the story clearly display:

> *Hvad jordisk er, vejres hen, forglemmes, kun Stjernen idet Uendelige veed det. Hvad Himmelsk er, straaler selv i Eftermælet, og naar Eftermælet slukkes—da lever endnu Psychen.* (118)

> (All that is earthly dissolves, and is forgotten; only the star in the infinite heaven knows it. What is heavenly shines in remembrance; and when remembrance fades away, Psyche still lives.)

The immortality awarded the mythological Psyche after her ordeal, is the immortality that Andersen so longed for—and got. But as pointed out by Meltzer: "Insistence upon the concept of immortality must always lead to the erasure of temporality, of difference, and therefore of history" (43). This story shows how dangerous this erasure of difference can be. What might have been intended as a eulogy over divine inspiration and a mourning and protest over the world's inability to recognize the true artist (also the theme of *Kun en Spillemand*) turns into a very profound questioning of the very existence and gender of the artist. The burial of the statue (in the text) is a symbolic gesture that protests the fact that art does not necessarily award immortality, fame, name and sex, and at the same time the text provides a complex story of presumed triumph of divine art itself.

NOTES

1. I wish to thank Carol Clover, Jette Lundbo Levy, Erik Østerud, Thomas Bredsdorff, and Niels Ingwersen for helpful comments in preparing this article. Also thanks to Allen Simpson for directing my attention towards *Psychen* in the first place.

2. H.C. Andersen: *Nabofamilierne*. Andersen's ironic view of *det Skønne* (beauty) is amusingly conveyed in this story, where an educational conversation takes place between a mother sparrow and her chicks: "'Jeg forstod meget godt hvad den Fugl sang!' sagde Spurveungerne, 'der var bare et Ord, jeg ikke forstod: Hvad er det Skønne?' 'Det er Ingenting!' sagde Spurvemoderen, 'deterbare saadanne et Udseende....' "[1:366] ("I understood very well what the bird sang!" said the chicks. "There was only one word I did not understand: what is beauty?" "It is nothing!" said mother sparrow, "it is merely an appearance").

3. Although I claim that sculpture, as presented in the text, occupies a position that renders it "radical other" to the written narrative, I must emphasize that the sculpture in question here obviously is a written one and not an unmitigated visual one. My claim therefore must be seen as part of an examination of the polysemy of the sculpture in the text. That is of its "borrowing" and "merging" of qualities inherently non-verbal into the verbal writing.

4. Unless otherwise noted all translations of Andersen's texts are mine. My translations will attempt exactness not poetic rendition.

5. In an entry in his diary on Sunday December 1, 1833 H.C. Andersen describes his viewing of Raphael in a matter-of-fact fashion: "Gik nu til Palazzo Farnazina, hvor Raphael med sine Disciple har malet Psykkes Historie i Fresko paa Loftet, Guilander med Blomster og Frugt slynger sig over vort Hoved og bag denne sees den deiligste italienske Luft med Guder og Genier. En Gruppe med Grazierne og Amor er ganske af Raphael" (Went to Palazzo Farnazina, where Raphael together with his pupils has painted the story of Psyche in a fresco on the ceiling. Festoons of flowers and fruits are twined above our heads and behind this the wonderful Italian sky with gods and spirits can be seen. A group of Graces and Cupid is completely by Raphael).

6. Here quoted from Warminski 48.

7. This "conflict" between sculpture and painting is also evident in *Improvisatoren*, where the marble sculpture signifies ideality, transcendence and purity while painting is

associated with sensuality and excess. Andersen's use of sculpture and painting is more complex than this seemingly simple dichotomy might indicate. A further study of this dichotomy is, however, beyond the scope of this article.

8. The gaze of Medusa can naturally be connected to the psychological problems of narcissism, to desire and the castration anxiety as Freud has taught us in his famous interpretation of the phallic Medusa. The sculpture in connection with sight, gaze, and the myth of Medusa, probably could be seen as a symbolic representation of a castration threat. A threat that was ultimately carried out in the destruction of the artist. The uncanny feeling of the double, that Freud discusses in his most prolific essay on visuality, "The Uncanny," could here be seen as the uncanny feeling that, we as readers, experience through the gliding meaning of the sculpture. We do not really know how to understand it. Of whom is it a double?

9. Susan Stanford Friedman writes in her book *Psyche Reborn*: "Psyche, the mortal woman whose search for Eros has frequently been interpreted as the soul's quest for divine immortality. The name "Psyche" comes from the Greek word for "soul," often portrayed in Greek art as a butterfly that leaves the body at death. Psyche is the spirit that survives physical decay to be reunited with the divine. But in the story first told by Apuleius and later retold by countless poets, Psyche must undergo severe trials culminated by the archetypal descent to underworld before she can rejoin Eros" (9).

10. René Girard writes in *Things Hidden Since the Foundations of Time*: "Narcissism is in fact the final manifestation of the idol worshipped by the Romantics. It gives its own mythological character away when it turns uncritically to the Narcissus myth, and interprets it as a myth of solipsism, while in reality the image behind the mirror (as in the story of the nymph Echo) conceals the mimetic model and the struggle between doubles" (377).

11 Here quoted from Françoise Meltzer, *Salome and the Dance of Writing* (73). The following paragraph is inspired by Meltzer's analysis of mimesis.

12. Interestingly enough there are many similarities between Sacher-Masoch's book *Venus im Pelz* from 1870 and *Psychen*. Cold, hard, "cruel," marble-women are the focus of desire for the male (masochistic) protagonists in both fictions.

13. Linda Hutcheon writes: "Part of Narcissus's characteristics, according to Ovid, was that 'he does not know himself'" (9). This adds an extra perspective to my analysis of the artist as Narcissus.

14. Camille Paglia sees the eye as an "Apollonian projectile." She states: "Fashion is an externalization of woman's demonic invisibility, her genital mystery. It brings before man's Apollonian eye what that eye can never see. Beauty is an Apollonian freeze-frame: it halts and condenses the flux and indeterminacy of nature. It allows man to act by enhancing the desirability of what he fears" (32).

1.5 Françoise Meltzer uses the term *radical otherness* in her analysis of the figural image in a narrative. She discusses the problem of how literature "augments, diminishes, and manipulates" a figural image, or rather its visual presence in the text. She asks, how does literature attempt "to reedit in a verbal form, something both visual and fundamentally nonverbal?" (2).

16. See Meltzer.

17. "Mimetic creation can be said to engage death," says Meltzer, "because the simulacrum of life, in its static presence, negates by its very stasis the life it depicts" (116).

18. Semantically the word 'abyme' (abyss) evokes ideas of depth, of infinity, of vertigo and of falling, in that order" (Dallenbach 8).

19. One might in fact, as Linda Hutcheon does, call it a *covert* narcissistic narrative. She writes:

> Overt narcissistic texts reveal their self-awareness in explicit thematization or allegorizations of their diegetic or linguistic identity within the texts themselves. In the covert form, this process is internalized, actualized; such a text is self-reflective but not necessarily self-conscious. (11)

20. I wish to thank Erik Østerud for calling my attention to Raphael's second burial during Andersen's stay in Rome.

21. A month later this Raphael-story proves to have involved a peculiar case of mimetic rivalry.

> *Ved Raphaels Beens Fremtagelse, havde Maleren Cambuccini faaet Eneret paa at male Gravstedet; Horaz Vernet vidste det ikke og tog Blyanten for at ridse det af, et slags pavelig Poletie forbød ham det, han blev forundret og sagde roligt, «men efter Hukommelsen tør man dog hjemme gjøre sig en Erindring derom," dette kunne man intet sige til. –/ Fra 12 Middag til 6 Aften malede han sig nu et smukt lignende Oliemalerie, han lod nu gjøre en Pladefor at trykkt den, men den blev tagen under Beslag, han skrev nu et heftigt Brev at han for 24 Timer forlangte den tilbage, da Kunsten ikke som salt og Tobak kunde bringes under Monopol, da han fik den brød han den og sendte den med et høfligt Brev til Camuccini og viiste ham at han ikke til hans Skade vilde benytte sig deraf, men C fik den godt sadt sammen igjen og leverede den atter med et venligt Brev og opgav ganske at udgive sin Tegning, nu fik Enhver Lov til at tegne Graven.* (234)

(At the exhumation of Raphael's bones, the painter Cambuccini was given the exclusive privilege to paint the grave. The painter Vernet did not know this and took his pencil to sketch it. A kind of papal police banned him from doing so. He became surprised and said calmly: "But from memory one can try to make an impression of it at home." This nobody could deny. –/ From 12 noon to 6 in the evening he now painted a beautifully resembling oil painting. He then ordered a plate to be made so he could print it. But it was confiscated. He now wrote a furious letter demanding the plate returned within 24 hours as art could not be monopolized such as salt and tobacco could. When he got it back he broke it and sent it with a polite letter to Camuccini to show him that he meant no harm and would not take advantage of the plate. But C. had the plate reassembled and returned it with a friendly letter and he gave up the plan to publish his drawing. Now everyone had permission to draw the grave.)

22. As Lacoue-Labarthe does, 127.

WORKS CITED

Andersen, Hans Christian. "Psychen." 1831. *Samlede Eventyr og Historier*. Vol. 3 Denmark: Gyldendal, 1982.
———. *Improvisatoren*. 1835. Copenhagen: Gyldendal, 1968.

————. *Hans Christian Andersens Dagbøger: 1825–1875*. Copenhagen: G.E.C. Gads Forlag, 1971–1977.

————. *The Diaries of Hans Christian Andersen*. Eds. Patricia L. Conroy and Sven H. Rossel. Seattle: U of Washington P, 1990.

Dallenbach, Lucien. *The Mirror in the Text*. Trans. Jeremy Whiteley and Emma Hughes. Chicago: U of Chicago P, 1989.

Drost, Mark. "Nietzsche and Mimesis." *Philosophy and Literature 10.2* (1986): 309–17.

Friedman, Susan Stanford. *Psyche Reborn: The Emergence of H.D.* Bloomington: Indiana UP, 1981.

Girard, René. *Things Hidden Since the Foundation of the World*. Trans. Stephen Bann and Michael Metteer. Stanford: Stanford UP, 1987.

Hutcheon, Linda. *Narcissistic Narrative: The Metafictional Paradox*. Waterloo, Ont.: Wilfrid Laurier UP, 1980.

Jardine, Alice A. *Gynesis: Configurations of Woman and Modernity*. Ithaca: Cornell UP, 1985.

Lacoue-Labarthe, Philippe. *Typography: Mimesis, Philosophy, Politics*. Ed. Christopher Fynsk. Cambridge: Harvard UP, 1989.

Meltzer, Françoise. *Salome and the Dance of Writing: Portraits of Mimesis in Literature*. Chicago: U of Chicago P, 1987.

Paglia, Camille. *Sexual Personae: Art and Decadence from Nefertiti to Emily Dickinson*. New Haven: Yale UP, 1990.

Perniola, Mario. "Between Clothing and Nudity." *Fragments for a History of the Human Body*. Ed. Michael Feher with Ramona Nadoff and Nadia Tazi. Vol. 2. New York: Zone, 1989. 3 vols.

Plato. *The Republic*. Trans. G.M.A. Grube. Indianapolis: Hackett Publ. Co., 1974.

Warminski, Andrzej. "Facing Language: Wordsworth's First Poetic Spirits." *Romantic Revolutions: Criticism and Theory*. Ed. Kenneth Johnston, Gilbert R. Chaitin, Karen Hanson, and Herbert Marks. Bloomington: Indiana UP, 1990. Pp. 29–49.

Winckelmann, Johann Joachim. *Reflections on the Imitation of the Imitation of Greek Works in Painting and Sculpture*. Trans. Elfriede Heyer and Roger C. Norton. LaSalle, IL: Open Court, 1987.

Hans Christian Andersen—
The Journey of His Life

Hans Christian Andersen's delight in travel is well-known, as is his talent for describing his progress through Europe and, briefly, the Near East and North Africa. His very earliest works, and his earliest successful works, were travel books or fiction inspired by the experience of travel in the middle of the nineteenth century. They show him integrating fact and fiction seamlessly, so that the reader comes to experience the world through his mind, with his sensitive eye for the significant and the insignificant detail of life in those days.

This present work is indirectly inspired by research into Hans Christian Andersen's work for the stage, an aspect of his career that has to a great extent remained unseen in the work of critics. Among his thirty stage plays is one originally written for reading rather than for performance: *Agnete and the merman* (*Agnete og Havmanden*, 1833). Written in Switzerland during his first long journey through Europe in 1833, it comes across as a strikingly personal and intense account of the nature of exile and the impossibility of making a proper return to one's homeland, once a decision has been made to leave it behind, even just temporarily.[1]

The student of Andersen's life and work soon becomes aware of the importance of travel and exile as themes both in the author's own career and in his written work. Both as a man and as an artist, Andersen was 'on the

From *Bulletin of the John Rylands University Library of Manchester*, vol. 76, no. 3 Autumn (1994). © 1994 by the John Rylands University Library of Manchester.

move' throughout his life, restlessly changing address both in real terms and metaphorically. There is, perhaps, nothing remarkable in this: it is in the nature of great men and women that they resist the temptation to settle, that they are constantly looking for new paths to travel. But in Andersen's case the significance is of a specific nature. He offers an opportunity to observe the artist's mind on the journey through the world.

Andersen is best known as the author of fairy tales for children, and his fame rests on a comparatively small number of the very best. In all, he wrote 157 and increasingly, as his career progressed, he changed the emphasis from children's tales to something much closer to the short story, which was gaining importance as a genre in nineteenth-century Denmark.[2] However, he never entirely let go of his young audience. After all, much of his fame in the later part of his career depended on it. This article will show that the travel motif acts as a guide through Andersen's career in much more general terms, and this can be taken as an indication of how important it was to Andersen's thinking.

A closer reading of his collected tales reveals that travel plays a part in almost twenty per cent of them.[3] This article will look at how the travel motif is developed in thirty-four of the tales, published between 1835 and 1874. It will also look at the different ways in which the travel motif is made to work for the story teller as he constructs the tales.

It soon becomes clear that it does so in a variety of ways. To a certain, limited extent it provides the plot for his stories. In this respect, the journey becomes a string of episodes, adding up into a full narrative. As in Homer's *Odyssey*, and as in countless folktales, the journey and its constituent parts are made significant for what they have to say both about the places where the travellers go and about the travellers themselves.

But more significant is the way in which Andersen uses the travel motif as part of the theme of a tale. Where this happens, it is possible to see how Andersen gradually moves away from an early reliance on folktale motifs to describe a pessimistic view of the life of the emotional and geographical exile, to a much more self-assured, realistic and cosmopolitan view of life, expressed in a more modern prose style.

At no time does he abandon the fairy tale entirely, in the sense that he continues to include elements of the irrational in many of his stories. This is part of Andersen's world view and fundamental to his art: everything under the heavens, be it animate or inanimate, has a voice, which the author hears and which informs his stories. Travel feeds into the stories in different ways, sometimes simply by providing casual detail to the description of characters, at other times by providing the actual key to characterization or even the actual physical environment in which the characters move. Travel as such is rarely of great importance in the tales. Andersen is not using them to sell the idea of travel as an important part of the development in the individual. But they do suggest, by their example, why it is so important, and that is probably how they can contribute to the lives of their readers.

Andersen wrote several autobiographies, starting with the first, hand-written one from 1832, *Levnedsbogen*[4] (*The book of my life*), written when he was only twenty-seven years old and three years into his professional career as a writer. Here, for the first time, he puts the view that God has, as it were, written the script for his life, providing him with direction and, perhaps more to the point, offered this son of poor parents unexpected and almost miraculous opportunities in the middle-class world of literature. 'Day by day, my life becomes more and more like poetry', he writes: 'Poetry enters into my life and it seems to me that life itself is a great marvellous poetic work. I feel that an invisible, loving hand guides everything ...'.[5] In later autobiographies, he was to update this image: 'My life is a beautiful fairy tale', he was to write, claiming that even a powerful fairy could not have guided him on the path of life with greater happiness and wisdom.[6]

There is no doubt that this is how he saw his life and it is certainly the metaphor which he, as a self-publicist, chose to use when presenting his life to his audience as a typical Romantic artist: the natural talent who had risen almost magically to international status as an artist. But the metaphor does not hold. Not only was magic obviously not involved: he earned his status by using his talent and he was given help by those of his contemporaries who could see that he deserved it.

A better metaphor for Andersen's life is that of the journey. Andersen remained single all his life and moved between a number of temporary addresses in Copenhagen until he settled in to his first real home in 1866, at the age of sixty-one years. The purchase of his first bed caused him great concern as he imagined that it would one day become his death bed. In fact, he died, still single, in the home of wealthy friends, some of the many who had invited him into their home for shorter or longer periods of his life; not because he was poor but because he was offered hospitality, often by top members of society, sometimes even by royalty.[7]

But somehow he remained 'homeless' in an existential sense. He left his poor background behind when he left for the Danish capital in 1819 and he never truly found another home of his own, except in the world of the arts. His relationship with the family of his benefactor, Jonas Collin, illustrates this excellently. Although Andersen saw a father figure in Jonas Collin and worked hard to get close to Collin's son, Edvard, he was never fully integrated into the family. Andersen accepted this: he was a public figure and he gradually came to accept that he had to live a public life, in other people's families.

Andersen travelled throughout his life. His first significant journey, significant because it changed his life, was the one that he made from his home town to the Danish capital in 1819. But he made many other journeys outside Denmark, from the first to the Harz Mountains in 1831 to his final journey in 1873, and he visited most of Europe. Andersen was not only a passionate traveller but also a professional one, and his experiences of foreign countries found their way not only into his fiction but also into actual travel descriptions. The earliest of these is *Skyggebilleder af en Rejse til Harzen og det sachsiske Schweiz* (1831, *Shadowy images of a journey to the Harz Mountains and Saxony*) where clear description of landscape mingles with humorous description of human behaviour.

His Grand Tour of 1833–34 resulted in a novel (*Improvisatoren* (*The improviser*), see below). His later, ten-month journey through Europe in 1840–41 inspired one of the great classics of nineteenth century travel literature: *En Digters Bazar* (1842, *A poet's bazaar*), where the reader experiences all aspects of human nature of contemporary transport systems in a manner that still inspires the reader to follow in the footsteps of their guide.

The two journeys to Italy and beyond were the great formative events in the author's life. The first took him out of himself and away from the limited Danish intellectual environment, into a quite different world of unexpected natural beauty and intellectual challenge. Italy was the Mecca of Danish nineteenth-century artists from all art forms, and in Italy Andersen found himself included in an international artists' community. *Improvisatoren* is clear evidence of the impression which Italy made on Andersen, its artistic maturity reflects the maturity that Andersen himself was reaching, as a man and as an artist.

En Digters Bazar is no less indicative of his development. By the 1840s, Andersen was a seasoned traveller and writer who was no longer just observing but also much more directly absorbing and conquering the world around him. The down-side of this professional development is, perhaps, indicated by his final two travel descriptions: *I Spanien* (1863, *In Spain*) and *Et Besøg i Portugal* (1868, *A visit to Portugal*) have greater journalistic than artistic merit. Here, the experienced writer was drawing on his craft rather than innovating.

But it is not so much the 'straight' travel description that is of interest here. Even taking into account that Hans Christian Andersen was always imaginative in his approach to the objective truth of the world around him, some of his works use travel in a stylized manner which throws clearer light on the way in which travel plays a part in the fairy tale.

In 1829, having completed his school education, Andersen made his official debut on the Danish literary scene with *Fodrejse fra Holmens Kanal til østpynten af Amager* (*Journey on foot from Holmens Canal to the east point of Amager*). This fantastic description of an imaginary, dream-like trip on New Year's Eve of 1828 is not only interesting because of its grotesque, surreal atmosphere: the appearance of the supernatural prefigures the later fairy tales. It is also important because it shows Andersen submitting the real world almost completely to his own creative imagination. The reader is taken on a journey through a known location by the author, but it is a journey which could only be made with the author, through his imagination. This becomes particularly clear when, at the end of the novel, Andersen uses the Modernist technique of printing a short chapter consisting only of punctuation.[8] By instinct, this author was a surrealist rather than a realist, and the contemporary reading public immediately took to his idiosyncratic style.

Andersen was to use this mode—the synthesis of reality and the imagination—in several of his travel-inspired works, notably in *Improvisatoren* (1835) and *I Sverrig* (1851, *In Sweden*). The approach is different in both, and both are different from *Fodrejse*.

Improvisatoren is an autobiographical novel, an inspired blend of two of Andersen's favourite subjects: his own unusual career, and the world outside his own country. It gave him an international reputation as a novelist, in advance of his fame as a writer of fairy tales, or 'romances' as they were often called in the previous century. *Improvisatoren* tells the story of a young man who rises from humble beginnings to artistic fame. Its success relied—and relies—on the fact that it is told through the mind of the main character and that we witness the colourful Italy of the early nineteenth century through his eyes. He had seen that Italy himself on his Grand Tour in 1833–34 and he chose to present his impressions in fictional form.

The eyes through which the reader sees Italy are those of a talented traveller and fiction writer. To students of Andersen's work, the narrator's point-of-view is always of crucial importance. It often says something very directly about how close the reader is to Andersen's own experience.

I Sverrig is a very different kind of work, but it is also testimony to its author's ability to operate with a range of literary technique. Like *Improvisatoren*, it is the fruit of the actual travel experiences of its author.[9] But *I Sverrig* is no ordinary travel description, any more than *Improvisatoren* is. Rather, it is a collage of impressions of a country that was then not well known in Europe, at least by travellers. The structure is episodic, a collage made up of a variety of linguistic media, using straight prose interspersed with fairy tales[10] and lyrical poetry. Andersen does not restrict himself to straightforward description of what he sees, although such descriptions are included: he ranges from realism to philosophy, using his Scandinavian sister nation as a springboard for all the many thoughts that travel may engender in a receptive mind.

What we have in these three works is evidence of Andersen's versatility and his ability to juggle narrative styles and levels of realism. They suggest that Andersen was not only crossing geographical borders on his way through Europe but also inhabiting a continent of the imagination, one without boundaries and with endless variety of landscape and experiences. It was this landscape which he was to travel in his fairy tales.

Andersen published his first fairy tales in 1835, in a small volume of *Eventyr fortalte for Børn*, 'fairy tales told for children'. He continued to write and publish them almost to the end of his life, the last collection being called *Eventyr og Historier*, 'fairy tales and stories'. The change in title to include the word 'stories' was deliberate and suggested Andersen's own changing priorities as a writer of short prose: he was increasingly seeing himself as a writer of short stories for adults, without leaving his young audience entirely behind. The truth is that audiences of all ages were always in the implied audience for his tales.

The four titles in the first volume included *The tinder box* and *The princess and the pea*. Both of them make use of the travel motif, but at this point that motif plays only a simple part in straightforward plots: the soldier in *The tinder box* is marching home from war, apparently without aiming for any particular address, and is intercepted by his destiny, in the shape of money, power and love. This is an adaptation of the story about Aladdin from the *Arabian nights*, which Andersen had known since childhood, and as such it is a rare example of Andersen borrowing an idea from the existing folk tradition.

The princess and the pea shows a prince engaging in a futile journey to find a real princess. Only after his return does such a princess journey to his home, appearing mysteriously out of the blue and settling down as his Queen.

Both these stories have the ring of the true folk-tale about them, their characters are clearly acting without rational motivation and their plots progress in ways that suggest the interference of non-human powers. They represent a particular strand in the use of the travel motif: one that stems from the folktale, where the journey is a recurrent and purely functional plot element, offering opportunities for purely functional, one-dimensional characters to meet challenges and complete tasks set by agents of the non-human world.[11]

The earliest tale to illustrate this use of the motif is also one of Andersen's finest: *The travelling companion* (*Rejsekammeraten*, 1835).[12] *Rejsekammeraten* is, in the true sense of the word, a 'classical' tale. It shows a young man reaching a turning point in his life: his father dies, he himself is uprooted and sets out on a journey that will ultimately lead to a new equilibrium in his life, in the same way as happens in *The tinder box* and *The princess and the pea*. To that extent, the plot of the tale is one that would be recognized by audiences and readers not only now or in Andersen's own time but as far back as ancient Greece, where the same plot is met in the *Odyssey* and in classical Greek drama. Throughout the story, the main character moves in a world that is only superficially like our own 'real' world: it is, in fact, suffused with the supernatural, in it witchcraft and magic both hinder and help the characters.

The final, happy end is contrived rather than probable in terms of modern realism, for this is story-telling as ritual, the plot is an acting-out of a transition from one stable condition to another. What Andersen has ultimately achieved with this tale is to show a young man undergoing the transition from boyhood to manhood, from living with his father to living, as an adult, with his own wife. He has been helped through this transition by a character with supernatural powers, and this character, the Travelling Companion, takes on the forces of darkness on his behalf.

Andersen is best known as a writer for children, but this is in reality also a tale of adolescence. For all that it involves the forces of evil, it also carries a comforting message: help is available, the main character does get through to the other side, stability will return. The traditional tale is particularly characteristic of Andersen's early tales, from the 1830s, although it continues to appear into the 1850s and 1860s.[13] It is given a variety of uses, from providing the structure for stories with deep metaphysical significance such as *The snow queen* (*Snedronningen*, 1845) to those that are much more straightforwardly amusing like *Clod Hans* (*Klods-Hans*, 1855).

Although Andersen himself refers to the stories told to him in his own childhood,[14] he only relied on the actual oral folk-tale tradition to a limited extent, composing most of his stories independently of known literary or pre-literary models.[15] Although he is often mentioned in the same breath as the Brothers Grimm, he was no folklorist. Rather, he was an author of 'Kunstmärchen', a modern Romantic. It is therefore necessary to look immediately beyond the folk-tale as such, to see in what other way he makes the folk-tale work for him. Part of the answer lies in the way he develops as an author of short stories. But at this early point in his career, he appears to have drawn on the folk-tale for other things.

Most obviously Andersen makes travel provide him with *plot*: it offers a reason for stringing a series of events together, events that shape the life of the main character(s). Thus, in *Inchelina* (*Tommelise*, 1835) the somewhat passive female main character passes through the hands of a series of potential husbands until she is carried off by the swallow to foreign parts. *The ugly duckling* (*Den grimme Ælling*, 1844) gives a similar view of a character passively developing into a more mature character, as a hostile world passes by.

The snow queen and *The story of a mother* (*Historien om en Moder*, 1848), by contrast, show two main characters making rather better use of their ability to travel, namely for a search for their loved ones. *The snow queen* and *The story of a mother*, like *The travelling companion*, are stories of human beings maturing, although in the case of *The snow queen* and *The story of a mother*, the process is intellectual or metaphysical rather than social or to do simply with ageing. It is not possible to say of stories such as these that they mainly exemplify a characteristic, conventional use of plot and character functions. These tales are far more sophisticated and their effect depends to a much greater extent on the use of symbolism. Although they *are* good stories, which work as entertainment at the surface, they invite interpretation that goes far beyond their story lines. At the story level, they have elements of the fairy tale, in that they include irrational and supernatural elements. But they also present themes of fundamental importance for human beings: the ability to love and, in the case of *The story of a mother*, the ability to let go of those we love.

At this point in his life, Andersen had made a reputation as a travel writer with *A poet's bazaar* (1842) and his experience as an observer of the world may explain why he was now capable of making better use of his plots. However, it is more likely that we are simply looking at a more mature writer in more general terms, for whom literature as such could be made to carry more meaning. Plot is now made to work harder, the individual events made to reveal more about the characters.

The use of travel as a means of structuring plot peters out in the 1850s along with the use of the folk-tale-like travel motif. It is likely that the two trends are linked. Andersen's tales were becoming increasingly realistic over the years and the focus moving increasingly away from plot structure to the reactions of the characters within the plots.

Andersen has rightly become renowned as a children's author, and the tales which most people now remember have become part of our collective unconscious, entering our cultural mythology. *The emperor's new clothes*, to mention just one obvious example, has provided countless public writers and speakers with ammunition for attacks on their opponents, and many of Andersen's tales have been published anonymously, adapted for children, proving that they are now themselves part of our narrative tradition, not even needing their author's name to survive.

Children are not naive and the universe which they inhabit is not one of simple, innocent bliss. Children know that and the most successful children's writers succeed by respecting that, as both Astrid Lindgren and Roald Dahl illustrate.[16] Andersen, too, reveals a complex and sometimes even frightening view of the world, both in his children's stories and in those intended for older audiences. The plots may lead us through landscapes peopled with devils and sprites before taking us up to the happy ending, and we do not forget that we had to see those landscapes as we travelled with the characters and that they are still there in the background as we learn that the main characters will live happily ever after.

The little mermaid (*Den lille Havfrue*, 1837) is a story of love that cannot succeed. That is, of course, not how it comes across in the recent animated version: Andersen's original tale commits the Mermaid to a fate of which the makers of modern mass entertainment dare not conceive.

Like its predecessor in Andersen's oeuvre, *Agnete and the merman* (*Agnete og Havmanden*, 1834), it tells the story of a character who follows her heart in a decisive existential choice, thereby unwittingly committing herself to a life in loneliness and exile. The little mermaid, like Agnete, chooses a partner who is so fundamentally unlike herself that a real relationship is not possible, no matter how great a sacrifice she is prepared to make. The story, revolving around this decisive moment when the wrong step is taken, evolves like a Greek tragedy from hubris to eventual nemesis.

A number of Andersen's tales show characters unable to engage in harmonious relationships, men and women shipwrecked by life, and this motif recurs from the earliest tales, i.e. *Inchelina* (1835) to one of the latest, namely *The wood nymph* (*Dryaden*, 1868). *The flying trunk* (*Den flyvende*

Koffert, 1839) provides a humorous example—the main character finds himself deservedly stranded abroad after an accident, but other examples leave little room for merriment. In *The garden of Eden* (*Paradisets Have*, 1839) the main character finds himself repeating the original biblical mistake, although without committing the original sin.

In *Under the willow tree* (*Under Piletræet*, 1853) a man who emigrates in order to escape from the romantic disappointment of his youth encounters the love of his youth abroad and dies as he tries to escape in the opposite direction, travelling home. *Ib and little Christina* (*Ib og lille Christine*, 1855) shows a woman destroying herself as she travels away to partake of sophisticated city life rather than the simpler and healthier provincial life which Ib could have offered her. And *A story from the dunes* (*En Historie fra Klitterne*, 1860) has a social misfit die, mad and alone, buried by the sanddunes in an abandoned church, after a life that starts and ends in shipwreck.

What is happening here? How does one account for this sombre aspect of Andersen's work? It is tempting to do what critics have so often done, namely to seek the reasons in Andersen's own life, and to a certain extent this makes good sense. Andersen was himself a 'misfit', he had left his poor childhood behind but he never truly seemed to arrive anywhere else, in spite of his international fame and comparative wealth. The fact that he never settled down in a love relationship, in spite of several involvements with various ladies, may have inspired his somewhat pessimistic view of love in the stories referred to here, where the characters are endlessly—and hopelessly—on the move.

One of the forest examples of how this motif is explored in the tales is *The steadfast tin soldier* (*Den standhaftige Tinsoldat*, 1838), whose main character only just has time to discover his love for the young ballerina before fate—or some other inexplicable force—casts him out into a hostile world from which he is miraculously and inexplicably saved, but only to be senselessly destroyed. What comes across in this story is that there is no sense to the universe, no apparent meaning or order, just casual and irrational changes of fate. Other stories in this group may not be quite so radical in their world view but they all share the feeling that we do not live in a safe universe.[17]

Andersen's treatment of the motif changes over the years, as he becomes more modern in his narrative style and can distance himself, perhaps, from his own personal experience. *A story from the dunes* shows tragic events in the lives of its characters, but they are the kind of events that you do tend to find in the nineteenth-century short story, where the sense of fate and of contrast between a person's young and old age is often what gives the short story its energy. In this particular story, Andersen moves close to the style of Steen Steensen Blicher, the father of the modern Danish short story. Like Blicher, Andersen gives his characters credibility by placing them in a recognizable universe, where events and people do, after all, seem probable even if their fate is extreme. In *A story from the dunes*, Andersen 'poses' as a nineteenth-century topographer, finding similarities between Arabia and Jutland.[18] There is still an element of the irrational in the story, but it has more to do with psychological irrationality than with the supernatural.

The homeless man, the exile who is out of his proper cultural environment, is still there but he is increasingly like a modern man. Characteristically, he still does not know what is hitting him, as is also seen in the case of the main character of *The ice maiden* (*Isjomfruen*, 1862). But by now the reader can see through the events and Andersen's technique is increasingly one of dramatic irony rather than the creation of alternative, 'parallel' worlds where nature and the supernatural interact.

At the same time as he was exploiting the existing thematic use of the journey in the traditional tale, he was also using it to express much more modern themes of alienation and exile. His inspiration may have come from his personal experience, but the real power of stories obviously depends on their reflection of a more general condition which his readers of all ages would be able to recognize and relate to, consciously or otherwise.

In about a dozen of his tales we thus meet characters who travel, perhaps because their instinct tells them to keep on the move, perhaps because fate hurls them along for no clear reason, perhaps because they are running away from their own anxieties or their own failure. But they do not escape: in Andersen's darker stories there is nowhere to hide, no home to go to.

To travel *is* to escape, perhaps from one's daily routine in order to go on holiday, perhaps to create a new life for oneself in new surroundings through emigration. There is, of course, that difference between the exile and the tourist—or the emigré—that the exile is not usually away from his home of his own free will. The exile is a refugee, unsettled, uprooted, only temporarily at his address, waiting for a chance to return. The tourist—and the explorer—engage in a more positive search for something different.

Andersen's later stories reveal a much more settled picture of the character away from home. Part of the change that happens in his narrative style is a greater emphasis on realistic details. Reality is always present in the fairy tales, whether through references to real locations or in details which more or less explicitly place the story in the reader's own universe. But in the later stories, reality becomes ever more obvious and in some cases the element of geographical and psychological realism brings Andersen's narrative close to the prose style of the short story writers of his own time.

This also suggests that the universe described in the stories—the world in which the characters 'live'—is becoming rather more manageable, because it is becoming easier to understand. This does not mean that the characters cope more easily with their world but that their problems are not always embodied in characters from another, metaphysical world. They are not necessarily any happier but they are more like 'real' people.

An example of a transitional story between 'exile' and the more realistic picture of the world abroad is *The pepperman's nightcap* (*Pebersvendens Nathue*, 1858), one of the best realistic stories among Andersen's many short tales. It tells the life story of a German merchant's representative, Anton, living in Copenhagen several centuries before Andersen's own time and making a living by selling spices (the 'pepper' of his title) on behalf of Lübeck and Hamburg merchants. The historical details of the story are interesting in themselves but the description of Anton's situation as an exile is more fascinating in this context.

Andersen takes his character's point of view, to the extent of describing German nature as being more attractive than Denmark's.[19] This may seem surprising to those who know Andersen as the author of some of the best-loved lyrical descriptions of the Danish countryside, but it is an indication of his cosmopolitan approach and it also says something about his ability to enter into the world of his characters. Andersen, after all, was also a playwright.

Because Anton is described with more psychological detail, his situation also calls to a greater extent on the reader's ability to observe and understand real events, and with Anton we move away from the well-known Andersen world of fairy tale to something that is closer to Andersen's contemporary Søren Kierkegaard. The focus is existential, the main character's problem cannot be solved by fairies or exacerbated by hostile trolls. His problem is one of living in a world that is in constant flux, one that changes constantly and which he is not equipped to understand. Andersen hints that modern nineteenth-century transport would have helped the character cope better with life away from home. At least now, in the 1850s, modern steam power has shrunk Europe to more manageable proportions.

Far from being an impoverishment of the tale, its existential emphasis becomes a sign of its author's versatility as well as, it may be assumed, some of his own experience of life. It is not a happy or desirable life, but as Andersen presents it, it does amount to a valid existence: the author is implicitly claiming to be presenting his reader with reality. Andersen describes his character's loneliness as seen through the character's mind: '... he didn't understand himself, he didn't understand the others; but *we* understand! You can be in somebody's home, with the family, and yet you do not strike root, you converse in the way you might converse on a stage coach, you get to know each other in the way you get to know other passengers on a stage coach, you bother each other, you wish that you were somewhere else or that your good neighbour were'.[20]

Realism never entirely takes over the Andersen fairy tale, but it grows in importance as an element in his narrative style and in a way it brings him closer to our own century, helps us to see that his world view is not that different from our own as well as allowing him to bring his talents as a creative writer and a travel journalist together.

One may wonder, at reading *The pepperman's nightcap*, whether it is a reflection of Andersen's true experience of 'homelessness'. The answer would probably be both a 'yes' and a 'no'. He may well have felt what his character does: 'Bitter is the life of the stranger in a strange country! You are only, noticed by others if you are in their way'.[21] What is more, the late twentieth-century reader easily recognizes the experience of living in a world in flux, where one's sense of belonging is constantly disturbed because modern technology keeps changing one's sense of what the world looks like. Feeling estranged has become one of the central experiences of life in our century and Andersen was ideally equipped to describe it well before it became commonly understood.

But at the same time he was also becoming used to it. The experience of homelessness, which he had had since childhood and which had become his both by choice and through necessity, had also become a strength. And so it is that late in life his attitude to rootless modern life begins to change. For one thing, foreign countries increasingly provide the setting for his tales or form part of the characters' world. Thus, *The ice maiden* (*Iisjomfruen*, 1862), *Psyche* (*Psychen*, 1862) and *The wood nymph* (*Dryaden*, 1868) are set outside Denmark. What is more, the author's attitude to life becomes increasingly cosmopolitan. His outlook, which is never narrow, becomes ever more worldly. He embraces, with enthusiasm, the concept of modern transport and he evidently understands that improved communication will also change the outlook of modern people. *The muse of the new century* (*Det nye Aarhundredes Musa*, 1861), *The wood nymph* (1862), *The bird phoenix* (Fugl Phønix, 1863) and *The thorny path* (*Ärens Tornevei*, 1863) are celebrations of life in a modern, cosmopolitan world. The 'Muse'—that of poetry—is a citizen of a world where, soon 'the Great Wall of China shall fall; the railways of Europe shall reach the closed cultural archives of Asia—two streams of culture shall meet and flow as one'.[22] *The thorny path* is an attempt to link the ancient Greek civilization with that of modern engineers, by listing some of the author's own heroes from world history. *The phoenix* is, again, creative writing as part of a timeless world-culture.

In *The wood nymph*, Andersen indulges in a description of the Paris World Exhibition of 1867 that combines his enthusiasm for the real, modern world with his fairy-tale style of writing. The story is described both through the eyes of the wood nymph, the dryad, who is granted twelve hours in human form, so that she can see modern Paris and the Exhibition; and through the eyes of Andersen himself and those of his readers: 'We are travelling to the Paris Exhibition. We are there! with speed, with a rush, entirely without witchcraft. We travelled on the wings of speed, at sea and on land. Ours is the age of fairy-tales. We are in the middle of Paris ...'.[23] Once the wood nymph goes sightseeing in this modern Paris, we find that the author's enthusiasm has not blurred his vision: this is both a Paris of human tragedy and of modern sewers, a Paris where hotels are decorated with fresh flowers and where pollution kills the trees outside.

In a sense, *The wood nymph* brings this journey through Andersen's fairy tales full circle. From using the journey as a conventional folk-tale motif, Andersen had reached the point where the journey was part of the shared experience of modern Europeans, an experience which seemed likely to reach modern people everywhere, tying them together in a shared world with a shared culture.

In his autobiography Andersen describes the city where he grew up, Odense, as being in some senses unchanged since the Middle Ages. His own background, his childhood, was rooted in the past. Towards the end of his life, in 1872, he published a fairy tale in which an old man, *Great-grandfather* (*Oldefader*, 1872), appears. 'Great-grandfather' himself comes from Odense and remembers its old-fashioned culture. But now, in his old age, modern technology enables his grandson Frederik to travel to America (by steamship), and the same technological age has provided the means (the telegraph) whereby Frederik is able to stay in contact with 'Great-grandfather'.

Andersen had himself travelled from the world of the Middle Ages to that of Modernism, in both art and culture. In his fairy tales, travel remained a central motif. It played different parts in the tales at different stages of his artistic career and in that respect it reflects changes in his life and in his art.

At an early age he set out on his life's journey, through an age of restless cultural, political and technological change. At the early stages, from 1835, travel was predominantly used in the way it happens in the folktale, as a conventional element in story-telling. But he soon began to explore travel at a more personal level in the tales, as a metaphor for homelessness and exile, reflecting his own dark vision of human life as a problematic journey.

But in the 1850s, a change takes place, a change which clearly reflects his own experience of travel and which may also reflect his own greater maturity as a man of the world: his outlook becomes increasingly cosmopolitan and his fascination grows for the technology of travel and foreign settings for his narratives.

He never loses track of the essential ingredient of the fairy-tale: its ability to merge the rational and irrational worlds. Nor does he ever forget that children are in the audience for the tales, after all writing tales specifically for children was one of his great achievements. But his view of the world changes and his readers—be they children or adults—are challenged to deal with ever more complex and advanced aspects of the world which they share with the author.

The great joy is that they have been allowed to go with him on his journey. Ivan Klima, remembering a school essay which he wrote in Theresienstadt, said that writing 'enables you to enter places inaccessible in real life, even the most forbidding spaces. More than that, it allows you to invite guests along'.[24] To this day, readers sense Andersen's generous invitation to go with him on that great journey of his life.

APPENDIX

Fairy tales considered for this investigation (the English titles in the list are those used in the Penguin *Complete fairy tales and stories of Hans Andersen*, trans. Erik Haugaard (Harmondsworth: Penguin Books, 1985):

1835	*Fyrtøjet*	The tinderbox
1835	*Prinsessen paa Ærten*	The princess and the pea
1835	*Rejsekammeraten*	The travelling companion
1835	*Tommelise*	Inchelina
1837	*Den lille Havfrue*	The little mermaid
1838	*De vilde Svaner*	The wild swans
1838	*Den standhaftige Tinsoldat*	The steadfast tin soldier
1838	*Lykkens Kalosker*	The magic galoshes
1839	*Den flyvende Koffert*	The flying trunk

1839	*Paradisets Have*	The garden of Eden
1842	*Metalsvinet*	The bronze pig
1844	*Den grimme Ælling*	The ugly duckling
1845	*Snedronningen*	The snow queen
1848	*Den lykkelige Familie*	The happy family
1848	*Historien om en Moder*	The story of a mother
1853	*Under Piletræet*	Under the willow tree
1855	*Klods-Hans*	Clod Hans
1855	*Et Blad fra Himlen*	A leaf from heaven
1855	*Ib og lille Christine*	Ib and little Christina
1858	*Flaskehalsen*	The bottle
1858	*Pebersvendens Nathue*	The pepperman's nightcap
1858	*Suppe paa en Polsepind*	How to cook soup upon a sausage pin
1859	*Et Stykke Perlesnor*	A string of pearls
1860	*En Historie fra Klitterne*	A story from the dunes
1861	*I Andegården*	In the duckyard
1861	*De Vises Sten*	The philosopher's stone
1861	*Det nye Århundredes Muse*	The muse of the new century
1862	*Isjomfruen*	The ice maiden
1862	*Psychen*	Psyche
1863	*Fugl Phønix*	The bird phoenix
1863	*Ærens Tornevej*	The thorny path
1868	*Dryaden*	The wood nymph
1872	*Oldefar*	Great-grandfather
1874	*Laserne*	The rags

NOTES

1. Hans Christian Andersen, *H.C. Andersen and Thalia: love's labours lost?* (Odense: Odense University Press, 1992).

2. Steen Steensen Blicher (1782–1848), clergyman, topographer and author, is the father of the Danish short story. Partly inspired by Sir Walter Scott, the Ossian tradition and folktales, he developed and perfected a style of pseudo-realistic narrative, often in regional Danish (Jutland) dialect. A number of stories are available in English translation (see Schroder, *A bibliography of Danish literature in English translation 1950–1980* (Copenhagen: The Danish Institute, 1982).

3. This investigation covers 34 out of 157 printed in Gyldendal.

4. Published in 1926. See H. Topsøe-Jensen: *Omkring Levnedsbogen* (1943).

5. Hans Brix (ed.), *H.C. Andersens levnedsbog* (1971), 19.

6. H.C. Andersen: *Mit eget eventyr uden digtning*, edited from the author's manuscript by H. Topsøe-Jensen (Copenhagen: Nyt Nordisk Forlag, 1942), 5. This is the Danish original of Andersen's first published autobiography, which appeared in German

translation as *Das Märchen meines Lebens ohne Dichtung* (Leipzig: Carl B. Lorck, 1847). Andersen's second autobiography, *Mit Livs Eventyr* (1855), uses almost identical twins to the passage quoted.

7. In 1857, he spent a month in Charles Dickens' home. See Elias Bredsdorff, *H.C. Andersen og Charles Dickens* (Copenhagen: Rosenkilde og Bagger, 1951). Andersen's many Copenhagen addresses are listed in B.H. Gjelten, *H.C. Andersen som teaterconnaisseur* (Copenhagen: Nyt Nordisk Forlag, 1982), 18.

8. Andersen uses a similar device in his first stage play, *Kærlighed paa Nicolai Taarn* (1829, *Love on St Nicholas's tower*), which suddenly becomes 'interactive', when the author invites the audience to decide how the play should end.

9. Andersen visited Sweden on several occasions, in 1837, 1838 and 1840. He spent three months in Sweden in 1849, before writing *I Seerrig*.

10. E.g. *Fugl Phønix* and *Poesiens Californien*.

11. See, for example, Terence Hawkes, *Structuralism and semiotics* (London: Methuen, 1977), 67 ff. VI. Propp is the proponent of this functionalist or syntagmatic analysis of the fairytale in *Morphology of the folktale* (Russian edition 1928, English translation 1958, revised Austin and London: University of Texas Press, 1968).

12. In fact, it is also his earliest fairy tale. He published the original version of this tale, *Dødningen* ('The dead man') in *Digte 1830* (*Poems 1830*). For the full text of *Dødningen*, see *H.C. Andersens eventyr*, ed. Erik Dal (Copenhagen: Det danske sprog- og litteraturselskab, 1963), 191 ff.

13. In this category we also find *The little mermaid* (1837), *The wild swans* (1838), *The flying trunk* (1839), *The garden of Eden* (1839), *The ugly duckling* (1844), *The story of a mother* (1848), *How to cook soup up a sausage pin* (1858) and *The philosopher's stone* (1861). Note that in this investigation a tale may exemplify several uses of the travel theme and may therefore appear in different categories.

14. See his preface from 1837, in *H.C. Andersens eventyr* (1963), i, 19ff.

15. See Elias Bredsdorff, *Hans Christian Andersen: the story of his life and work* (London: Phaidon Press, 1975), 310 ff. On Andersen's use of the folk-tale see also Paul V. Rubow, *H.C. Andersens eventyr*, second edition, 1943 (Copenhagen: Gyldendal, 1967).

16. See Alison Lurie, *Not in front of the grown-ups* (London: Sphere Books, 1991). For a discussion of Andersen and children, see e.g. Dot Pallis; 'H.C. Andersen's børneverden i eventyrene', *Anderseniana*, iv (1985–86), 297 ff.

17. *The shadow* (*Skyggen*, 1847) depends on similarly irrational events, although in this instance the travel motif moves to the background of the story in favour of the drama that develops between the man and his shadow, as the latter to take over his identity.

18. H.C. Andersen, *Samlede eventyr og historier* (Copenhagen: Gyldendal, 1972), ii, 386.

19. After Denmark's defeat in 1864 in the war against Prussia, such a liberal gesture would have been much less acceptable. The passage in question is the following: '"Great is the beauty of the Danish beech forest!" they said, but to Anton the beeches at Warburg rose even more beautifully' (*Samlede eventyr og historier*, ii, 204.)

20. *Samlede eventyr og historier*, iii, 208.

21. Ibid.

22. *Samlede eventyr og historier*, iii, 40.

23. *Samlede eventyr og historier*, ii, 277.

24. Ivan Klima, 'A childhood in Terezin' in *Granta* (1993), no. 44, 200.

War

Andersen's trip to Britain had done nothing to improve his reputation in Denmark—rather the reverse. Goldschmidt's *The Corsair* had carried a sarcastic piece about 'Andersen, the Lion', accompanied by biting cartoons depicting him as a grovelling toady. Edvard Collin had shown William Jerdan's enthusiastic report of Andersen's visit to the editor of *Berlingske Tidende*, a Danish newspaper named after its founder in 1745, suggesting that he might reprint it from the *Literary Gazette*. He was met with a firm refusal—not, the editor explained, through any malice, but because Jerdan had equated Andersen's greatness with that of Jenny Lind, and such a ludicrous overstatement would make him a laughing-stock in Denmark.

This assessment seems to have been right, for Andersen had only been back in Copenhagen a few hours when a mortifying incident occurred. Looking out of his window, he saw two well-dressed men pass by:

> They saw me, stopped, laughed, and one of them pointed up and said in such a loud voice that I could hear every word, "Look! There's our orang-outan who's so famous abroad!"

By contrast, the modest Jonas Collin had been made a titular privy councillor, and H.P. Holst, who had been Andersen's somewhat reluctant

From *Hans Christian Andersen: The Fan Dancer.* London: Allison & Busby (1998). © 1998 by Alison Prince.

companion in Rome before Andersen's Greek trip, had been knighted for his services to poetry.

On 4 November, Felix Mendelssohn died. His disintegrating health had been partly responsible for Jenny Lind's preoccupied mood in London, for she knew, as Andersen must also have done, that the composer had been so distressed to hear of the sudden death of his beloved sister in May of that same year, 1847, that he himself had lost consciousness, having suffered a stroke from which he never fully recovered. Although he had written the F minor String Quartet that summer during a period of remission, a further attack in September led to his death in under two months. Jenny Lind, grieving for him even before he died, had told Andersen in London that she would never be the same again.

Ahasuerus appeared on 16 December 1847. If Andersen had intended this ambitious verse drama to be a clinching proof of his status as one of the world's great writers, it failed abysmally. He had talked to Oehlenschläger about the idea before he started writing, and the wise old professional had warned him not to attempt it. 'There are such things as form and limits, and one has to respect them,' he advised—but Andersen had ignored him. When he sent Oehlenschläger a copy of the finished book, it earned him a sharp reproof:

> The whole work makes an unpleasant and disorderly impression on me; you must forgive me for putting it so bluntly ... the entire structure consists of aphorisms, fragments, sometimes stories, all of which are loosely connected. It seems to me that there is too much pretension and too little achievement in this poem.

Andersen reproduced his long letter in its entirety in *Mit livs eventyr*, but persisted in defending *Ahasuerus* as a new stage in his development. Early in January 1848, the king asked Andersen to come and take tea with him, and bring something to read. It was not an unusual request, for he had long been on easy terms with the older man who could have been his father, but this time, as Andersen read, he knew that his listener's vitality was failing, and realised with distress that this might be the last time the two of them would meet. Christian VIII was suffering from kidney cancer. Some theorists hold that an early diagnosis of this lay behind his sudden decision to ensure Andersen's welfare in 1844, on Als during the last holiday he took—and now, his remaining days were running out.

The king died on 20 January. He had ruled for only nine years, a steady, far-sighted monarch who had wisely retreated from the nervy absolutism of his predecessor, Frederik VI. They had been good years for Andersen, whose relationship with the king was warm and familiar. He put no thoughts on paper, but Christian VIII remained in his mind for a long time, referred to months later with regret.

The king's death cut the bonds on the demand for democracy which had been swelling in Denmark as it had in the rest of Europe. Christian VIII had been riding this turbulent force with a light hand, yielding to the liberalism of such men as Anders Sandøe Ørsted (brother of the physicist who so strongly influenced Andersen), well aware that his predecessor had come close to causing an embarrassing high-level rebellion in his move to censor the press, which he had been forced to drop. Had Christian lived longer, the new Constitution which was being prepared might have been less confrontational; as it was, his son 'Fritz' (Frederik VII) was left to sign a document which attempted, hopelessly, to bind the duchies of Schleswig and Holstein to Denmark.

The revolutionary urge which was infiltrating Europe in the wake of the French upheaval was essentially nationalistic in character, and the southern duchies seized the opportunity of Christian's death to demand their independence.

Frederik, often written off as 'the mad king' had none of his father's rational intellectualism. He had charm and could always say the right thing to the right person, which caused him to be known in his own time as Frederik the Popular, but he was essentially a lightweight, quite unable to withstand the huge cultural and political authority of Germany. As tension between the two countries rapidly worsened, Andersen, like almost every educated Dane, grieved that the land of Goethe and Schiller and the great composers was closing off and becoming a hostile camp. For years, young Danes of the upper classes, together with the odd maverick like Andersen and Thorvaldsen, had assumed it a vital part of their education to study in Munich or Dresden, Dusseldorff or Weimar, or at least to become familiar with these places on the long trek to Rome, and now, impending war threatened to block off this great cultural hinterland and set friend against friend.

On 22 February, revolution broke out in Paris for two violent days, followed by an uprising in Vienna on 13 March. Widespread famine throughout Europe brought the desperation of starving people to explosion point, and Schleswig-Holstein followed the Viennese example two days later when it staged armed insurgence. Two men whom Andersen knew well were leaders of the revolt; one was the Prince of Nør and the other was his brother, the Duke of Augustenborg, who went to Germany to enlist military support for the rebel movement. Andersen watched in horror as the Prince of Nør, too impatient to wait for the results of his brother's mission, launched an armed attack on the Danish garrison of Rendsburg. German troops supported him, precipitating a war which would rumble on for the next three years.

Lord Palmerston, whom Andersen had met in London, is reputed to have remarked years later that only three men ever fully understood the Schleswig-Holstein conflict; 'One was Prince Albert, who is dead, the second was a German professor who went mad. I am the third—and I have forgotten it.' For Andersen, no such levity was possible. To him, it was an agonisingly intimate war, and the thought of Weimar was particularly painful. Only six months previously, on 4 October 1847, he had written an ecstatic letter to Carl Alexander about his recent visit. Following his trip to Britain had come

> the beautiful days at Ettersburg, with our reunion, our life together there, and our parting. Yes, yes, my noble friend, I love you as a man can only love the noblest and best. This time I felt that you were still more ardent, more affectionate to me. Every little trait is preserved in my heart. On that cool evening, when you took your cloak and threw it round me, it warmed not only my body, but made my heart glow still more ardently.

With the death of Christian VIII, Andersen had suffered a great loss of warmth and friendship. The visits to Amalienborg stopped, and there were no invitations from the new king, a man three years younger than Andersen himself, to come and read.

Carl Alexander's father, the Grand Duke, awarded Andersen the Order of the White Falcon in February 1848, as if in a token of faith before the conflict which was boiling up. At almost the same time, Andersen, together with Oehlenschläger's son William, was honoured with the Swedish Order of the North Star. Oehlenschläger himself gave Andersen as a personal present the miniature replica of his own Danish North Star, confirming his affection and admiration despite his criticism of *Ahasuerus*. Andersen was touched by all this, but the assurances of friendship which they represented seemed a frail defence of decency in the face of what was happening all round him. The Prince of Nør's intervention had led to the Battle of Schleswig on 24 April, leaving countless dead and wounded, and ten days later, Andersen wrote to Carl Alexander in anguish:

> Denmark, my native country, and Germany, where there are so many whom I love, are standing opposed to each other in enmity!

Your Royal Highness will comprehend how much all that pains me! I believe so firmly in the nobility of all men, and feel certain that if they only understood each other, everything would blossom in peace ... How is it in Weimar? When shall we meet, my noble friend? Perhaps never again! And as I think this, all the dear memories of every hour of our life together, the warmth of our meetings, flash through my mind, and my heart melts.

In a kind of horrified fascination, Andersen set off for Glorup shortly after writing this letter. The manor was not far from the scene of the action, and his journalistic instincts prompted a first-hand view of what was going on. A week before the disastrous battle had taken place, he had written a vivid account of Denmark's preparations for war and sent it to Jerdan, well aware that it would be printed in the *Literary Gazette*. In this piece, he had been forthright about the treachery of the Duke of Augustenborg who, despite his support for the German attack on the Danish garrison, had turned and fled in the thick of battle, enraging the troops on both sides. The Moltke mansion of Glorup, on Funen, just north of Schleswig, was visited frequently by officers who had taken part in the action, and Andersen's diary was full of appalling details:

> Heard a good deal about the battle; the men shot in the chest or head lying as if they were asleep; those shot in the abdomen had been almost unrecognisable because their faces were so convulsively distorted with pain. One had lain literally 'biting the dust' with his teeth; his hands had been clutching at the turf.

Some of the stories were about men whom Andersen knew personally. The artist Johan Lundbye, thirty years old, died with tragic absurdity as he leaned on his rifle, which went off when a passing farmer happened to trip over it. Lieutenant Host wept as he told the story.

The defeated and disorganised Danes were scattered across the countryside and found scant hospitality from frightened villagers who feared Prussian reprisals if they offered food or shelter. The invading troops were pillaging their way across the land, and Andersen wrote on 24 May to his publisher, Richard Bentley, in the hope of stimulating British sympathy:

> You will know that the Prussians have penetrated into the country itself, have occupied Jutland and are daily requisitioning foodstuff, wine and tobacco, are sending out troops to take away

whole herds of horses, cloth from the factories, in short, they are
oppressing this poor country in the harshest possible way,
impounding the civil servants if they refuse to give in to their
demands. And just in these last few days—this really is the limit—
they have levied a forced contribution of four million rixdollars,
to be paid before May 28th, otherwise it will be extorted by the
power and terror of war! Jutland cannot pay this sum, not even
half of it can be found; so the Prussians intend to plunder and set
the towns on fire. That such things can happen in our time, that
such things can happen in civilised nations, seems to me like a
nightmare.

He went on to make a passionate appeal to Britain for help, and it may have
been that his intervention had some effect on public opinion, for, having seen
Sweden and Norway lend their support, the British government, together
with Russia, weighed in on the side of Denmark. The Prussian leaders
prudently withdrew their troops and refrained from pressing the demand for
four million rixdollars, and an armistice in September brought about a fragile
and uneasy peace.

In that same month, Andersen's new novel, *The Two Baronesses*, was
published in England, two months prior to its appearance in Denmark.
While in London, he had realised that the only way to stop the pirating of
his work in unauthorised translations was to corner the market with an
original publication, and from that time on, this became his standard
practice. That international copyright became established was largely due to
the campaigning of Charles Dickens, but it was Richard Bentley who had
prompted Andersen to his self-protecting course of action.

Andersen himself sent Dickens a copy of his new book. He had already
sent him his latest collection of tales, dedicated to Dickens and entitled *A
Christmas Greeting to my English Friends*, but this had elicited no response,
and neither did the new book. Until prompted by Andersen nine months
later, the great man remained silent. It may well have been that he found
himself unable to say much about *The Two Baronesses*, even if he read it, for
the book is completely lacking in all the qualities which Dickens regarded as
valuable. Its storyline is wandering and confused, without humour or
identifiable characterisation, and its heroine is so closely modelled on Jeanie
Deans in Scott's *Heart of Midlothian* as to border on pastiche. Andersen's
diary records his reading of this novel on 17 May 1848, early in the writing
of his own book.

As a mosaic of elements from his own life, *The Two Baronesses* holds a certain interest to present-day readers. The usual theme of making good from poverty-stricken origins is there, together with the friendships between young men, a shoemaker called Hansen, a girl who wears Hansen's red boots, a childhood dream of living in castles, a child with a wonderful voice and a reference to the magnificent acting of Johanne Heiberg. It may have been Jonna Drewsen's pending elevation to the rank of baroness through her engagement to Henrik Stampe which had sparked off the idea of a contrast between the young woman of non-aristocratic background and the older, more secure one, but numerous role-models have been suggested. Whatever its origins, the plot is so diffuse and lacking in organisation that it fails to hang together. Despite these shortcomings, the book was lighter in tone than Andersen's previous novels, and proved popular. Heiberg even went so far as to send its author his congratulations.

During the summer months of 1848, discontent continued to simmer in Schleswig-Holstein, the German-speaking inhabitants having been denied their wish to break away from Denmark, and Andersen saw that the armistice could not hold much longer. He wrote to Carl Alexander, voicing his fears that the duchies, already unwilling to abide by the terms of the peace settlement, would explode into further violence—'then we will have no postal connection in winter at all'. His concerns were always essentially personal.

Without apparent awareness that his friend's allegiances lay with the other side, Andersen's letter went on to give a description of the Swedish detachment that had been billeted on Count Moltke of Glorup while he had been there. He made it sound more like a cultural delegation than an army. There had been, he said:

> a colonel, eight officers, a chaplain, a surgeon and forty bandsmen, besides a large number of soldiers ... the officers are still cultured and mostly talented men (I met a pianist among them, a friend of Liszt). Every day the band played during dinner, and there were promenade concerts for the whole neighbourhood in the long avenues of the garden.

The Swedes had not actually engaged in the war, since the armistice had been declared shortly after their arrival, but they gave a hand with the harvest in the absence of so many Danish men, and were warmly welcomed.

At the end of that troubled year, Andersen was commissioned by the Royal Theatre to write a play for performance at its hundredth jubilee gala. After his years of struggle and disappointment in the theatrical world, it was a touching gesture of confidence, and Andersen produced a patriotic piece called *The Groundwork of Art*, in which he claimed that Denmark's greatness lay in her collective intellectual power rather than in military strength. It was an elegant explanation of his country's losing situation in Schleswig-Holstein, and the play ran to great public acclaim.

On 3 April 1849, as Andersen had feared, the fragile peace broke down and Denmark was again at war with Germany. This time, he had no desire to be a witness, and instead headed north to Sweden, leaving Copenhagen on 17 May. He stayed away for four months, finding himself heralded with much celebration wherever he went. He had only one unnerving moment; when taken to visit an insane asylum, the minister in charge of it asked on hearing Andersen's name, 'Will he be staying here permanently?' If meant as a joke, it was less than hilarious, and Andersen, morbidly sensitive on the subject of madness, could find no reply.

In the renewed fighting, the Danish forces were again losing heavily, as might be expected when the sympathies of the population lay with the opposing side, and Andersen found himself touched personally by the conflict as letters from his beloved friend in Weimar ceased to arrive. Finally he heard that Carl Alexander had himself led a contingent of troops into battle, and recognised at last that the man he cared for so deeply must be counted among Denmark's enemies.

Following a further defeat in a battle on 6 July, an armistice was again declared, and Andersen ventured to write to his friend. In a letter dated 18 August, he commented that the young duke had 'certainly experienced sad days this summer'. He did not post the letter until 8 September, by which time he had added a rash postscript:

> Your noble heart, and every noble German heart which loves the truth, will feel that Denmark is blameless and good, and has suffered injustice ...

Carl Alexander felt no such thing. In a letter written shortly after the latest armistice, he had, as Andersen told Edvard, stressed that their friendship should have nothing to do with politics. It was a clear warning not to overstep the mark, and Andersen did his best to keep his patriotic feelings out of their continued correspondence, even though the armistice broke down once more.

On 14 November 1849, he wrote a song called 'Poetry' for the public celebration of Oehlenschläger's seventieth birthday, little suspecting that the man he had admired so long was almost at the end of his life. At eleven o'clock on 20 January 1850 'at the same hour of the same day as Christian VIII' Andersen noted, Adam Oehlenschläger died, with immense dignity. He kissed his family goodbye and assured them that he felt no pain, and when Andersen saw his body, he commented that the jaundice which had killed him had conferred 'the appearance of a bronze statue rather than of a corpse. The forehead was beautiful, youthful and clear.'

People from all walks of life followed the poet in a long procession to his burial-place at Frederiksberg, where he had been born. Once again Andersen ('and old Grundtwig' as he told Carl Alexander in a long letter) had been commissioned to write suitable words, and Andersen's funeral song was set to music by Christophe Weyse. In the same letter to the young duke, he had spoken with excitement about H.C. Ørsted's newly published book, *Soul in Nature*, which revealed the world to be 'so splendidly great, so intelligible, so sacred'. Ørsted, though renowned for his innovative practical work in physics, was based very much in the tradition of Goethe, writing about natural phenomena with a perceptive curiosity which is only beginning to re-emerge in our own time from an age of artificial and restrictive division between the arts and the sciences.

On 2 February, the marriage between Jonna Drewsen and Henrik Stampe took place, and Andersen's diary contained no comment. On his forty-fifth birthday, 2 April 1850, he wrote to Carl Alexander with a long description of his new verse play, *Ole Lukoie*, which had just been staged. The eponymous hero is a figure not unlike the legendary Scottish Dream Angus, a bringer of the heart's desire to the sleeping mind, and the plot addressed the question which was beginning to trouble Andersen so much; when a man has all he could wish for, why is it that he still senses an inner emptiness and despair?

The play was widely misunderstood. Andersen quoted in his letter a critic who had taken the point to be a political one and assumed the author to be rebuking those who held 'false notions of a perfect equality in worldly circumstances for all'. Nothing could be further from the truth. As always, Andersen's concerns were purely personal, and while he retained a fellow-feeling for the underdog, he showed no signs of envisaging a society free of the gradients which were so material to his life and to his writing. The dismaying blankness which accompanied his success came from realising that admiration is no substitute for love. Edvard was lost to him, reduced to the status of a sensible and supportive friend, and the continuing war had made Weimar and Carl Alexander seem remote. His play was parodied in the newly established Casino Theatre, a popular and irreverent rival to the Royal, and Andersen wrote in distress to Ørsted's daughter, Mathilde. Ørsted himself replied, pointing out that 'almost all men of distinction are subject to attacks of that kind'. Very gently, he told Andersen that *Ole Lukoie* was not the best thing he had ever done, and cautioned him on no account to try to defend himself.

Andersen took his advice—but by the summer, he was sinking into depression. At Glorup, his fellow-guests made it clear that they knew about his friendship with the Hereditary Grand Duke of Weimar, and needled him constantly about this and about his effeminacy. His diary entries in June record a multitude of provocative remarks. '"Isn't that a handkerchief from Schleswig-Holstein?"'. '"You're not writing to the Duke of Weimar, are you?"'. On 25 June, he had a particularly bad time:

> Mr Lindegaard was boorishly witty at my expense—talked about my courage with bulls and so forth, and later, at home, about my having made the cloth flowers for the chandelier. I ignored him, but felt uncomfortable about it. Afterwards ... Countess Scheel came out with some drivel—that I was supposed to have said I didn't have the heart for war but would go along as a troubador! I was angry to have such nonsense pinned on me and objected to such 'unnatural talk'.

The next day, he went out to pick forget-me-nots for Miss Raben and Countess Moltke, and felt a little better, but toothache began to plague him, with an abscess which had to be lanced. 'Melancholy;' he wrote on 1 July, 'my progress as a writer is a thing of the past.'

Four days later, as Andersen was out walking alone in a 'dark and sombre mood', a servant rushed up with the news that there had been a cease-fire:

> Tears sprang to my eyes; I ran in to His Excellency; saw the announcement on the leaflet sent to us from Nyborg by the merchant Suhr. It isn't official; I don't dare give myself over to my joy.

The peace treaty was signed on 2 July 1850. 'Peace! Peace with Germany!' Andersen wrote to Carl Alexander. 'It rings through my heart.' He rushed on to voice his hope that he could visit Weimar again, and lamented that Beaulieu had entirely ceased to write to him.

His letter met with a hostile silence. Andersen seemed unaware that Germany had technically lost the war, since the treaty had given Denmark continuing, though conditional, rule over the duchies. The Schleswig-Holstein insurgents ignored the cease-fire and continued to fight on against the Danish troops, but without their Prussian allies they had no real hope of victory, and were finally crushed in January 1851. Their defeat left the duchies in a state of sullen resentment, under a Danish hold much weakened by conciliatory clauses in the peace treaty—and Germany was biding its time, well aware that the business had not been concluded. In such continuing tensions, Andersen's gushing letters to Weimar must have seemed blunderingly insensitive, and Carl Alexander remained silent.

Home concerns occupied Andersen. Jette Wulff, an intrepid traveller despite her small, deformed body, embarked on 12 September on a year's trip to the Danish West Indies aboard the brig *Mercurius*, of which her brother Christian had just taken command. Like several Danish women of the time, she was a skilled painter, depicting landscape and genre scenes with a fluent, easy technique and clear perception. Shortly after her departure, Andersen began sitting to another woman artist, Elizabeth Jerichau-Baumann, for a portrait.

On 7 November, Copenhagen University honoured H.C. Ørsted with a celebration of his fiftieth jubilee as a lecturer there. At seventy-three, with an untidy shock of white hair and an enthusiasm for the mystery and excitement of physics which was as strong as ever, he was adored by his students, who staged a torchlight procession for him. Andersen described the whole thing in yet another letter to the silent Carl Alexander, chatting excitedly about the second part of Ørsted's *Soul in Nature* and its effect on his own latest book, *In Sweden*. He added that the Moltkes' son, Jerichau, who had served as a hussar in the Danish army, had died of typhus. The silence from Weimar continued.

As the unofficial war finally came to an end in January, Andersen watched the victorious troops returning to Copenhagen, exhausted rather than triumphant. His publisher, Reitzel, gave him thirty copies of the book of patriotic songs Andersen had written during the war, including the famous *In Denmark I Was Born*, for distribution to the soldiers. Andersen gave them to the wounded men first, then to the youngest, and lamented that he had not enough. What the men said is not recorded.

There was a waspish reference to this public benevolence in Meier Goldschmidt's new publication, *North and South*, but it was caused in part by a foolish discourtesy of Andersen's towards the editor. He had been invited to Goldschmidt's house on 12 February for a celebration of Ole Bull's birthday but decided not to go 'as I so often do', he admitted in his diary. The indignant Goldschmidt took him to task for sending no apology or excuse and accused Andersen of being jealous that somebody other than himself was being feted.

It was the kind of social gaffe which Andersen, ever locked within his own concerns, was particularly prey to. Now that the victory celebrations were over, the anticlimax was setting in, and there was little to distract him from his growing bleakness. On 21 February he wrote, 'No joy about the future. The wreaths and garlands have been taken down; only a few hang here and there like flowers after a ball.'

An old friend, Emma Hartmann, died on 6 March, and a worse blow followed three days later. H.C. Ørsted, after only a few months in the country residence provided for him, caught a cold which led quickly to a chest infection, and he was dead in a matter of hours. A great procession went to his house and laid a silver wreath on his coffin, then the mourners carried it on their own shoulders to the University, where he lay in state until his burial on 18 March, very close to the main door of the University, in the courtyard which separates it from the Church of our Lady. Andersen's new book, *In Sweden*, came out the next day, as if in tribute to the man who had so heavily influenced it.

Ørsted's death deepened Andersen's sense of solitude, and he sent the still-silent Carl Alexander a bust of himself, following this by a letter to Beaulieu-Marconnay in which he asked tentatively whether a visit to Weimar might be possible, or whether his pro-Danish views might make him unpopular. Beaulieu reacted like a poked lion, snarling that if Andersen was so one-sided as to consider Denmark right in all things, he had better stay away. Recovering himself, he added that his correspondent would of course be welcome as 'a dear, worthy poet with whom one may go for a walk but not discuss politics'.

Andersen forwarded this sharp reply to Edvard Collin for advice, and received a closely reasoned response tinged with sheer fury. Beaulieu should not forget, Edvard said, that his token support of a democratic uprising in Schleswig-Holstein must be set against a regime of press prosecutions, civilian oppression and political imprisonment in his own country. Denmark had been forced to oppose 'German arrogance', and the fact that the new Danish government of the duchies was described in Germany as a 'Casino-Cabinet' showed a continuing contempt:

> It might perhaps interest Herr Beaulieu to learn that there are four noblemen in the Cabinet, among them two counts, and that the President of the Council is one of our highest and most distinguished aristocrats.

Edvard, as a deeply conservative civil servant, had an ingrained respect for aristocracy and regarded the radical changes which were sweeping Europe as utterly distasteful. Describing himself as 'an official of the *ancien régime* and no friend to democracy', he was outraged that Beaulieu should regard himself as a virtuous progressive where Schleswig-Holstein's affairs were concerned, and hoped that Andersen would utterly refuse to be regarded by such a man as 'a dear, worthy poet with whom one may go for a walk but not discuss politics'. His repetition of the phrase showed how offensive he found it, and he offered to make his entire letter available to Andersen to send to Beaulieu as it stood.

Andersen could not take such a drastic step. It would have meant the final breaking-off of all contact with Weimar, and while Edvard would have thought this a good thing, Andersen could not face it. He wrote in conciliatory terms to both Carl Alexander and Beaulieu, explaining that he had merely feared that the 'lower orders' might show some ignorant prejudice. He had no fear of coming into conflict with 'the cultivated classes', he went on:

> We have so many other interests in common which are dear to us, so much that is good and beautiful to talk about and entertain ourselves with, that I would unhesitatingly come to my friends.

A slightly stiff contact was resumed—but Andersen abandoned any thoughts of going to Weimar that year. Nevertheless, after the restrictions imposed by the war, he was chafing to go abroad again, and on 17 January, set off on a modest European journey. This time, he took with him Ingeborg Drewsen's youngest son, Viggo, knowing by now that loneliness was a constant hazard of his travels.

Viggo, now twenty-one years old, found Andersen's fussiness over details irritating and, with the impatience of youth, probably seldom understood why his companion seemed so set in his ways and easily upset. For Andersen, the journey was a disturbing one. He was troubled by the evidence of warfare that lingered in the embattled duchies and 'did not breathe freely until all Holstein, including Hamburg, had been left behind'. To travel through Germany without visiting Weimar was equally painful, and by the time the pair got to Prague, Andersen was suffering from persistent and excruciating toothache. In Dresden, Viggo headed for home alone, leaving Andersen to stay with his old friends, the Serres, at Maxen.

In the autumn of the same year he was made an honorary professor of Copenhagen University, to his great delight, and through the winter of

1851–2 he worked on a new volume of stories. The bulk of what are now considered his classic fairy tales had by now been written, but he continued to produce short pieces which have much to say on the sad comedy of human life and his own experience of it.

A week before Christmas, he wrote to Jette Wulff, who was now in America. She had told him the voyage was perfectly easy, and urged him to come over and sample the delights of the New World. 'You can travel about with the Lind,' she suggested. Jenny Lind was indeed about to start an American tour with that great showman, Barnum—but Andersen would not cross the Atlantic. He had always been afraid of long sea voyages, which Jette knew, but he fell back on the excuse that he could not afford it. He was interested, however, in the question of his books circulating in the States in cheap and un-paid-for editions, and gave Jette strict instructions to bring sample copies back with her.

He was still obsessed with the idea of going to Weimar, and in March 1852 wrote a politely insistent letter to Carl Alexander, fishing for an invitation. It duly came, and he set out in mid-May, full of nervous hope. The visit was not a great success. He stayed with Beaulieu, a little surprisingly in view of their previous correspondence, but was only one of several guests, and found the atmosphere difficult. Beaulieu was now married, with two children, and had his cousin staying with him. This young man, Ernst Beaulieu-Marconnay, had been an officer in the Prussian army and still suffered from the effects of a severe head-wound, complaining constantly of pain and sometimes almost fainting, and in fact died three years later. He was a walking reminder of the war, and Andersen found him unnerving. 'He is lying in the room outside mine,' he wrote in his diary on 23 May, 'I'm completely shut in by him, and the thought occurred to me that he might go mad during the night and come in and murder me. Can't lock my door.' He spent some time during the days that followed in listening to the young man reading his poems aloud and admitted eventually that he could be quite pleasant, but he never quite recovered from his first impression that Ernst was sinister and not to be trusted.

Carl Alexander himself proved elusive. His first meeting with Andersen had taken place on the neutral ground of his mother's house, and although the two men had embraced and kissed as old friends would expect to; he seemed otherwise occupied for most of the visit, only seeing Andersen on formal occasions, with other people present.

There were substantial reasons for his preoccupation. The Empress of Russia, Alexandra Feodorovna, arrived during Andersen's stay, necessitating a shift round of rooms. Her husband, Tsar Nicholas I, was the brother of the

Grand Duchess of Weimar. The Empress was frail and almost blind, having to be carried upstairs. Andersen found it pitiable and, as he admitted in a letter to Ingeborg Drewsen, slightly absurd that such a frail invalid should be head of a country 'the size of the surface of the moon'. He was not feeling welcome, and increasingly occupied his time with visits to artistic friends, and on 25 May wrote with some astonishment of Liszt, who was living in sin with the Princess of Wittgenstein, that the pair of them seemed 'like fiery spirits blazing, burning—they can warm you at once, but if you get too close, you will be burned.'

Liszt was full of enthusiasm for the music of Wagner, which Andersen failed to admire, as he made clear in *Mit livs eventyr*.

> In Wagner I see an intellectual composer of the present day; he is great because of his understanding and his will; he is a tremendous innovator, rejecting everything old, but I feel that he lacks that divine element which was granted to Mozart and Beethoven.

He sat through a performance of *Tannhäuser* and remarked in his diary that the music was competent but lacking in melody. 'What Weber or Mozart couldn't have done with it!' he added, in a somewhat comic lumping-together of unlikelihoods. *Lohengrin* failed to change his opinion. When Liszt came bounding into his box at the theatre to demand what he thought now, Andersen merely said limply, 'I feel half dead.' He was happier with Flotow's light opera, *Martha*, with its indisputably tuneful theme-song, 'The Last Rose of Summer'.

Despite its evident shortcomings, Andersen wrote rapturous descriptions of his Weimar visit to his friends. At the end of three weeks he moved on, and in Munich he met King Maximilian of Bavaria, generally known as 'King Max', together with the old king, Ludwig I, Max's father. Andersen went on a boat trip with them to their island villa, and after dinner sat chatting with the younger monarch on a bench. He then joined Viggo Drewsen in Leipzig and travelled with him to Milan. Rather strangely, he wrote from Frankfurt on the way home to Beaulieu, saying that he would have liked to call again at Weimar, but his companion 'wished to return home without making a stay anywhere'. It seems doubtful that there had been a specific invitation, but Andersen could not stop worrying at the Weimar question, as if he could somehow shake it into the real welcome he so desperately wanted.

In Frankfurt, some German friends tried to take him to Homberg, where the Duchess of Augustenborg was anxious to see him, but here Andersen dug his heels in. He could not forgive that family for its involvement against Denmark during the war, and wrote in his diary on 14 July, 'they have brought misfortune and unhappiness to my native land. I'm not judging them, but I cannot bear the thought of meeting them.'

In the spring of 1853, Andersen arranged a large-scale deal with Reitzel for four thousand copies of his *Illustrated Stories* and two thousand of his *Collected Works* to be reissued. It was to be his last meeting with the publisher, who died shortly afterwards and was succeeded by his son. In May he went to Sorø for a long stay with the Ingemanns, and wrote to Jette Wulff on 5 June about the daily good-natured wrangles with the poet about the meaning of creativity:

> He sets poetry high above science, but I don't. He admits that our time is a great era of inventiveness, but only in the field of the mechanical and the material, which is constantly expanding. I think of this as a necessary support for what is spiritual, a great branch from which poetry can blossom ...

The Ørsted influence was still strong. Two days previously, Andersen had written in great excitement to Carsten Hauch about the electric telegraph which had just been installed between Elsinore, Copenhagen and Hamburg, due to open for public use the following year. Andersen had stood beside Peter Faber, the operator, and heard him contact Elsinore with the news that a great poet was in his office—whereupon a whole stanza of one of Andersen's earliest poems had come back from that distant place. It was, Andersen said, 'as if I stood under the wingbeat of an eternal, mighty spirit'. He added that, had he discovered science twenty years ago, he might well have followed that discipline, which could have been 'a better one'.

A few days later, cholera broke out in Copenhagen. It was an appalling epidemic, causing nearly five thousand deaths during the summer months, and Andersen fled for safety to Jutland. There, he heard that Carl Alexander's father, the old Duke of Weimar, had died, leaving his son to inherit the title. 'In the new activity of your life I shall probably hear from you less often,' he wrote in his letter of sympathy and congratulations, 'but I firmly believe in you, and that I live in your thoughts as you have grown into mine.'

During the two months of his self-imposed exile, Andersen began work on an extended version of *The True Story of My Life*. This new autobiography was to occupy him for the next two years, and would eventually appear as *The Fairytale of My Life—Mit lies eventyr*.

By the time Andersen thought it safe to return to Copenhagen, the epidemic had killed Edvard's mother-in-law, Oline Thyberg, and also a cousin on old Mrs Collin's side of the family, Emilie Hornemann. The newspapers declared the city to be free of the disease, but Andersen, ever fearful and hypochondriac, lived for some time in the dread of being stricken down.

His sensibilities were deeply offended in January 1854 when he read a book called *Mimona*. This was the work of a young actress known as Clara Raphael, her real name being Mathilde Fibiger, and it dealt uninhibitedly with incest and other sexual aberrations. Andersen was deeply shocked that a young woman could, as he wrote to Ingemann, 'live, think, write and read about something like that'. Such confrontation with female interest in sex repelled him, and he described the book as 'bestial'.

That year, he took Viggo's younger brother, Einar Drewsen, with him on a trip to Germany and Italy. In Vienna they dined with Jenny Lind, now married to Otto Goldschmidt, who had gone out to America to be her accompanist there. He had converted to Christianity in order to appease his wife's increasing religiosity, and the first of their three children, a little son called Walter, had been born in the previous September. Jenny had now become convinced that to sing in a theatre was sinful, and restricted her appearances to concerts and oratorios sung in churches. Andersen remarked that it was 'a sin against the spirit, an abandonment of the mission God gave her', and his disappointment soured his mood and may well have added to the difficulties of his relationship with Einar, who became fretful and unwell. Andersen did not tolerate other people's malaises easily, and in Munich the pair of them quarrelled. Whether by pre-arrangement or as a result of their falling-out, Andersen went on alone, first to visit King Max and then to Weimar, and this time found a warmer reception.

For all Carl Alexander's cordiality, politics lurked not far below the surface, and when Andersen was asked to visit the Duchess of Augustenborg and resume the friendship, he flatly refused. Carl Alexander accused him of bearing a grudge, pointing out that ladies were above politics, but Andersen was not to be moved.

In the spring of the following year, he was fifty. Oddly enough, it was a muted birthday; after a meal with the Drewsens he went home and spent the evening correcting the proofs of *My Life's Fairytale*. He was living at this time in a couple of rooms in Nyhavn, an adequate base for such tasks, but essentially he remained as homeless as a stray cat, shifting from one hospitable house to another and travelling abroad at least once a year. No longer young, he retained extraordinary stamina, seeming unaware that few people could cope with such constant moving about, and yet he fretted obsessively over every ache or itch or stomach upset. At Christmas he had gone home from the Collins' house because of a stye on his eye and had sat alone, holding a compress over the affliction. Winter was always a bad time for him, and he looked forward to the better weather which heralded another travelling season.

In June, after attending the funeral of Neils Gade's wife, Sophie, he set off again, and while passing through Nuremberg, heard that King Max and his queen were in the town. He at once put off his journey, as he wrote to Jette Wulff:

> and as soon as the Majesties heard that I was here, I was received most warmly, most beautifully. We dined at the castle in the large banqueting hall, where the wood panelling is beautifully carved, walls and windows medieval, and immediately outside, the old town lay down below in the sunshine.

Andersen had arranged to meet another young member of the Collin tribe in Munich, this time Edgar, the nineteen-year-old son of Edvard's elder brother, Gottlieb. Edgar's mother, Augusta, was the sister of Andersen's friend from his days in Rome, Fritz Petzholdt, who had been so tragically killed. With this young companion, Andersen spent four days in Wildbad—and discovered to his alarm that the Prince of Nør was also present. 'I saw him from behind,' he wrote to Jonas Collin—'I do hope we won't meet!' He managed to avoid this enemy of Denmark, and headed for a far more congenial meeting, though one which filled him with some nervousness. Edvard and his wife, together with their son, Jonas, then fifteen, happened to be visiting a spa in Wildbad, and Carl Alexander had also come to the town in order to see Andersen, bringing with him Karl Schiller, son of the poet. This rather oddly assorted company was to meet, and Andersen was well aware of Edvard's feelings about Weimar and its rulers.

He need not have worried. Whatever Edvard's private opinions, he was nothing if not diplomatic. He was also a royalist, and was much taken with the duke, telling Andersen afterwards that he would like to know Carl Alexander better. Relieved, Andersen went on with Edgar into Switzerland, where they climbed Rigi-Kulm.

On return to Zurich, the pair spent half an hour with Wagner. The composer was then living in exile from Germany, having been much involved in the revolutionary movement, but Andersen, with his customary political blindness, seems not to have understood the implications, or even to have realised that it was Liszt who, because of Wagner's poverty and lack of recognition, had personally funded the productions of *Lohengrin* and *Tannhäuser* in Weimar.

At the beginning of September, Edgar had to go back to Copenhagen, and Andersen missed him. He was upset, too, by meeting a Dane who told him that *My Life's Fairytale* newly published in Denmark, had been badly reviewed. His diary recorded that he felt 'physically and spiritually ill', and he fled to Weimar to take refuge with Beaulieu, Carl Alexander still being away. It was not a happy visit. The weather turned cold and Andersen was bored and chilly. 'I have my winter clothes on and sleep with a down comforter. Not in a good mood.' Peevishness exudes from his entry on 11 September 'At home alone at the tea-table with Mrs Beaulieu-Marconnay.'

In practical terms, however, the stay was a productive one. Andersen talked to Liszt about staging his two musical plays, *The Raven* and *Little Kirsten*, in Weimar, and Beaulieu helped him to translate *Little Kirsten* into German, promising that it would appear early the following year.

Back in Copenhagen, Andersen found that his autobiography had not received the savaging he had feared. His sharpest critic, in fact, was Jette Wulff, who had seen the book in proof form. She was even more critical than the Collin family of her friend's hobnobbing with the nobility, for whereas the Collins' objections sprang from a respect for the social divisions and a feeling that one should know one's own place, hers were briskly political. Her nature, she told Andersen, was 'definitely democratic and egalitarian', and his liking for the aristocracy baffled her. Before the book's publication, she had written to him with some severity:

> I am surprised when someone like you, Andersen—recognising that God has given you special gifts—that you should feel happy and honoured to be placed—well, that's what you say here—at the table of the King of Prussia or some other high-ranking person—or to receive a decoration of the same kind worn by the greatest scoundrels, not to mention a horde of utterly insignificant people. Do you really place a title, money, aristocratic blood, success in merely mundane matter, above genius—spirit—the gifts of the soul?

Jette, the daughter of an Admiral who was also a renowned man of letters, had a well-founded confidence underpinning her refusal to be impressed by the trappings of wealth and class, and could not see why her admired friend was incapable of the same mental freedom. For Andersen, disillusion about the follies of the rich was more than outweighed by the sense of security he derived from each mark of acceptance he was given, not to mention the possible implications of an actual royal connection. His was the classic paradox of the self-made man, simultaneously measuring himself in terms of the favours he could win while resenting the power of those whose approval he sought.

As if to mark how far he had come, he sent a copy of *My Life's Fairytale* to Fedder Carstens, the teacher who nearly half a century ago had patted his cheeks and protected him from the rough boys and then so abruptly disappeared. One can only wonder anew what memories had stayed in Andersen's mind to prompt such a gift. Carstens had clearly been important to him.

In the following year, 1856, Jette Wulff left Denmark again on a further transatlantic voyage—but this time, she was overtaken by tragedy. In America, her much-loved brother, Christian, died of jaundice. Jette made her desolate way home alone, leaving Christian to lie in his grave in South Carolina.

Andersen, by contrast, seemed increasingly concerned with petty detail. He had begun another novel, titled *To Be Or Not To Be*, in which he was exploring the question of Christian faith, floundering a little as he grappled with the holism of Ørsted's thinking in the great man's absence. As if in recoil from these large ideas, his mind took refuge in trivia; his diary entries plunged into a long saga about being overcharged for some postage stamps, and another stye on his eye reduced him to 'sitting with half a boiled egg on my eye; can't get out at all, can't read and have difficulty in writing'.

Little Kirsten had been staged as promised in Weimar during January, and Andersen, who had been travelling between manor-houses for some months, set off in June for another visit to Germany. He stayed with the Serres in Maxen, and found that a fellow-guest was the author Karl Gutzkow. Andersen had met Gutzkow the previous year and described him as 'cold, cautious, not very charming'. The dislike was clearly mutual, for Gutzkow at Maxen missed no opportunity to pour scorn on the Dane's work and to imply that he was effete. On 17 June Andersen recorded furiously that his enemy had been 'so tactless as to ask me whether I had ever been in love—one couldn't tell from my books, where love came in like a fairy; I was myself a sort of half-man!'

Gutzkow's point was a valid one, as Andersen knew. His objection is to the tactlessness rather than to the accusation itself. As a man of over fifty, craggy and yet dandified, he had begun to look what would nowadays be recognised as 'an old queen', but he relied on the decencies and inhibitions of the time not to say so—and, perhaps, to refrain from forcing his own recognition of his nature. The status of poet had long protected him from any such incursions into his privacy, and he fought off Gutzkow's attack with an intensity that left his hosts distraught. 'Mrs Serre was crying, said she'd like to thrash Gutzkow, who was now chasing her dearest friends away. Serre came and spoke with me in an effort to restore harmony ...' Some kind of uneasy truce was achieved, but Andersen took himself off a couple of days later and fled to the more reliable Weimar.

To Be Or Not To Be was published on 20 May 1857 in simultaneous German and English editions with the Danish. It is one of Andersen's least readable novels, mulling inconclusively over the religious conflicts which he himself could never quite resolve. The simple Lutheran belief inherited from his mother was at odds with a kind of instinctive Judaism, whether present by blood or not, which made him feel it his duty to play the hand of cards dealt by God as successfully as possible. At a deep level, he felt as his father had done, that there was nothing supernatural about Jesus Christ, and his chosen hero, Niels Bryde—a name very close to that of his composer friend, Niels Gade—worries his way through the almost plotless book, pausing only to express his dislike of Kierkegaard, Grundtvig and dogs.

Andersen dedicated the new novel to Charles Dickens, with whom he had kept in touch sporadically since his visit to London a decade ago. Writing to his fellow-author in sending him the book, he described it as marking 'a stage in my development which I have not previously reached'. He also took up a polite invitation issued by Dickens the previous autumn, announcing that he would like to visit him in the coming summer of 1857.

NIELS KOFOED

Hans Christian Andersen and the European Literary Tradition

INTRODUCTION

All literary activity is determined mainly by three factors: the author's individual talent, the times, and the historical tradition. The most important of these factors is, of course, the author's talent, but also the ideas and the taste of his age have an impact on his writings and provide the direction they are going to take. The third factor, tradition, contains a large complex of social and cultural components that both deliberately and unconsciously form the author's career and the character of his work. In addition to the author's social milieu there is the national background that sets the stage and delivers the scenario.

Most writers of some importance intend to address their contemporaries and countrymen directly. Some of them even make a virtue of being rooted in their nation and their age, not caring for an international reputation. They do not aim beyond their country and their compatriots, which make up the very center of their life. They take an interest in their own time and its people, they may be patriots and portrayers of their own society, but their curiosity stops at the national border.

The artists who have crossed those boundaries are often either involuntary emigrants or those, who have made mankind itself the center of their works. These are the true metaphysical artists, who endeavor to

From *Hans Christian Amdersen: Danish Writer and Citizen of the World.* © 1996 by Editions Rodopi B.V.

transcend frontiers and break down the barriers between national origin and international society. They openly declare themselves as members of all humanity and adapt their works to this goal. Among them are two Danish artists, the writer Hans Christian Andersen (1805–75) and the sculptor Bertel Thorvaldsen (1770–1844). Both of them recognized early on that they had to transcend national borders to bring their talents to fruition. They preferred the larger European stage to the smaller Danish setting. By doing so they not only deepened their relationship to contemporary society but to the European tradition as well. They became great Europeans. The taller the tree and the more widespread the crown, the deeper and more ramified do the roots become as well.

The roots of Andersen's work are seated partly in Danish literature, partly in the larger European tradition. Andersen was by no means erudite, but he was well educated and above all a restless reader during most of his life, an assiduous theatergoer, an art lover, a singer with a fine sense of music, and an avid traveler. He had a better knowledge of Europe's geography, history, and culture than almost any other Dane of his day, and any other European for that matter. He counted kings, princes, and ordinary citizens in many European countries among his personal friends, and was familiar with nearly all its capitals and larger cities.

YEARS OF FORMATION AND UPBRINGING: 1805–1830

Hans Christian Andersen's first encounter with literature was listening to his father reading aloud in the evenings from the comedies of Ludvig Holberg (1684–1754) and from tales in the *Arabian Nights*. He also built his son a puppet theater for which the boy made the clothes for the puppets himself. Afterwards Andersen made up small plays and put them on his stage. He even taught the puppets their lines and staged performances. Andersen's second encounter with literature took place when he visited his grandmother at the old people's asylum in Odense. Here he found the old women sitting in the spinning-room singing folksongs and telling folktales. This childhood world endowed with impressions from the life of the Danish working class later emerged in Andersen's tales and novels.

When Andersen was about seven years old he was sent to a school for the poor, where he sat absent-mindedly in the classroom losing himself in daydreams and was said to have a screw loose. Although he was hardly able to read, he came across a number of major works in world literature, such as *Medea* and *Ariadne on Naxos*.[1] Andersen exploited these works with a view to his puppet theater, but as he could not form the lines for his plays on his own he added sentences from the catechism. Already when Andersen was eleven he was an eager reader of all kinds of literature. He read Shakespeare's plays, for instance *Macbeth* (1605) and *King Lear* (1605), in a bad translation, and Shakespeare's imaginative power appealed to him much more than Holberg. Andersen's world of fancy was from the outset directed toward the supernatural tale. Life itself was a tale and he himself an adventurer.

When the Royal Theater in 1818 paid a visit to Odense, Andersen was given a walk-on part, and he became familiar with the singspiel *Cendrillon* and the plays of the Danish romantic Adam Oehlenschläger (1779–1850). It was certainly because of these guest performances that Andersen made up his mind to leave his native town and seek his fortune in Copenhagen as soon as possible after his confirmation in 1819.

Thanks to his unique frankness, Andersen soon succeeded in finding a number of influential benefactors, for instance the composer C. E. F. Weyse (1774–1842) and the director of the singing school at the Royal Theater, Guiseppe Siboni (1780–1839). He also gained a footing in several highly-placed families of the time, those of Hans Christian Ørsted (1777–1851), the famous physicist, Peter Frederik Wulff (1774–1842), naval officer and a man of letters who was also a competent translator of Shakespeare, and Jonas Collin (1776–1861), the state secretary of finance and the right hand of King Frederik VI. As secretary of the Royal Foundation named *Ad usus publicos*, and as a member of the board of directors of the Royal Theater, Collin held all the possibilities for young Andersen in his hand. In spite of not possessing much knowledge of literature and fine arts himself, he was nevertheless a competent high government official who was eager to support talented artists, and in fact both Thorvaldsen and Andersen profited from his benevolence.

Collin pleaded Andersen's cause before the king, who granted him a scholarship for the grammar school at Slagelse, from which Andersen later transferred to Elsinore (see Chapter 1). After years of misery and adversity, Andersen completed his studies at the University of Copenhagen in 1829 with a minor degree in philology and philosophy, but all attempts to get him to continue his studies failed. Instead, he made his official debut in 1829 with a book entitled *Fodreise fra Holmens Canal til Østpynien af Amager i Aarene 1828 og 1829* (A Walking Tour from Holmen's Canal to the Eastern Point of Amager in the Years 1828 and 1829).

Having been admitted to the grammar school, where he received a comprehensive training in Danish, history, religion, mathematics, as well as Greek, Latin, German, French, and Hebrew, implied for Andersen a passage once and for all from the working to the middle class. The aim of the school's curriculum, whose principal was the well-known scholar of classical languages and minor poet Simon Meisling, was to provide a good knowledge of the classical languages and literatures, an insight into theology, ethics, and the history of Europe, and a proper mastery of modern languages. Even the natural sciences were taught. If one reads some of Andersen's still extant essays from the school,[2] one is struck by the great number of general philosophical and theological subjects dealt with. There can be no doubt that the training Andersen received in the classroom formed the basis for his literary activities. He was introduced to a large complex of problems and motifs that make up the very core of European civilization.

As a student at the university Andersen continued his general education without choosing a professional study. He managed to maintain a dual existence as student and writer. During his first year at the university he completed *Kjærlighed paa Nicolai Taarn* (Love in Saint Nicholas Church Tower), a poorly written parodic vaudeville with which he made his debut as a playwright in 1829, satirizing, in particular, the Danish romantics Oehlenschläger and Bernhard Severin Ingemann (1789–1862).

All his compulsory schooling conflicted with Andersen's self-esteem as a creative artist, adding to his feelings of insecurity. He became an eager reader of contemporary literature. Ever since his arrival in Copenhagen he had borrowed books at a lending library, and early on developed a broad familiarity with Danish and European literature, from the tragedies of Shakespeare, and the eighteenth-century comedies of Holberg and rhymed comical tales of Johan Herman Wessel (1742–85), to the romantic five-act play *Aladdin* (1805) by Oehlenschläger, his tragedies based upon Scandinavian mythology and history, and the historical tragedies *Blanca* (1815) and *Masaniello* (1815) by Ingemann, all of which are echoed in his early works. Andersen dreamed of becoming an actor and a playwright. He wanted desperately to live the free life of an artist, and this side of his character appears in his literary production before his adult works were begun. Already at the age of seventeen he had written three unpublished plays and published his first book, the pseudonymous *Ungdoms-Forsøg* (1822; Youthful Attempts), and he had no intention of giving up his free, untrammeled existence.

Rather, Andersen's true university was nature, man, and the countries he visited, as Ingemann, his elder personal friend and literary guide through more than 40 years, once wrote to him in a congratulatory letter.[3] The base of Andersen's European formation was first and foremost Shakespeare, Walter Scott, and Goethe. As a student at the grammar school at Elsinore he subscribed to a series of Goethe's works, and the first novel he ever read was

Scott's *The Heart of Midlothian* (1818), which appeared in a Danish translation in 1829 by Caspar Johannes Boye and made a great impression on him; but Andersen must have been familiar with Scott before that time. *Youthful Attempts*, published under his nom de plume, Villiam Christian Walter, contains among other texts a story "Gjenfærdet ved Palnatokes Grav" (The Ghost at Palnatoke's Grave), which has a Scottish touch. By means of magic Andersen tied up his destiny to the two great Englishmen.

By having chosen Shakespeare and Scott as his immediate models, Andersen wanted to indicate that he was going to become a playwright and novelist himself. His first book never sold well and the main part of the whole printing was pulped. This was an experience to which he referred many times in his later works. However, strong hands caught hold of the youthful writer and helped him start again. Andersen had succeeded in making friends even among members of the royal family and the government, and he had submitted to the will of his benefactors.[4] At the same time a struggle with his surroundings began that left its mark on him. His openness and indiscretion made him enemies. Already on his first evening in Slagelse in 1822 he had read *Alfsol*, a tragedy eventually published in *Youthful Attempts*, and "The Ghost at Palnatoke's Grave" aloud to Meisling, expecting to find at least some kind of appreciation, but already at this point the hostilities between the free artist and the representatives of the educational system began that later on became a main theme in Andersen's life and literary works.[5]

Andersen needed help, he aspired to knowledge and good manners and was completely dependent on helpful people and the surrounding community; but at the same time he was unwilling to enter into a compromise with his dreams. If he wanted to attend a performance at the Royal Theater in Copenhagen, he would hike back to Slagelse on foot about fifty miles in the snow, while reading Shakespeare's *The Tempest*.

In Copenhagen Andersen became a frequent guest with the Collin family. He learned to move in the best circles and was regarded as one of their own children. Here he adopted the easy-going tone of the Copenhageners and acquired the art of being a good-natured tease. Also P. F. Wulff, residing at Amalienborg, the royal castle, often invited Andersen to his home, where he formed a life-long friendship with his daughter, Henriette, who was a cripple endowed with a talent for painting and a taste for adventure. Besides these, there was a circle of talented scientists and writers employed at Sorø Academy, located in the small Zealand town, where Andersen would stay with Ingemann and his wife.

Thus the first chapter of Andersen's biography is the account of a child from the proletariat, who with the assistance of influential people makes his way to the top. Just as poor students in those days were admitted regularly to the dinner tables of the well-to-do, so Andersen circulated between a number of families. Here he adopted the bourgeois way of life, which became the ideal of a society moving toward democracy. The poor provincial yearned for all the experiences of drama, dance, music, and literature that the times had to offer. Here the myth of the self-made artist who had freed himself from all constraint had its origin, and from now on Andersen insisted on making his living solely as a writer. He was never employed in private or public service, and had to face the hard fact of addressing a very small readership.

DENMARK'S LITERARY AND CULTURAL SITUATION AROUND 1830

At the turn of the nineteenth century there was no literature of true significance in Denmark. Only the representatives of the Enlightenment still exerted a considerable influence, and among them Knud Lyne Rahbek (1760–1830) a writer, critic, and a professor of literature, occupied an important position. He and his wife Kamma held a literary salon at "Bakkehuset," their beautiful, small estate in Frederiksberg, outside Copenhagen. In their living room the youthful talent of the time gathered, and here the transition from the classicism of the previous century to the romanticism of the nineteenth was made. The house looked more like a home for young writers from the provinces than a center of cultural high life. In the lounge the new generation, which later on made up the glittering circle of men and women of the so-called Golden Age in Danish cultural history: Oehlenschläger, Nicolai Frederik Severin Grundtvig (1783–1872), Henrich Steffens (1773–1845), Johan Ludvig Heiberg (1791–1860), Ingemann, and Andersen, introduced itself to the host and hostess.

Whenever a new era is inaugurated in the history of literature, its activities do not restrict themselves to a limited field such as music or poetry. The new ideas penetrate all the spheres of civilization with a reorganizing will. The aesthetics of romanticism were rooted in eighteenth-century philosophical debates and inquiries into art, poetry, and beauty, and Denmark with its geographically strategic position as the gateway to the North has over the years functioned as a catalyst for various trends coming from Germany, England, and France being adopted by the other Scandinavian countries, transforming them according to national standards and capabilities. So it also happened with the romantic movement.

Philosophical romanticism, also called Universal Romanticism

(*Universalromantik*), began in Berlin shortly before the turn of the century. It reached its climax in Jena with the publication of the periodical *Athenäum* (1798–1800), published by Friedrich Schlegel, the movement's foremost theoretician, and his brother August Wilhelm, and ended with the latter's lectures in Berlin between 1802 and 1804. The Schlegel brothers, the philosophers Johann Gottlieb Fichte and Friedrich Schelling, the theologian Friedrich Schleiermacher, and the poets Ludwig Tieck and Novalis belonged to this group and were even joined by the Dano-Norwegian scientist and philosopher Henrich Steffens (see above).

The ideas of Universal Romanticism were rooted in the philosophy of the eighteenth century and in the political ideas of the French Revolution. It therefore differs considerably from the later two phases of romanticism: the national German romanticism with its center in Heidelberg, and late romanticism, when democratic and popular ideals came into fashion in close association with vigorous waves of nationalism. During the first period the chief goal of the movement consisted in a unification of philosophy, religion, and poetry. In the second phase the goal shifted to a position that became decisive for the remainder of the movement: a fusion of medievalism, nationalism and Christianity.

In the conflicts between the adherents of the revolutionary ideas of Universal Romanticism and the conservative wing of writers fighting for monarchy and church, to which eminent novelists like Scott and Victor Hugo belonged, we find the essential clash of interest. The common good of mankind was a central concept of the early romantics, and in a way one may consider National Romanticism an answer to the horrifying events of the French Revolution and the long period of political and social unrest that followed in the wake of Napoleon. The rebirth of the national state resulted from military defeat and from new possibilities of economic progress.

The romantic movement meant not only a break with the patterns of eighteenth-century classicism as an expression of a world of balance and stability, it also occasioned a rebellion on behalf of the northern "Gothic" Europeans against the predominance of southern, classical civilization. Remnants of tribal conflicts are in fact visible in all the essential disputes of the period. Scandinavian mythology and folklore made up an inexhaustible treasure of motifs and themes. Fichte's *Reden an die deutsche Nation*, delivered during the French occupation of Germany in 1807–08, the attempts of Danish poets to awaken the populace after England's attack on the Danish fleet off Copenhagen in 1801, the shelling of the capital by the English in 1807, and the peace treaty of Kiel 1814 forcing Denmark, which had formed an alliance with Napoleon, to cede Norway to Sweden, gave rise to a Nordic and a specifically Danish patriotic movement based on a broad, popular foundation. Not since the days of the Lutheran Reformation in 1536 had there been a stronger German influence in Denmark than during these years when prolific writers such as Oehlenschläger and the poet Jens Baggesen (1764–1826), an eminent representative of the previous century and of great importance to the development of Danish–German relations during these years, even tried to establish themselves as German writers in an attempt at breaking the narrow boundaries of the national state. Never has the struggle of a small European nation to survive as an independent state of multi-national character—and benefiting greatly from this diversification—left such indelible marks on its domestic life.

It was not until the start of the third stage of romanticism in the 1830s that other tendencies took the lead. The dramatic poems and novels in verse by Lord Byron and the lyrical poems by Heinrich Heine delighted the Danes with their frivolous tone. The fight for a Scandinavian renaissance on a Christian foundation did not harmonize with an aristocratic contempt for law and order. Byron and Heine came into fashion and a new aesthetic taste for more liberal ideas on the relations between the sexes and on religion was adopted by the middle class. This new audience demanded local color in the so-called vaudevilles, musical comedies with a sprightly intrigue, and novels dealing with everyday life. All the great and naive passions of historical heroes were to be replaced by descriptions of a newly established and self-conscious bourgeois world carried out with refined sensibility and piquancy.

This third phase of romanticism, which to some extent reflects the belated breakthrough of romanticism in France and the other Romance countries, has been named "poetic realism." In the period from 1825 to 1850 the key words of the era strongly influenced by the philosophy of Friedrich Hegel became: idea and spirit. Both in the arts and in philosophy as such, the times may be characterized as the era of Hegel. Johan Ludvig Heiberg, the Danish critic and playwright, became an enthusiastic adept in Hegel's thought. Hegel, the master philosopher himself, was professor at the University of Berlin from 1818 to 1831, and he exerted a strong and long-lasting influence on Danish writers. From Heiberg and Søren Kierkegaard (1813–55) to the naturalist critic Georg Brandes (1842–1927) there runs a current of philosophical rationalism and idealism that stood in opposition to positions held by the older school of romanticism. The break with this speculative trend came partly from the minister and poet N.F.S. Grundtvig, who fought it based on ecclesiastical and historical views, partly from Ingemann and Andersen, who were wholeheartedly romantic poets and anti-academics eagerly concerned with folklore and the popular cause.

As an adept of Molière, Holberg, and Hegel, Heiberg was an eminent representative of the German and French school advocating such genres as the vaudeville and the satirical or Aristophaneic comedy, yet at the same time the public developed an interest in modern prose based on the sentimental English romanticism of the late eighteenth century represented by writers such as Laurence Sterne, Tobias Smollett and Samuel Richardson. The Ossian poems of James Macpherson and the novels of Walter Scott had been translated and published during the first decades of the nineteenth century, and it was mainly due to their impact on Danish writers that there was a new wave of prose writing beginning in 1824 with Steen Steensen Blicher's (1782–1848) *Brudstykker af en Landsbydegns Dagbog* (Fragments of the Diary of a Parish Clerk) and Pout Martin Møller's (1794–1838) *En dansk Students Eventyr* (unfinished, publ. 1843; The Adventures of a Danish Student)—as was, in fact, happening all over Europe. In Denmark such writers as Ingemann, Blicher, Møller, and Andersen all passed from a stage of lyrical poetry to a new stage of writing novels, tales and stories.

When Andersen arrived in Copenhagen in 1819 this change was already being prepared. By virtue of his unique ability to adapt himself to the life style and bourgeois culture of his time, he succeeded in less than ten years in acquiring a knowledge of classical formation that at the time was the foundation of all education, and he managed to gain a knowledge of the romantic poetry that was the favorite reading matter of the 1820s.

During the transitional period between national romanticism and poetic realism, there was a wealthy and educated middle class in Copenhagen that was instrumental in making the city a cultural center. Political activities were limited, since the country was still governed by an absolute monarchy, so instead all the attention of the populace was directed toward an aesthetic and fictional world in which imagination and emotions could move unimpeded. After the French Revolution and the turmoil of the Napoleonic era, there was an urge to cultivate the muses. The peace-loving Danish population made up an affluent and interested public eager for poetry and the fine arts. Interest in the theater came to the fore, and even though there was not a first-rate playwright to be found among the writers of the day, there was a rich repertoire for the stage performed at the Royal Theater. All writers were courting the dramatic muses, so it comes as no surprise that Andersen should start his career trying to become an actor, a dancer, and a singer. In the long run his shortcomings in these arts prepared him for life's disappointments, but throughout his life he kept the stage door open. This was what he had been born to, he claimed, but for the time being he was only a supernumerary and a keen observer of the Copenhagen proletariat that lived in a quarter next to the theater and of the middle class that had confided in him. In Andersen's first autobiography, he writes about a visit to the Wulff family in December 1825:

> It was indeed a strange transition to come from Meisling's home to that of P.F. Wulff. Here everything was pure elegance, everything fine and pretty—I arrived there in the evening.—Oh, it appears so vividly to me! I was received so affectionately as if I were a child of the house. When I felt sated and refreshed, the servant took me to my bedroom, I got two rooms facing the square, and before I went to bed I was presented with three volumes of Shakespeare, nicely bound. I felt so imbued with heartfelt gratitude, so happy—I have still kept some leaves of a diary from this stay in the city, which I had written that very same evening. "I would walk out there on the big square five or six years ago; no one knew me in the whole city and now I can really have a good time with my Shakespeare staying with a loving and respected family.—Oh God! This is like *Aladdin*, I too am sitting inside the castle looking down. Good God! No, you will not let me down. I could kiss you!"[6]

In this remarkable scene from the royal castle of Amalienborg, dream and reality are connected like interwoven threads: Shakespeare and Oehlenschläger in one cloth. *Aladdin*, Oehlenschläger's youthful play (see above), was the very quintessence of an adventurous life, a myth of the chosen hero, the spokesman for the people in opposition to the royal court. Here was a story about the poor, fatherless boy, who refuses to serve his apprenticeship, a good-for-nothing, dreaming of a great, unexpected fortune. This five-act play in Shakespearean blank verse had not only inaugurated the Golden Age in Danish literature, but had also given true expression to the fairy-tale myth of the child of fortune, chosen by the gods, a youngster having the courage to carry his good blessing and to implement his most daring schemes.

Andersen, identifying with Aladdin, made his tale a leitmotif in the drama of his own life. When people would mock him for his peculiar appearance, he would clench his fists in his pockets saying: I am going to prove that I am not the simpleton they take me for! Just wait! Some day they will stand up and bow to the triumphant poet—the genius of the world, who will be seated on Parnassus beside Homer, Dante, Shakespeare, and Goethe." Andersen told this tale time and again. His very first tale,

"Fyrtøiet" (1835; The Tinderbox), is the story of Aladdin transformed into a retold folktale. In "Den grimme Ælling" (1844; The Ugly Duckling) *Aladdin* has been changed into an animal fable. In Andersen's novels and in his tales and stories he repeated and varied the theme of his life numerous times, developing it and enlarging on it, turning it into a universal song about poetry being of common interest to all mankind. He even considered the fairy-tale genre to be the underlying structure of all good novels and the universal genre of a coming global civilization.

At the same time Andersen was an unhappy student, who in his principal saw his worst tormentor. The evening before he returned to Slagelse from his Christmas holidays at Amalienborg he wrote:

> All the last day [of my visit] I felt so miserable; but in the evening I was presented with a copy of Boye's new play *William Shakespeare* to read aloud to the Wulffs; it made a strange impression on me. It was taken right out of my soul; I thought it was my own story, so while reading it I burst into tears, but I also felt strengthened by it.[7]

When Andersen was sent to the grammar school in Slagelse, Ingemann had already settled in nearby Sorø. He and his wife Lucie (née Mandix) who was a painter, took care of the young boy, and many years later Andersen gave the following description of their friendship:

> Yet the most happy event to me was on a Sunday when the forest was bursting into leaf, to travel on foot the ten miles from Slagelse to Sorø; the town is situated in the middle of the forest, surrounded by a lake; there is an academy for the nobility founded by Ludvig Holberg.—Here I paid a visit to Ingemann, the poet, who recently had married and been appointed to the position of lecturer. He had received me kindly in Copenhagen, and here, if I may say so, the reception was even more cordial.[8]

On January 28, 1826, Andersen records in his diary that he has paid a visit to Sorø Academy, and here Carl Bagger (1807–46), one of his friends who later became a novelist, showed him his collection of books: Shakespeare, Scott, Byron, Oehlenschläger, and Ingemann. This was the very core of modern reading material. Andersen writes: "He offered to let me take what I wanted," adding: "but I had read it all."[9] From his stay in Elsinore as a grammar school student, a collection of quotations from the works of such writers as Goethe, Schiller, Oehlenschläger, E.T.A. Hoffmann, and Jean Paul has been preserved,[10] indicating some of Andersen's favorite writers of the period.

Ingemann could also be included among Shakespeare's admirers. As a writer he belonged to the patriotic and historical school of national romanticism, and in his dramas he was deeply influenced by the romantic wave of enthusiasm for the Elizabethan theater, which had started in Germany some years before. Ingemann enjoyed a great reputation as a writer of historical novels and poems dealing with the establishment of Denmark's Baltic empire during the Middle Ages. At the same time Ingemann was very familiar with German romantic poetry and the romantic literary tale. As a teller of tales himself, he had started by imitating Tieck and Hoffmann, and after his return from Italy in 1819 he had published a volume entitled *Eventyr og Fortællinger* (1820; Fairy Tales and Stories).

Ingemann's chief opponents were the representatives of the Copenhagen intelligentsia, such as Heiberg and the critic and librarian Christian Molbech (1783–1857). Heiberg had derided Ingemann for his dramatic dramas written in a Shakespearean style, and Molbech had disqualified him as a writer of historical novels. In spite of embittered feelings Ingemann was never petty-minded and accepted Andersen's flitting between these Copenhagen circles and the provincial and historical setting of Sorø. Andersen had initially been successful in trying to place himself as a follower of Heiberg. Bagger, his friend from school days, had also eagerly tried to persuade him to produce satirical and humorous works. In 1829, when Andersen published *A Walking Tour*, he and Bagger met every Sunday together with a third friend, Frederik (Fritz) Petit, in the so-called "Serapion Brotherhood," named after Hoffmann's collection of stories *Die Serapions-Brüder* (1819–21), Andersen showing up regularly with a large sheet of paper sticking out of his pocket. As a writer *in spe* he aimed at creating fanciful arabesques in the style of Hoffmann. What he had learned from Ingemann, talked about with Bagger and read in Hoffmann, he tried to summarize in this small book, which as a medley of travelogue, autobiography and fairy tale contains all the basic elements and forms of his creative power.

A Walking Tour cannot be labeled a travelogue in the literal sense of the word, for the walking tour undertaken by the poet on New Year's eve from the center of Copenhagen and through the Amager gate to the Sound is a journey taking place within himself, a humorous, self-ironic, narcissistic mapping of confused mental life. Of course, the model could be found in Hoffmann's *Die Abentheuer der Sylvester-Nacht* (1813–15) and *Die Elixiere des Teufels* (1815–16). All the far-flung world of imagination from the depths of the oceans, the abyss of the heart, the temple of poetry, the interior of the earth and airships in the sky, is unfolded in this book. The reader encounters Doctor Faust, Emperor Octavian, Saint Peter, Aristophanes, Shakespeare, Cervantes, and Carlo Gozzi. Andersen presents the whole repertory of his reading, "partly old classics, partly little-known works, from which the petty poets of the present day sometimes steal an arm, sometimes a leg, now an eye, now a heroic arm in order to scrape together a fairly tolerable hero and heroine they can pass off as their own."[11] The young author, who was just about to free himself from the straitjacket of the grammar school, is like Hercules at the crossroads. On one side he has a street vendor, called the Amager Woman, a plain woman of the people and of the flat island outside Copenhagen, a land of cabbages and potatoes, representing the old world of classicism and rationalism; on the other side he has Louise, a hollow-cheeked girl from the morgue, the muse of romanticism. Everywhere the poet's ego is confronted with a splitting up of things and their phantoms, and it consequently appears as his own double. A good many of Andersen's fairy-tale motifs are found as germs in this small book, which like the immature work of any great writer reveals the true character of his talent.

   A Walking Tour is first of all a marvelous display of feelings and imagination—a capricious display with poetic motifs and a scanning of limits from aesthetic, moral and religious points of view. It is also a disguised encounter, similar to that of the revivalist preacher Grundtvig (see above), with the orthodox circles that wanted to control him, but failed to make him a member of their congregation. Andersen defended himself, fighting back,in order to retain his freedom as a talented, young artist, but still the most crucial test seemed to be due recognition by Heiberg and his circle. On the other hand Andersen could hardly realize that his propensity for satire and persiflage would also offend older romantic poets such as Oehlenschläger and Carsten Hauch (1790–1872). It was the same case with Andersen's debut as a playwright. *Love in Saint Nicholas Church Tower*, his first vaudeville, which in any case turned out to be a trifle that should never have been performed, nearly cost him his friendship with Oehlenschläger because of its satire of his historical tragedies and dramas of fate.

   The basic genre in Andersen's early production is the arabesque, which at that time was conceived as a form permitting the artist to give a full expression to a capricious imagination, and which according to Andersen's own statement seemed to be made for him. When Islam banned not only all depictions of the deity, but of humans and animals as well, artists learned how to encircle the pages of the Koran with ornaments of foliage and fruit in the most fanciful ways. As adopted by Christian artists, this decorative technique was extended to include living creatures, and eventually the arabesque was adopted as an original form in the world of European fine arts and literature. The core of the literary arabesque as a piece of short prose is the episode, the free flight of fancy and a structuring concept. As to the work of Andersen he had a clear concept of this genre, adding a good memory, a sense of reality, a clear understanding of his objective, and an ability to improvise as necessary conditions. Friedrich Schlegel, the chief theoretician of German romanticism, had introduced the theory of the arabesque in 1798[12] and he associated the concept of fairy-tale fantasy with poetic abundance and ironic ease. Even Edgar Allan Poe adopted the genre later on, making the grotesque narrative a valid expression of emotional contradiction.[13]

Thus Andersen's first production during the years from 1829 to 1835 became a test of the possibilities and limits of his talent. Heiberg had an open eye for the young writer's aesthetic qualities when stating:

> The author finds himself in the same position as a painter, who before daring to take up stricter compositions practices with the arabesque, for even in the arabesque the elements are casual, heterogeneous and indifferent to one another, but the originality and the grace with which they are fused give it artistic value.... *A Walking Tour* should be evaluated as a musical fantasy.[14]

In the ninth chapter of *A Walking Tour* the narrator, Andersen's alter ego, pays a visit to the Pantheon of poetry. First he lingers in the antechambers with several figures, and finally enters a large hall with a number of living spirits. In the four corners the princes of poetry, Aristophanes, Shakespeare, Cervantes, and Hoffmann are seated. Even Tieck and Gozzi are present in the hall. At last the narrator meets a lovely small boy with colorful butterfly wings, who clasps him in his arms and flies into God's heaven. Together they walk on a bright rainbow, until he abruptly awakes from his dream. "Did I snatch you away, son!" cries a brutish female voice. It is the Amager Woman—an allegorical representation of reason and classical education—catching the narrator in a fowler's net and putting him into a cage. Andersen looks at himself as in a mirror in order to define his own identity as a writer. He makes a double movement in releasing himself and all possible models and being reborn as a child with all its spontaneous freshness. He is certifying his literary vocation as a classicist and as a romanticist as well.

It is strange that Goethe is not among the poets in the Pantheon. Research aimed at the models for Andersen's youthful works have focused mainly on the influence of Scott, Hoffmann, and Heine. Heinrich Teschner[15] has proved Andersen's dependence on Heine as a lyrical poet; Elias Bredsdorff[16] has dealt with Scott's influence, and Helge Topsøe-Jensen points to Andersen's collection of quotations in foreign languages.[17] These sources allow us to get some idea of his reading. Among the best-known writers are Oehlenschläger, Ingemann, Baggesen, the Swedish poet Esaias Tegnér, Gellert, Gozzi, Seneca, Herder, Schiller, Goethe, Jean Paul, Wieland, Tieck, Hoffmann, and Novalis. The quotations have not been translated and appear in many languages: Danish, Swedish, German, English, French, Greek, Latin and a single one in Hebrew. Of 196 quotations in all, twenty-six are by Goethe. The main emphasis is on German literature, because German was the only foreign language Andersen could read with effortless ease, but we should not forget that Shakespeare and Scott were mostly read in translation. From 1821 to 1828 thirty-three translations of Scott's novels were published in Denmark, and Shakespeare's plays and Byron's poems also appeared in great number. A popularity similar to that of Scott's novels was only reached by the literary dandy, Edward Bulwer-Lytton, who was widely read and held in high esteem even by Andersen.

YEARS OF FRUSTRATION AND ADVERSITY: 1830–1835

Having published the collection *Digte* (Poems) in 1830, which also contained his first tale "Dødningen" (The Dead Man), Andersen had succeeded in firmly placing himself in the minds of the reading public as a promising young writer. He enjoyed the favor of most critics and earned a living, but immediately there began a long period of disappointment and adversity, that would prepare him for a larger world than Denmark.

In the summer of 1830 he met a beautiful girl on Funen. She was the sister of his fellow student and friend Christian Voigt; her name was Riborg and she was the daughter of a well-to-do businessman in Fåborg. She was already engaged to a young forester, but as her parents did not care much for her fiancé, Andersen felt he had a fair chance. The following autumn Riborg showed up in Copenhagen and paid him a visit. Andersen was as much occupied with her brother Christian as with her. He studied the poems of Ludwig Uhland together with Christian and fell deeply in love with his sister. The strange situation led to a serious crisis in Andersen's life. After a period of hesitation he proposed to Riborg and was rejected. One day Andersen had presented her with a short poem entitled "Til Hende" (To Her), which was originally part of his libretto *Bruden fra Lammermoor* (1832; The Bride of Lammermoor) after Scott's novel. Set to music by Edvard

Grieg, this poem which begins: "You have become the sole thought of mine," is sung in recital halls around the world, usually in its German translation as "Ich liebe dich." Andersen could now join the long line of unhappy lovers like Johannes Ewald (1743–81), Grundtvig, Ingemann, and Kierkegaard.

Not only in his private life did Andersen have a stroke of bad luck; his attempts at reworking two of Scott's novels, *The Bride of Lammermoor* (1819) and *Kenilworth* (1821), into opera libretti were ruthlessly criticized after a few performances at the Royal Theater, in spite of the fact that the latter contains some of his best lyrical poems, set to music by Weyse. All of a sudden Andersen found himself in the middle of a literary feud, labeled as gifted with talent but without discipline in a pamphlet by the poet and playwright Henrik Hertz (1798–1870) entitled *Gjenganger-Breve* (1830; Letters of a Ghost), a poetic manifesto defending Heiberg's aesthetics. Being very susceptible to any cold winds blowing down from the Danish Parnassus and still suffering from his unhappiness as a rejected lover, Andersen went on his first journey abroad in the summer of 1831.

Before leaving Denmark, Andersen had asked Ingemann for guidance, and in a letter written on New Year's Eve 1830 he took Ingemann into his confidence: "My health is pretty good; but yet I don't feel satisfied, I am not any longer the man I used to be, I feel that I am growing older, I feel that life has something far deeper than I dreamed of before, and that I shall never, never become truly happy here."[18] In times of despair Andersen hung on to his friend, fifteen years his senior, who could speak of the Danish critics from experience. Ingemann's help consisted in his willingness to acknowledge Andersen's character and his unique talent. From the outset he had recognized the genius of the fatherless schoolboy, guiding him as a writer, strengthening his self-reliance and letting him follow partly in his footsteps until he outpaced him as a storyteller. Ingemann had all the experience in love affairs, in the theater, and as the object of harsh and unjust criticism that Andersen now was to experience himself. In times of trial Ingemann stepped in, cautioning him about making Byron his ideal. The way Ingemann responded in this matter, trying to deter Andersen from adopting a Byronic lifestyle, behavior in sexual matters and radical religious views may lead us to suspect that he might have met with Byron himself during his long stay in Italy 1818–19, but in this respect evidence has to be found in his literary remains. At any rate Ingemann could neither endorse the formalism that he found in Heiberg's and Hertz's works, nor could he approve of their demands for greater correctness of orthography and grammar. Instead he pointed to Andersen's childlike fantasy, his depiction of everyday life and his fascination with death as being essential subjects of literature.

In his autobiography Andersen has summed up his essentials literary development up to 1830:

> Among my young friends in Copenhagen there was at that time Orla Lehmann, who later on has been brought to the top of public favor in Denmark's political life.... His father was German; this language was much used in their home, and here Heine's poems had come to delight young Orla; he was staying in the countryside near Frederiksberg Castle; I came out to see him and he shouted with joy one of Heine's stanzas: "Thalatta, Thalatta, du ewiges Meer!"—We read Heine together, the afternoon and evening passed, it got so late I had to stay there overnight, but this night I had come to know a poet who seemed to sing out of my soul; he displaced Hoffmann, who as one may see from *A Walking Tour* had the greatest effect on me at that time.—In my youthful days there are only three writers, who as it were have spiritually got into my blood, with whom for a while I have shared my life, and they are Walter Scott, Hoffmann, and Heine.[19]

Ingemann, who had gone on his great educational journey to Germany and Italy in 1818–19, always remained a luke-warm European. Thus he wrote to one of his friends in 1818:

> I like the Germans most of all next to Danes and Norwegians, whom you come across almost everywhere; every city and country is swarming with stuck-up Englishmen. The French like France itself "hab ich mit Löffeln gefressen," and between you and me the Italians are not worth many scudi. All husbands are cuckolds here; as you may well know they feel honored by this fact and are too ignominious for being jealous.

The further Ingemann traveled in Europe, the more Danish he felt: "I will live and write in Danish," he wrote. "One may well discuss literary relations in Germany and the benefit of foreign theaters, etc., for the sake of appearances. All in all I don't give a tinker's damn for it."[20]

In spite of this outburst, Ingemann had formed important and long-lasting friendships in Germany with Adelbert von Chamisso and Tieck, hereby paving the way for his protégé Andersen. When the latter went abroad for the first time in the spring of 1831, Ingemann had furnished him with letters of recommendation to his friends abroad. Tieck especially was well acquainted with Denmark and Danish literature, and had already received Oehlenschläger some years before and also met Ingemann in 1819, who on his way back from Italy had spent a whole month in Tieck's home. Ingemann had competed with Tieck in telling stories and tales, and he claimed that there could be no other German poet he would rather be with than Tieck. Whereas Oehlenschläger, who during his stay in Germany in 1805 and 1806 met often with Goethe, feeling quite attracted to his personality and the Weimar school of neoclassicism and eventually falling out with the representatives of romanticism, Ingemann succeeded in establishing very good relations with Tieck, Friedrich de la Motte Fouqué and Adelbert von Chamisso. By virtue of his influence, Andersen immediately got a foothold in Germany, staying with Tieck in Dresden and then Chamisso in Berlin. At Andersen's departure Tieck wrote a few lines in his album and inaugurated him as a true poet by profession by kissing him on both cheeks.

Goethe's sarcastic remarks about young Oehlenschläger being one of these sons of the North who behave like a dancing bear[21] had no bearings on either Ingemann or Andersen, whose first journey to Germany nearly assumed the character of a homecoming. On his return to Denmark, Andersen published a travelogue entitled *Skyggebilleder af en Reise til Harzen det sachsiske Schweitz etc. etc., i Sommeren 1831* (1831; Shadow Pictures from a Journey to the Harz Mountains and Saxon Switzerland, etc., etc., in the Summer of 1831), in which he appears as a true disciple of Heine. The book created a sensation, but the author frequently suffered from financial worries and felt increasingly downhearted as to his future in Denmark. Fits of deep despair lay in wait for him at all times. "What is to become of me?" Andersen wrote to Ingemann going on to say: "I look forward to nothing, hope nothing, only write, because I have to, I can't help doing it. This world would be so beautiful, if only everybody would let their heart play a greater role than it is allowed to do."[22]

One of Andersen's problems was an increasing sense of inferiority. Throughout his entire adult life he carried the burden of his social heritage, and to this lack of a clear social identity one may add a failing or uncertain sexual orientation. He felt attracted to both sexes, and he found excellent excuses for not marrying. In a society with clear gender roles he could easily have run the risk of becoming superfluous, had it not been for his distinguished talent as a writer. His travels abroad were a necessity, because he escaped from his literary adversaries at home, which he feared more than anything else. Consequently he rarely felt homesick, but felt a strong and continual urge to travel, which in the long run drove him to more and more extended journeys all over Europe. Enclosed with his application for a travel grant in December 1832, directed to the Royal Foundation *Ad usus publicos*, were many letters of recommendation. Oehlenschläger praised his lyrical talent, Ingemann his sense of nature and descriptions of popular life, and Heiberg found his humor similar to that of the famous comic writer Johan Herman Wessel.

Getting financial support for a grand tour of Europe by the Royal Foundation, to so many Danish painters and writers used to be a crucial event in their artistic development. As for Baggesen, Ingemann, Oehlenschläger, and Andersen, a stay for one or two years in Germany, France, and Italy not only helped to bring them abreast of the times, but it also enabled them to establish networks of international significance. By keeping their fingers on the pulse of their times, they responded to current changes in art, literature, and politics. Baggesen's stay abroad fell during the French Revolution, Oehlenschläger experienced the turbulent period of early romanticism and the French occupation of Germany by Napoleon's troops, Ingemann breathed the sacred air of the Holy Alliance and felt the wave of conservatism in the wake of the Vienna Congress of 1814–15. Obvious parallels can be drawn between Ingemann's and Andersen's careers. They were both awarded the royal grant when they were twenty-eight years old, they stayed abroad for about eighteen months, and they followed the same itinerary, which went from Copenhagen to Kiel and Hamburg and then on to Cologne and Strasbourg. The next stop was Paris, where they both stayed for a couple of months, continuing to Switzerland on they way to Italy. After an extended stay in Rome they traveled to Naples and the Gulf of Sorrento. On their homeward passage they visited Florence, Venice, Vienna, Munich, Dresden, and Berlin.

Ingemann taught Andersen how to travel. He instructed him about museums and famous architectural sites, told him the names of sculptors and painters he ought to go and see in Berlin, and he gave him addresses of art galleries and personal friends, such as Chamisso, Friedrich de la Motte Fouqué, both of them renowned writers of fairy tales, and Johan Christian Dahl, the Norwegian painter, who resided in Dresden. The highlights of Ingemann's journey had been the encounter with the historical places in Germany, where he met the fascinating compound of the German medieval and romantic periods that was a true reflection of himself. From Italy he brought his tragedy *Tasso* (1819) back to Denmark, and with it a work within an essential genre in German and European literature: the drama dealing with art itself and the life of artists.

Whereas Ingemann brought his tragedy of *Tasso* and the German romantic literary tale of Hoffmann, Tieck, and Novalis back to Denmark as conspicuous results of his long stay abroad, it seems to be the travel book, the prose novel, and the fairy tale that first and foremost provided Andersen with a reputation as a distinguished writer. In the years 1829–33 he had tried his hand at lyrical poetry, drama and short story, but without experiencing a real breakthrough. When he felt most dejected, he was not met with caring sympathy, but rather with an unsentimental severity. Before his departure on his next journey abroad in the spring of 1833, he received a letter from Ingemann including the following passage:

> What up till now has most prevented your development as a poet, has undoubtedly been the misfortune that with far too much confidence and an almost childlike affection you have thrown yourself into the arms of this large, many-tongued and fickle audience and into the millpond of empty social intercourse before knowing what you really wanted and were capable of doing.... You should care a little less about the poet and his laurels and more about poetry! Don't cut the songbird open to collect the golden eggs at once.[23]

This letter probably dates from the end of December 1832 and led to a stop in their exchange of letters for nearly two years. Ingemann had been anxious to see his protégé develop according to his true character and peculiar talent and not just to go along with the requirements of any school or the general demands of the time. He therefore warned him against his urge to flatter his readers and to submit to the judgment of his critics. Andersen continued to do both, knowing better than Ingemann how to address his readers and his contemporaries, but his seductive attitude also had its share in his fate as a Danish writer.

A SPIRITUAL REBIRTH: ANDERSEN AND ITALY: 1833–35

In the course of his life Andersen undertook thirty journeys abroad which, apart from his travels to Asia Minor in 1841 and Morocco in 1862, all went to one or several European countries. His knowledge of Europe was unequaled in his age, and although traveling life at that time was troublesome and sometimes even dangerous, Andersen spared no pains to achieve his objectives. For him traveling became a lifestyle and an existential necessity. "To travel is to live!" he simply declared.[24]

Life itself was a journey and he himself a pilgrim destined for immortality.

Andersen's educational journey from 1833–35 was by far the most important. He left Copenhagen on April 22, 1833, passing through Lubeck on his way to Hamburg. A couple of months before his departure from Copenhagen he had written to Henriette Wulff. "I have remained a child ever since I was young. I have never known what it is to be a youth! ... It is an inveterate idea I have that only by getting tom away from my actual surroundings will I ever amount to anything; if I must stay here, I will perish!"[25]

It became a tour of cultural formation, on which Andersen kept a diary over all the places he visited, and, in addition, made skillful drawings of the scenes and monuments he saw. Two-thirds of the pencil drawings left by Andersen come from this journey. Diaries, letters, and drawings were the raw material for this incessantly active artist, always on the lookout for unusual events and particulars of interest. His journey was intended as a cure, transforming and developing his character and at the same time providing him with material for new writing. In Paris Andersen joyfully celebrated his regained freedom, but he nevertheless also felt a lack of letters from Denmark. During the three months he stayed in Paris, he became acquainted with Heine and Victor Hugo, but went in vain to see Eugene Scribe, the famous playwright. In a letter to Christian Voigt of June 26 Andersen mentions that he had been admitted to a society named "Europe littéraire." In spite of his determined will to avoid Heine, this was the first writer he met there. Heine approached him kindly, claiming that in his view Oehlenschläger was the greatest poet in Europe. When Heine called on him at the hotel a few days later, Andersen was not in, and he continued to avoid him. "I think one has to be on one's guard against him," he adds. Still they got along on friendly terms, although Andersen did not sympathize with Heine's revolutionary ideas.[26] On the whole he had some difficulty in eradicating Denmark from his mind, and during his entire stay in Paris he worked regularly on *Agnete og Havmanden* (1834; Agnete and the Merman), a lyrical drama in five acts based on an old Danish ballad.

Late in the summer Andersen left Paris for Switzerland, where he stayed in Le Locle in order to finish his play in rural quiet. He wanted his work published in the same size and color on the cover as Goethe's *Faust* (1808) and Oehlenschläger's *Aladdin* in order to express his gratitude and to emphasize the importance of his drama. On September 5, 1833—on the fourteenth anniversary of his first arrival in Copenhagen—he crossed the border to Italy. In a way this became his second rebirth. This time Andersen was born as a European and an adult writer who shed the slough of childhood. A new landscape and a different art world met him as he traveled through Lombardy and stood in contemplation before the Medicean Venus in Florence. The everyday life, delight in nature, and the art of the Renaissance appealed more to him than the world of antiquity.

Andersen arrived in Rome on October 17 and was kindly received by the members of the Scandinavian Club, which met regularly at the "Caffé Greco" close to the Spanish Steps. At that time Antonio Canova was everyone's favorite sculptor, but his obvious successor was Bertel Thorvaldsen, one of a group of Northerners bringing Scandinavia to the forefront of European art. In the 1820s the romantic movement had its breakthrough in Paris. Now the new generation of romantics arrived in Rome, and they were bound to conquer, if only because of their age. The French romantics were born in the decade of 1795–1805 and included writers such as Honoré de Balzac, Victor Hugo, Alfred de Vigny, and George Sand. These young people were the generation of the "Empire" and had, as Alfred de Musset put it, been conceived between battles and attended school to the sound of rolling drums.[27]

Andersen's life fitted in perfectly with this up and coming generation, and he happened to be in Paris and Rome at the right moment. Like these writers he became a strong anti-Bonapartist. Taking their cue in this respect from François René de Chateaubriand, they repudiated both the Republic and the Empire, and they embraced the old monarchy with its link to the medieval past. Apart from the fact that Andersen, unlike Ingemann, did not admire the Middle Ages, he remained an advocate of absolute monarchy, but also deliberately tried to avoid getting involved in politics.

For a couple of months Andersen lived happily in Rome, but just before New Year he received a letter from Jonas Collin informing him of the death of his mother, and a few days later another letter from Edvard, Jonas's son, in which he could read a scathing criticism of *Agnete and the Merman*. In a furious state of mind Andersen went to see Thorvaldsen, whom he found in his studio working on a bas-relief named *Justice on the Rolling Chariot*. Andersen took it as an obvious sign of relief to his tormented soul. Here the master himself stood in front of him all smeared with clay, consoling the unfortunate author by saying: "Feel your own strength; don't let yourself be led by the judgment of the masses; and go calmly on."[28] Andersen was still furious, but nevertheless he immediately set to work on the first chapter of what was to become his first novel, *Improvisatoren* (1835; The Improvisatore).

After having spent the carnival season in Rome, Andersen went to see Naples and Amalfi before returning to Rome at Easter. On his departure from Italy in April of 1834, Andersen did not carry many manuscripts in his luggage: a few poems, the diary, the drawings, and the initial chapters of *The Improvisatore*, which within a year should turn out to be the turning point of his career. Two of the most important models for this novel were Scott and Madame de Staël-Holstein. "As Walter Scott, if I may say so, depicted the highlands and its people, I portray the landscape and the people of Hesperia," Andersen wrote to Henriette Hanck, his friend in Odense.[29] About his other model he wrote the following to Ludvig Müller: "Madame Holstein's *Corinna* seems to me a guide wrapped up in ordinary novelist's chatter and some very sensible discourse. Heine, who never really crossed the Apennines, might as well have written the whole story in Hamburg."[30] After his return to Denmark Andersen confided to Henriette Wulff that he worked every day on his novel and that he had read Dante, Virgil and "a great many folios about art and Italy."[31] In the final account Andersen ended up using all his models and materials including Goethe and his two volumes *Italienische Reise* (1786–87) and *Zweiter römischer Aufenthalt* (1788), which he read during his stay in Munich before he returned to Denmark.[32]

Behind *The Improvisatore* lie also Dante's *La Divina Commedia* (c. 1307–21), Tasso's *Gerusalemme liberata* (1581), Virgil's *Aeneid* (publ. 19 B.C.) and even Goethe's comprehensive diaries. The description of the Roman carnival is based directly on Goethe's account of the saturnalia, but Andersen had also personally participated in the festivities. He had experienced the street life of Rome on his own, using his eyes and his ears as hardly any Danish writer before him and committing his impressions to his diaries and letters, from which he later transferred all the best passages directly to his novel. Add to this a comprehensive reading of relevant European literature, old and modern, with an unerring eye for the useful elements of the texts, and one may conclude that Andersen's entire production comprises a synthesis of travels and travel experiences transformed into drawings and notes greatly enriched by sparks of his brilliant imagination. This is how a professional writer is incessantly working. Not only did Andersen borrow motifs and details from Goethe's diaries, he also followed in the footsteps of his admired model. Being a traveler from the North trying to regain his spirit in the same way as Goethe, he emphasized the cultural and allegorical contrast between Rome and Naples by letting Antonio, the novel's principal character, go through the same existential crisis as Andersen himself. For Andersen and Goethe, Naples appears to have been of crucial importance in their spiritual development. In *The Improvisatore* and in his overpowering tale "Skyggen" (1847; The Shadow), Andersen lets his main characters experience the decisive moments of truth in this city. Andersen's novel is not only a travel book, but also a novel dealing with love and the religious and ethical aspects of making a career as an artist. Therefore the tension between Rome, the seat of the church, history, and learning, and Naples, the city of art and love, plays a predominant role.

Each of the three novels Andersen published during the years 1835–37 after his return from Italy marks a peculiar phase in his struggle for identity as an artist and for his integrity as a moral individual with roots in a proletarian soil. That is the very reason why Andersen's climb up the social ladder seems more difficult than Goethe's fight for his moral and artistic integrity. All of Andersen's novels are predominantly stories of realistic defeat and dream fulfillment, and consequently very different from his tales and stories. *The Improvisatore* is an example of the poetic and sentimental realism following upon Scott's historical novels in the 1830s, but the relationship with Goethe's *Die Leiden des jungen Werthers* (1774) and *Torquato Tasso* (1790), his Italian drama, in which Goethe describes the incongruities between the artist and the surrounding society and life in general, is even more conspicuous. *Torquato Tasso* has been called "ein gesteigerter Werther" and the split between Tasso, the poet, on the one hand, and Antonio, the government official, on the other, between the dreamer and the practician, has been transformed in Andersen's novel into a class conflict between the poor, fatherless Antonio and young Bernardo, a member of the nobility. To elucidate his problem Andersen makes use of a complementary delineation of character. He introduces his persons in pairs, imitating a pattern in European epic tradition that goes back to ancient mythology. Antonio, who is a student of theology at a seminary in Rome, feels coerced to abandon his hope of becoming a priest and turn to an artistic career because he experiences religion as the brutal force of a punishing father, whereas Bernardo, as his complementary opposite, enjoys full freedom of mind. As the young Andersen, like Goethe his model, could not reconcile himself to the surrounding world, he let his problem pass on from one novel to the next. It was not until he discovered the fairy tale, in which the lines of demarcation between the two opposite worlds of reality and dream are obliterated, that he found a sanctuary where he could survive. The fairy tale became a pantheon in which both the child and the adult could be seated together.[33]

On his way back to Denmark from Italy, Andersen stayed in Austria for about a month. In Vienna he went to see Joseph Sonnleithner, who invited him to dinner. Thanks to Andersen's talent for establishing contacts with people of influence, he was also introduced to other Austrian writers. In Sonnleithner's home, where many Danes would come, he met the playwright Franz Grillparzer, who sat beside him at the table. He seemed rather fragile of health, Andersen observed in his diary, but was also very pleasant.

Andersen also was very much attracted to the Viennese theater, going to the Burgtheater as often as he could. He was especially fond of the way in which August von Kotzebue was performed, because in his view Kotzebue held the position of being the Eugène Scribe of the eighteenth century, a writer of little imagination but capable of writing a good dialogue. Andersen also met Johanna von Weissenthurn, the famous actress, who also became a celebrated playwright. She was a great admirer of Oehlenschläger, with whom she had become acquainted during his stay in Vienna in 1817.

During his stay in Vienna Andersen also read Grillparzer's *Das goldene Vließ* (1822). In his diary he calls the play a masterpiece, which will put Grillparzer among the finest playwrights in the German language.[34] Meanwhile he became better acquainted with Ignaz Franz Castelli, whom he considered to be genuinely Viennese in his good nature, humor, and loyalty to the emperor. Andersen went to see Castelli several times and made him one of the characters in his novel *Only a Fiddler*. He also became familiar with Ferdinand Raimund's and Johann Nestroy's popular comedies and fairy-tale plays, and gained an impression of the easy-going and fantastical humor of the Viennese singspiel. He felt so pleased by the performances he attended that he returned with a copy of Raimund's comedy *Der Verschwender* (1834) in order to translate it, but it was not until fifteen years later he succeeded in introducing a fairy-tale comedy of his own, *Meer end Perler og Guld* (1849; More than Pearls and Gold), in Denmark.[35]

All the European countries that Andersen had visited left ideas for coming works in his mind. In France it was Hugo's novels. In Italy it was the art of the Renaissance and the great epics of the same period that most appealed to him. In Austria it was the singspiel and the popular farce that impressed him. To establish a clear context between landscape, nationality, character, and fate seems to be the formula of Andersen's creative writing in these years. Politics and history never appealed much to him. His knowledge of contemporary literature, its favorite topics and forms and, above all, a personal contact with writers, painters, composers and other important people mattered most to him. His diaries and letters testify to his continual activity in mixing with people who might be useful to him.

The closer he got to Denmark, the more Andersen dreaded his homecoming. Immediately before arriving in Copenhagen he wrote in a letter to Henriette Wulff: "Well, now I am flying toward my Gethsemane, to Judas kisses and cups of bitterness; but this, of course, is quite poetic; as a poet I am held to be a butterfly, and they are supposed to be most beautiful when wriggling on the pin."[36]

THE BREAKTHROUGH IN 1835

Andersen's homecoming turned out to be much better than he had expected. He arrived in Copenhagen on August 3, 1834, and after staying a few days he went to Sorø in order to visit Ingemann and his wife. Here he calmed down after his journey and set to work on *The Improvisatore*, which was published in April 1835, a few weeks later followed by the first small volume of tales. In the three novels, *The Improvisatore*, *O.T.* (1836), and *Kun en Spillemand* (1837; Only a Fiddler) Andersen succeeded in making the transition from the historical novel of the 1820s to the realistic novel of the 1830s dealing with contemporary topics. By doing so, he underwent the same development that such writers as Balzac and Charles Dickens made in the same decade.[37]

There had been two essential characteristics in the romanticism of the 1820s. One was the sense of *couleur locale*, local color, which Scott had evoked through his nostalgic and retrospective novels, the other was the sense of the supernatural, which Scott had in common with Hoffmann and Tieck. After 1827, when Goethe proclaimed the existence of a coming world literature (see below), the supernatural came into fashion all over Europe, and it was not until this year that romanticism, which had prevailed in the English, German and Scandinavian literatures for nearly three decades, had its breakthrough in France. After this time literature was neither really classical nor romantic any longer; it was simply modern, because the freedom of the individual, the ideals of political democracy, and a newborn sense of the lower classes were brought into focus. In *O.T.* Andersen commented on his own narrative techniques with the following words:

> Our tale is no figment of the imagination, but a picture of the reality in which we live, blood of our blood and flesh of our flesh. We are going to see our own days, to meet people of our own time. Still it is not only the everyday life, not only a lingering look at the mosses of the surface. We shall contemplate the whole tree, from the roots to the scented foliage—but the tree of reality cannot sprout up with the same rapid growth as the one of imagination, like the magic tree in Tieck's *The Elves*.[39]

Andersen seems to have been very conscious about his own double role as a spokesman for poetic realism and for the use of unrestrained imagination in literature. As a novelist he wanted to be true to his own social background and the difficulties he had experienced on his way upwards, but he also knew that an author's freedom of speech is limited in a small society. Actual conflicts always had to be disguised somehow or other. Andersen wanted to tell the truth, but he would have to paraphrase it by subtle means. All of his novels deal with the development and identity of character based on autobiographical material. They describe young men and women and their struggle for independence in a world of social and moral restraint. In *O.T.*, in which the capital letters denote either *Odense Tugthus* (Odense Jail) or *Otto Thostrup*, the name of the principal character carrying the two letters branded on his shoulder, Otto is brooding over a somber secret. In this respect Andersen pays a tribute to his time by mixing reality with romance. He continued to give a complacent display of his own character in *Only a Fiddler*, in which Christian, his alter ego who is born with a great talent for the violin, perishes because nobody cares to support him. Andersen loved to describe the offspring of the pariah in his novels: Jews, gypsies, and orphans. The social outcast and the rootless emigrant were his favorite characters. He was one of the first writers who dared to describe the loneliness and misery of modern man irrespective of age, sex, nationality, and social class. The setting of the third part of *Only a Fiddler* is Vienna, and is full of local color. Naomi, one of two principal characters in the novel, is described as an example of a female cosmopolitan, an emancipated Jewish woman detached from her natural surroundings. Time and again Andersen asks the same question: What happens to human beings breaking away from their ethnic background, social class, and native country? One might suspect that Andersen would be fascinated by the Kaspar Hauser case, which took place these years. On December 28, 1833, he included, however, only a brief notice of Hauser's death in his diary.[39]

Andersen deliberately built his novels on stark contrasts and let his characters move around in a Europe with which he had just become familiar. From time to time he failed to live up to his own demands for realism, as he neither dared nor was able to delve into the deeper moral layers of his characters. "In a small country like ours, it is good for an author to be unknown. Here we stand upright close together watching every crease of the clothes; the personality turns the scale," he said.[40]

Whereas in *The Improvisatore* Andersen deploys all his skill to paint a colorful picture of Italy, *O.T.* is, according to his own statement, a French seed.[41] Otto Thostrup, who is fighting his obscure past and his intense feelings of social inferiority, cherishes deep sympathies with the French. He is characterized as a resolute devotee of the Revolution and a secret follower of Napoleon. In this hero, Andersen intends to glorify the struggle against the enemies of enlightenment and revolution by claiming that his story is not mere fancy but based on actual fact. Yet in spite of this claim Otto is a typical hero of the day possessed by a melancholy of the same sort as could be found in Byron's most desperate verse. Andersen knew exactly where to set the bounds between an author's diplomacy and boldness. Even if *O.T.* involved a private and very painful conflict in his life, namely his ambivalent feelings toward and fear of his half-sister Karen Marie (see Chapter 1), who might have ruined his career, he did not dare to give full expression to all his innermost problems. In order to make a career in a society dominated by the middle class, Andersen would have to suppress his sexuality and the memories of his social background. Yet his awareness of such sensitive spots added something to his presentation of the subject: "In front of the audience, in public, I have taken every step of my career as a writer; it has been a show, where the plate has passed around to provide food for the artist."[42]

It was the novels that put Andersen on his feet again as a writer. He published three novels in three years and had them all translated into German through his friendly connections in Germany. On April 20, 1835, he wrote to Henriette Wulff:

> *The Improvisatore*, my novel, has now appeared in Danish.— Never yet has any work of mine gripped the masses so intensely. Hertz called on me in order to thank me for the pleasure, assuring me quite nicely that many people who did not otherwise like me were here devoted to me. Ingemann says that it marks the transition from youth to manhood in my writing.[43]

Apparently Andersen straightened himself up because of his good fortune. By reversing a trend of general dislike of his writing, he had come to a turning point in his career, especially as his novels also gave him a provisional economic security. The fact that he now let his journeys result in novels and fairy tales was not a mere coincidence. During his stay in Italy Andersen had changed from a lyrical poet into a modern writer of prose and a storyteller. With this change he attained a position from which he could assert himself internationally. While abroad he had been tempted to free himself of all loyalties to his native country, in the same way as the shadow splits from its master in the tale of "The Shadow." Disparities at all levels— philosophical, moral, and psychological—tormented Andersen and added to his feeling of isolation. Even the conflict between a deep-rooted patriotism and an ever increasing yearning for a larger world, between nationalism and cosmopolitanism, would become a main theme of his literary work, since the tension between the narrow and oppressive environment at home and the freer conditions of life abroad is felt more deeply in a small country than in a larger one. This conflict is thus distinctly reflected in the careers of such Scandinavian writers as Andersen, Henrik Ibsen, and August Strindberg.

In the nineteenth century the highway to European fame for Scandinavian writers went through Germany. Andersen wrote in his German autobiography from 1847:

> From Germany came the first strong approval, or perhaps overestimation of my book, and I bowed like a sick man before the sunshine, gratefully happy, for my heart is grateful. I am not what "The Danish Monthly Review" condescended to subscribe to and publish in its criticism of my novel "The Improvisatore," an ungrateful person demonstrating in my book a lack of gratitude toward his benefactors.... From Sweden praise later resounded, all the Swedish newspapers that I caught sight of were in panegyrics over my work, which in recent years has been received just as warmly in England, translated by the poetess Mary Howitt. As has been related and written to me, the same good fortune has been allotted me in Holland and in Russia, where the book has been translated into the native languages. Audible recognition came from abroad.[44]

After the publication of *The Improvisatore*, Andersen consciously aimed at addressing a European public, deliberately setting some of his novels in France, Germany, Austria, and Switzerland. He wrote to Henriette Hanck: "I want to become the best novelist of Denmark! In my nook the few souls around me will recognize that I am a true poet; if I had been French or English, the world would mention my name; now I am getting dropped and my songs with me. No one listens to them in poor distant Denmark."[45]

There is no lack of histrionic and high-flown statements of this kind in Andersen's letters, nor was he ever short of humor and a keen sense of comic details, but like all other novelists of the time he loved melodrama and sentimentality. Only when it came to discussing his position and vocation as a writer belonging to world literature did he lose his self-irony. The struggle had been too hard, the obstacles too many and the critics too unjust toward him, that he could not help being embittered. Still he worked unremittingly to realize the myth of Aladdin. He was the Aladdin of literature preparing the way for the new Aladdin, who in his turn would reconcile natural science with religion. In the course of time Andersen felt more and more inclined to refer to an enigmatic election haunting his intellect:

My life is really a poetic story, surely I am a poet! The son of the poor washerwoman running around in the streets of Odense in his wooden shoes has already come so far that he is treated like a son in the home of one of Denmark's most estimated men and has friends among honorable and wonderful people. One *has* to mention me as one of the good writers of my time, but I want even more! God granting me sufficient strength, I want to be mentioned among Denmark's *best* writers together with Holberg and Oehlenschläger! But there is one more leap to take, a great leap upwards, I really sense it, although I don't like to talk about it. The good Lord must take me by the arm; it's no use my just lifting *my* legs. But cheer up! A great writer here and a greater one still in the next world, that is the image of my hopes, and it is a bad soldier who doesn't think of becoming a general, as the proverb says.[46]

By gradually extending his ambition to fit his new possibilities, Andersen currently updated his demands for a high position.

In the summer of 1837 Andersen paid a visit to Sweden, going by boat on the Göta Canal to Stockholm, where he was well received and became acquainted with several distinguished Swedish writers. On the boat he had met Fredrika Bremer, a prolific novelist and female emancipator. Very soon she became his personal friend. Andersen was enthusiastic about Sweden and flattered the Swedes by praising Stockholm as the Naples of the North, and the cathedral of Uppsala as Notre-Dame de Paris. In the 1830s the relations between Sweden and Denmark were still rather cool as a result of the numerous wars fought over the centuries between the two countries. Some of these hard feelings might be due to a sort of hereditary mistrust between neighbors.[47]

At the same time as he promoted his own production, Andersen worked to enhance international understanding, openly professing his belief in the incipient pan-Scandinavian movement, the so-called Scandinavianism that grew out of student gatherings in Denmark and Sweden in the 1820s and 1830s.

With the publication of *Only a Fiddler* in 1837, Andersen was on his way to becoming a European celebrity. While staying in Denmark he received a visit from Count Conrad Rantzau-Breitenburg, a cabinet minister, who was a Holsteiner by birth. The count called in person at Andersen's modest residence and asked what he could do for him, and the following year Andersen was granted an annual stipend for the rest of his life. In his autobiography he dated the turning point of his career to May 28, 1838, the day on which the king had signed the grant. After that day Andersen was no longer compelled to write for lack of money. He had in fact become independent of his benefactors. It was *Only a Fiddler*, his third novel, which decided the matter. This novel roused a great deal of enthusiasm in Germany, and Andersen could not help taking advantage of telling his detractors who he was. Besides he had Ingemann on his side. The latter wrote in a letter to his young friend: "Now let the critics say what they want! Our aesthetic criticism is like an ostrich; it gapes as if it were going to swallow up the swan of poetry, which from the very instant it flew out of the egg has surpassed it."[48]

With this passage Ingemann presented Andersen with the basic metaphor for his tale "Den grimme Ælling" (1844; The Ugly Duckling). He invited him emphatically to join him in his fight against speculative philosophy and the whole world of conceited and semi-educated critics. "Devotion to poetry and feeling for it is not a rare phenomenon," Ingemann added, "but very few are good judges of it."[49] Although Andersen agreed with Ingemann in his popular taste and liberal ideas, he made no attempt at concealing the fact that an ardent desire and an almost insatiable greed for recognition, which hardly any human court could guarantee, were the true incentives for his activities. He confided his conviction thus to Henriette Hanck:

> I am looking for a literature suitable for my time and instructive for my spirit; an ideal picture is emerging vaguely in my mind, but its outlines are so shapeless that I cannot render it distinct myself. It seems to me that every great poet has added a link, but no more than that, to this huge body. Our age has not yet found its poet. But when will he appear? And where? He has to describe nature as Washington Irving does, to comprehend the age as Walter Scott could, sing like Byron, and yet originate in our time like Heine. Oh! I wonder where this messiah of poetry will be born? ... I was born to be a poet, I feel, and I am aware of the fact that everything comes into my life as poetry, and still I want more![50]

From Chamisso Andersen learned how estimated he was in Germany as a novelist, but at the same time his situation at home was aggravated. The more European he became, the less popular he was with his compatriots. The hardest blow was directed at him by the philosopher Søren Kierkegaard, whose first book in its abstract Hegelian style, *Af en endnu Levendes Papirer* (1838; From the Papers of One Still Living), contained a furious attack on Andersen and his novel *Only a Fiddler*. The varying degrees of the effect on the novelist's mind caused by Kierkegaard can be examined in Andersen's diaries and letters, where he describes himself as going around in a state of feverish lethargy. Christian, the hero of *Only a Fiddler*, Kierkegaard claimed, is not a genius but a sniveler. He has no outlook on life, no philosophy of his own and for that reason no personality either. In Denmark everybody agreed in denouncing Kierkegaard's critical lampoon, but nevertheless it gave birth to two of the most obstinate myths about Andersen: his obvious lack of character and his deficiency of true interest in intellectual matters.

If Andersen had been able to rise above the general disregard of his opponents by ignoring the judgments of his critics and the whims of his public, he would have been in a stronger position, but ever since his childhood he had been used to submitting to the country's rulers and the reigning men of letters. His attempts at approaching the speculative Hegelian Heiberg-Kierkegaard camp had been turned down definitively, and the leading representatives of romanticism, writers like Ingemann, Blicher, and Hauch, who believed in a literature based on sincere feelings and a vivid imagination, were living outside the capital.

Although he maintained strong ties with the Collin family and had many friends in the Copenhagen middle class, Andersen's endeavors to become a Danish playwright were never crowned with success. His most ardent wish never came true, and in the eyes of the Copenhagen theatergoers he appeared more or less as a minor dramatist visited by fiasco. Since his debut in 1829 Andersen had been a steady supplier of plays to the Royal Theater but had only a few successes, in particular *Mulatten* (The Mulatto), a romantic drama that premiered on February 3, 1840. Heiberg did not have a good word to say about him. Even his wife, the celebrated actress Johanne Luise, could never recognize Andersen as a playwright because she did not consider him sufficiently masculine. The relationship between Andersen and the Heiberg family turned into a lifelong and at times rather embittered fight, which Andersen lost in spite of his rare talent for diplomacy. If he had been met with a more forthcoming attitude from the theater, which held a monopoly on the Danish stage, romantic drama might have been more successful in the history of Danish literature. No other Danish writer had a more comprehensive knowledge of the European theater of his time than Andersen, who could state: "If I must be classed with a certain school and not be allowed to establish one of my own, I would have to be considered as something between Victor Hugo and Casimir Delavigne."[51]

During his first visit to Paris, Andersen had become familiar with the theater of French romanticism. In May 1834 he had attended a performance of Hugo's *Marie Tudor* (1833) in Munich, and he seriously considered translating the play into Danish; nevertheless all his attempts at transplanting contemporary French drama to the Danish stage failed. Andersen's knowledge of the French language was not sufficient. While he was staying in Paris in 1833 he did, for instance, read his first novel in French, Hugo's *Notre-Dame de Paris* (1831), but as he admitted it gave him a lot of trouble.[52]

On the whole, cultural relations between Denmark and France were slight during these years. Xavier Marmier, a young French writer, decided to remedy the situation. During a stay in Denmark in 1837–38 he succeeded in acquiring a good knowledge of the Scandinavian countries and their history, and his *Histoire de la littérature en Danemark et en Suède* (1839) became a unique introduction to Danish cultural life for the French reading public.[53] When Andersen on his second visit to France in 1843 wanted to see Hugo, Marmier brought about the meeting, and now the Danish writer was warmly received and presented with a free ticket by his host to attend a performance of *Les Burgraves* (1843). "The play did not really amuse me, I didn't understand it," Andersen wrote in his diary.[54] Strange to say that Marmier had not only prepared the way for his Danish colleague in France by writing an article about him in *Revue de Paris* in October 1837, he had opened a path for him in Denmark as well, where no one at the royal court had ever noticed him until Marmier presented his article to Prince Christian, who later ascended the throne as King Christian VIII. "At his own request I have given [Marmier] a sketch of my life," Andersen wrote Henriette Hanck. "'But may all of Europe know about it?' he asked, and I was—as you would say—vain enough to add: 'I belong to the world! Just let them all know, what I am thinking and feeling'."[55]

The first time Andersen had paid a visit to Hugo in his fashionable apartment at Place des Vosges in 1833, he was not familiar to him at all, but being a colleague Hugo had put his own name on the top of a piece of paper, fearing that his signature might possibly be abused. "In the hall there was a picture of Notre Dame [de Paris] on the wall and on the floor a small gypsy child was running about, apparently one of the good Victor's," Andersen then wrote in a letter to Henriette Wulff.[56] During his second stay in Paris ten years later Andersen wrote in his diary:

When I called on Victor Hugo, he was away, his wife asked me to wait for him, she would write an answer to Marmier. I came into a small room, decorated in rococo, Gobelin tapestries with gods of love, kings and ladies! Some kind of sofa just like those antique choir stalls stood along the wall. Victor Hugo's daughter, about 11 or 12, was seated here having lunch while reading a comedy, she was dark and pretty; the maid put the parrot into a cage. Madame Hugo is, beautiful, looks Spanish, she was very kind.[57]

A few days later, when Andersen had lunch with the French celebrity, Hugo had read Marmier's book and familiarized himself with the caller.

In 1843 the thirty-eight-year-old Andersen had already become a man of European renown, who by means of letters of recommendation and personal contacts had beaten a path to all the important people and places. On April 25, 1843, he wrote in his diary: "At one o'clock I rode out ... to see David [d'Angers], the sculptor, a plain, straightforward man, like a Danish peasant, in his blue smock and Greek cap, we crossed a beautiful garden in front of his studio; he was working on a bust of Victor Hugo."[58]

Andersen also paid a visit to the poet Alphonse de Lamartine in his aristocratic apartment, where many servants dressed in livery received him and one of the large rooms was decorated with a life-size portrait of the poet himself. Even Alfred de Vigny became his friend, and Andersen also went to the theater together with Alexandre Dumas *père*. He was moreover invited by Elisabeth Rachel, the famous actress, who appeared as Racine's Phèdre at the Théâtre-Français during the season, and at an evening party he was introduced to Balzac, "to whom I paid some compliments. He was a short, broad-shouldered, stocky fellow," Andersen wrote ingenuously in his dairy on March 25.[59]

In all respects the 1840s became years of incredible success on a European scale. Andersen's novels had rapidly been translated into several languages. *The Improvisatore*, first published in 1835, appeared in a German translation the same year, in Swedish in 1838, in English and American editions in 1844, in Russian in 1845, in Dutch in 1846, in French in 1847, and in Czech and Polish in 1857. The same was the case with *O.T.* and *Only a Fiddler* and already in 1847 his *Gesammelte Werke* began to come out in Germany.

Andersen continuously set out on long journeys in order to promote his work and international understanding by making himself visible to his readers and admirers. Wherever he went, he immediately looked up well-known painters, sculptors, writers and composers. Acting as an intermediary and a propagator of Danish culture seemed to him an obligation he enjoyed fulfilling. His patriotic feelings flourished beautifully when he went abroad. His capacity for social contact must be seen as a direct consequence of his artistic talent. There have indeed been other great geniuses that have turned their backs on the outside world and been unwilling to address or even to like their public. This was never the case with Andersen. As a writer and a human being he loved his audience. He was to some extent a deliberate simpleton, who with disarming ingenuousness and a mediocre skill for speaking foreign languages headed straight to the cultural centers of the nations of Europe and made friends everywhere. In Germany he attended concerts with Franz Liszt and paid visits to Felix Mendelssohn-Bartholdy and Robert Schumann. He felt deeply inspired by the painters he met in Rome and borrowed motifs from the biblical paintings by Wilhelm von Kaulbach for his epic poem, *Ahasverus* (1847; Ahasuerus). Having a more direct knowledge of his European contemporaries in art and music than any other Danish writer of his age, Andersen realized instinctively the important role played by the great historical and religious epics in French and German romanticism.[60]

In Denmark Andersen was a welcome visitor at many manor houses in the countryside and he made friends with several aristocratic families, but he spent most of his time abroad during these years. In 1844 he went to Weimar to be introduced to Carl Alexander, hereditary grand duke of Saxony-Weimar-Eisenach. Standing in the chapel of the cemetery between Goethe's and Schiller's coffins he said the Lord's Prayer, begging God to let him become a writer worthy of these two men. In Leipzig he spent an evening together with Robert Schumann, and afterwards he went to see Jacob Grimm in Berlin, who for a change had never heard of him. Here he also met the scientist Alexander von Humboldt and the French-German composer Giacomo Meyerbeer.

Through his letters, diaries, pocket calendars, his so-called almanacs and autobiographies we can follow Andersen day by day, sometimes even from one hour to the next. We may watch him at famous tourist resorts with his sketch book in hand; we see him alone in his room at the hotel and as a European celebrity in the opera house or at the royal castle, always persecuted by his shadow, which like a permanent toothache containing bitter vestiges of poverty and underclass life together with the scars of his unremitting efforts to reach his goals, would cause him pain. All the travels that Andersen undertook during his lifetime were made up of equal parts of recreation, work, education, and escape. Traveling was a part of his character, he liked to think of himself as a migratory bird. As a storyteller Andersen wanted to find and confirm himself in an endless striving toward the Absolute, but also in a most earthly desire for fame. He wanted to reach all the peoples and nations of the world, and in this he departed from the norms of his contemporaries. His travel books are not just descriptions of the countries he had visited. Analyses of their political systems and social conditions did not really interest him as such. If anything, these books were rather a hunt for pictures, a search to express the soul of a country by painting genre pictures, by rendering fragments of everyday life to which is added a touch of fresh sense impressions, light, colors, and fragrance.

As a model for his travelogue *En Digters Bazar* (1842; A Poet's Bazaar), Andersen initially had planned to use Lamartine's *Souvenirs d'un voyage en Orient* (1835), but ended up rejecting it because over the years he had learned to rely on his own eyes.[61] His travel books were in fact complex outlooks on life. Always being on the watch for the poetry of the instant, as Andersen put it, he sought the transcendent experiences behind the phenomena, in which the genre picture assumed a shape of myth or symbol. He wished to open up perspectives of cultural and philosophical importance and make them visible to his readers, but as he had a completely concrete mindset, he acted rather as a painter, trying to accentuate all the picturesque elements and the local color of the country in question. Above all, he wanted to write a condensed prose fraught with a maximum of meaning. His weakness was his lack of talent for logical analysis and cohesive characterization. The truth he found only appears in glimpses and in small details. The sweeping panoramas are rare. One finds the best example of Andersen's artistic technique in his travel book *I Sverrig* (1851; In Sweden), in which the river navigation on the Göta Canal through Sweden is both a realistic depiction of waterfalls, floodgates, and landscapes, and an imaginary trip into the world of myth and legend as well, dealing with the one great topic of true interest to him: the relationship between faith and knowledge, the myth of the end of civilization and its rebirth as expressed in the tale of the phoenix, the bird that is burnt to death and thereafter arises from its own ashes.[62]

For this reason the presentation of Andersen's development as a writer and his personal view of life are closely connected with his journeys, because traveling for him consisted in a double activity: an exploration of the outside world and a search for the human being within. In the course of the 1830s Andersen had managed to conquer Germany and Sweden. In the 1840s France and England were added to his sphere of interest. One of the highlights in his career was when Alfred de Vigny, a writer of great elegance, on April 26, 1843, called on him in the small room on the fifth floor in which he lived during his stay in Paris. However he also received a letter from Denmark the very same day informing him that *Agnete and the Merman* had been laughed to scorn on the opening night at the Royal Theater in Copenhagen. Deeply hurt, Andersen exploded with rage, cursing the small country he had been condemned to live in. On April 29, 1843, he wrote in a letter to Henriette Wulff.

Here, in this large, foreign city, Europe's best known and the noblest spirits lovingly surround me, meeting me as a kindred soul, and back home the boys go about spitting on the best creation of my heart!—Indeed, even if I have to be judged after my death as I am judged in life, I shall say: "The Danes can be evil, cold, satanic!"

Before closing the letter Andersen added the following: "However, I am probably expressing myself characteristically for a booed-at writer."[63]

The conflict between the valuation of Andersen in Denmark and abroad became critical in these years. The growing nationalism and the social and political revolutions in Europe ran counter to his international and enlightened outlook. Andersen was to some extent a Russeauean optimist regarding democracy as an ideology suitable for bringing about ethnic, social and cultural equality, and he could never approve of the romantic concept that the borders of nations, states and languages should coincide as a condition for a democratic constitution. It seemed quite natural for him that Danes, Norwegians and Germans had been living happily together within the same state since the Middle Ages. But Andersen's attempts at gaining influence in Germany and later in England were met with doubt in Denmark. *De to Baronesser* (1848; The Two Baronesses), a novel that was inspired by a stay on the North Frisian island of Föhr, to which Andersen had been invited by King Christian VIII and his queen, Caroline Amalie, is with its descriptions of the tidal areas and the Frisian islands the last picture of Denmark within the setting of the United Monarchy, before it was dissolved as a result of the defeat in 1864 (see below).

During the mid-1840s the Golden Age in Danish literature reached its zenith. Andersen and Kierkegaard wrote their most significant works, Grundtvig, Ingemann, and Blicher contributed to its bloom with hymns, poems, and short stories, and Frederik Paludan-Müller (1809–76) published his great epic poem *Adam Homo* (1842–49). This impressive display of talent was subsidized by an absolute monarch, Christian VIII, a man of letters himself who took a great interest in art and literature. This prosperity appeared in many ways paradoxical and inversely proportional to the decline in the political influence of the monarch, as absolutism as a form of government was about to be replaced by the first democratic constitution in 1849.

For Andersen it was a period of restless traveling. In 1845 he celebrated Christmas in Berlin together with the Swedish singer, Jenny Lind, his beloved and admired female friend, whom he had met a couple of years before in Copenhagen and fallen hopelessly in love with. Having been invited as a guest to the Prussian court and receiving the Knighthood of the Red Eagle by King Friedrich Wilhelm IV, Andersen could now parade at balls with a rapier and a three-cornered hat. In Weimar he was frequently asked to the court of Grand Duke Carl Alexander of Saxony-Weimar-Eisenach. On one occasion he read aloud the tale of "Den lille Havfrue" (1837; The Little Mermaid) in Goethe's house at Frauenplan, where also Jenny Lind made her voice heard with songs by Mendelssohn.

For many reasons Andersen's journeys became an odd mixture of triumph and escape, often followed by fits of depression. During his long stay in Naples the following summer of 1846 he suffered severely. While he was sitting in his room working on his autobiography, he was overwhelmed by the excessive heat and fell ill; but in spite of heavy strokes of indisposition which are recorded in his diary, Andersen was inspired by his feverish hallucinations and the idea of his tale "The Shadow," a complex and inexhaustible text, inspired by Chamisso's *Peter Schlemihls wundersame Geschichte* (1814), appeared to him in a delirious dream.

The following year, 1847, Andersen visited England for the first time, where he met Charles Dickens on July 16. He had felt encouraged to undertake this journey by the propitious reception of his novels in England. *The Improvisatore, O.T,* and *Only a Fiddler* had all been published in English in 1845, and the English edition of *The Two Baronesses*, was, in fact, published two months before the novel appeared in Danish. After 1846 his tales and stories also began to appear in English. "Your name is now an honoured one in England," his first translator Mary Howitt had written him in July of 1845,[64] and there is plenty of evidence to prove that Andersen acquired a popularity in England that was unrivaled by any foreign author. He was accepted as the literary lion of the season and received by the aristocracy of the country.

Andersen also made a journey to Scotland. In Edinburgh he went to see the prison and the monument to Walter Scott. He made a trip to the Highlands to visit the scene where Scott's story *The Lady of the Lake* (1810) and novel *Rob Roy* (1818) took place, and on several occasions he was greeted with the honorable name of "the Danish Walter Scott." So he immediately started reread *The Heart of Midlothian*, which was the first book by Scott he had read as a schoolboy in 1824, and whose plot he had used in *The Two Baronesses*. Andersen held the opinion that he was more clever than Scott in depicting nature, but he also admitted openly that his own capacity as a portrayer of characters, a delineator of settings and an antiquarian lagged far behind his beloved idol. As a novelist Andersen lacked a breadth of outlook and the faculty of calmly advancing the narration. He was so much the better at short prose, which corresponded so well to his nervous and restless temperament.

In spite of his conspicuous dislike of politics, Andersen was frequently overtaken by violent events. In 1848 the February Revolution broke out in Paris, and in the same year Denmark's Three-Year-War against the duchies of Schleswig and Holstein, which desired independence from Denmark, started. The political realities had an impact on the cultural life, and the times no longer felt disposed toward literature and fine arts, but toward political action. In *Ahasuerus* Andersen tried to gather his ideas about the crucial events of world history. This poem was intended to become an epic dealing with the genius of mankind—a despairing and deeply split consciousness of belief and doubt embodied in the contradictory characters, Columbus and Ahasuerus. But Ingemann accused Andersen of turning his back to the current situation by letting his historical poem conclude with Columbus' discovery of the new world. He was himself far more pessimistic about the future of humanity. *Ahasuerus* was completely rejected and ignored by the Danish critics. Still the formation of a new world order fighting the folly of its surroundings, the old world constantly denying the new, and the indispensable and yet conditional faith in progress, were all to become the main theme of Andersen's works during these years of mature writing. There is indeed a straight line of coherent ideas from *Ahasuerus* to the religious and philosophical novel *At være eller ikke være* (To Be, or Not to Be?) from 1857.

The protracted war, the general political unrest and the cholera epidemic in the early 1850s kept Andersen back in Denmark for several years. When he resumed traveling abroad, the reason for doing so might have been his fear of the Danish critics. As Andersen had published his autobiography, *Mit Livs Eventyr* (The Story of My Life) in 1855, full of unrestrained feelings of bitterness against what he considered to be a persecution of his person and an underrating of his exploits, he looked forward to meeting his friends abroad. During his stay in Weimar Grand Duke Carl Alexander had embraced him and kissed him on both cheeks. "Tears came to my eyes," he wrote in his diary on June 23, 1856; "I was thinking of a time, when the poor shoemaker's and washerwoman's son had been kissed by the nephew of the Tsar of all the Russians, how the extremes were meeting."[65]

Without taking a clear political stand, much less becoming a socialist, Andersen was still increasingly concerned with issues of poverty; but at the same time he had no way of reconciling his social background with the elitist views held by him as an artist of international reputation. He appeared to be a simpleton in the eyes of the English aristocracy, yet while he might have been a harmless storyteller for children on one hand, still he was a subtle and humorous challenger of society on the other, convinced that truth did exist and would prevail in the long run.

Taking his point of departure in the German novelist Wilhelmine Canz's novel *Eritis sicut Deus* (1854) and some academic lectures given by D. F. Estricht, a well-known German zoologist of the time who wished to combat the German school of materialistic philosophers led by the zoologist Carl Vogt, the physiologist Jacob Moleschott and the physician Ludwig Büchner, Andersen set out to write his novel *To Be, or Not to Be?*, which was to make his name reverberate throughout Europe.[66] In Weimar he had attended a performance of the second part of Goethe's *Faust* (1833) in 1856 and had reread the whole tragedy. On May 2, 1857, *To Be, or Not to Be?* appeared in Denmark, having been published in England a short time before. Prior to its publication Andersen had gone to England as Charles Dickens' guest. The latter had informed him in a letter that after having finished his novel *Little Dorrit* (1857) he wanted to see him at Gad's Hill, his country house outside London, and as Andersen did not dare to await the reception of his own ambitious novel at home, he preferred to absent himself in due time.

In his letters to all his friends in Denmark Andersen was vocal in his praise of Gad's Hill, but as a guest he was also sensitive of a hint of matrimonial tragedy behind Dickens's seemingly idyllic family life. Andersen was mainly concerned with a concert that he had attended in the Crystal Palace, where 2,000 performers had presented Handel's *Messiah*. In his view the Crystal Palace was the next thing to Aladdin's palace in the *Arabian Nights*. Meanwhile he became quite upset by the negative reviews of his novel sent to him from Denmark, and he let himself be consoled by his renowned English friend, who advised him to be less vulnerable and more proud.

From England Andersen set out for Weimar in order to participate in the festivities that were going to take place on the occasion of Grand Duke Carl August's centenary. In Weimar he was offered the position as Goethe's successor, which he declined. On his way back to Denmark, Andersen suffered from severe depression on account of his fear of a cholera epidemic in Kiel. His homecoming was felt as an ignominious defeat in contrast to all his experiences abroad.

In 1858 Andersen paid another visit to Switzerland. In his view Switzerland was one of the countries that meant most to him. In the contrast between the Lake Lucerne, the green lake of the mountains, and the idyllic Sorø Lake, where Ingemann's house was located, he saw a kind of explanation for a part of his own life story: the loss of an idyll and the struggle to regain it. Among the snow-covered mountain peaks of the Jura Mountains he had finished *Agnete and the Merman* in 1833. To him Switzerland could have symbolized the country where bottom and peak are present together in a synthesis of euphoria and despair, ascent and fall. Now at the top of his career he returned to the country of his youthful hopes and aspirations in order to continue dreaming about greatness on the mountain top and death in the glacial valleys. Tales like "Sneedronningen" (1844; The Snow Queen) and "Iisjomfruen" (1861; The Ice Maiden) have themes closely associated with a Swiss setting and scenery. In Andersen's vivid imagination huge icicles and organ pipes produce the same kind of music.

Until the last years of his active life Andersen continued to travel to Germany, Sweden, and Spain, including a trip to North Africa and a stay in Portugal. Often these trips were true triumphal processions during which he was presented with many marks of honor, but they were nevertheless all put in the shade by the occasion in Odense in 1867, when he was made an honorary citizen of Odense and the town was lit up as had been foretold by a fortune teller in his childhood.

In a travel book from 1863, entitled *I Spanien* (In Spain), Andersen depicts his experiences of the nature, people, and culture in this large country which he visited in 1862. Andersen had crossed the border to Spain on September 6, the very same date he arrived in Copenhagen in 1819 and in Italy in 1833. Spain had in fact always played an important part in his imagination as a magic and fabled land hidden behind the Pyrenees. Already in 1838 he let Spain emerge in his poem "Dette har Zombien gjort" (The Zombie did it); and even earlier in his singspiels *Spanierne i Odense* (1836; The Spaniards in Odense) and *Skilles og mødes* (1836; Parting and Meeting), dealing with all the disorder caused by the Spanish troops in Denmark during the Napoleonic Wars, this nation played a part in his creative mind. To this list of works inspired by Spain should be added the romantic tragedy *Maurerpigen* (1840; The Moorish Maid), telling the story from the Middle Ages about the conflict between the Moors and the Christians and influenced by the Spanish national epic *Poema de mio Cid*. Even in his Jutland tale "En Historie fra Klitterne" (1859; A Story from the Dunes) a series of Spanish pictures can be found.

THE SOURCES OF ANDERSEN'S FAIRY TALES

Andersen's world fame does not rest on his novels, travelogues, poems, and plays. Although it was the novels that first made a name for him as a writer of European standing, this would only rank him among writers like Oehlenschläger and Ingemann, who were also considered to be among the best of the romanticists. Had it not been for his small, insignificant and modest-looking booklets of tales and stories, his writings would have fallen into the kind of oblivion, into which nearly all classic works of literature sink unless they become part of a compulsory syllabus in high-school education. As a novelist Andersen does not measure up to either Scott, Dickens or Balzac. As a writer of tales and stories, however, Andersen is unique and to some extent without real competition.

When in May of 1835 Andersen published the first collection of *Eventyr, fortalte for Børn* (Tales, Told for Children), containing "Fyrtøiet" (The Tinderbox), "Lille Claus og store Claus" (Little Claus and Big Claus), "Prindsessen paa Ærten" (The Princess on the Pea), and "Den lille Idas Blomster" (Little Ida's Flowers), he did not suspect that he was thereby forming the basis for his fame. He was simply not aware of the fact that tradition, his individual talent and the times agreed to an exceptional degree in his case. Already the first four tales reveal Andersen's eminent skill at writing short prose and the versatility of his treatment of topics and themes.

The sources of Andersen's tales and stories are manifold. First of all there is the anonymous folktale; next there is the German literary tale by writers such as Tieck, Arnim, Brentano, Chamisso, and Hoffmann, which had flourished throughout the romantic period; furthermore Andersen's own life story, and finally modern technology and natural science, a source pointed out by one of his closest friends, the physicist Hans Christian Ørsted. In his tales and stories Andersen exploits the entire treasure trove of motifs and themes to be found in European literature as well as in Greek and Roman antiquity, and he also found inspiration in Arabic, Persian, and Indian narrative.

One of the secrets behind Andersen's success may have been the fact that in his development as a writer he accomplished a transition from poetry to prose, from writing in verse for an educated reader to a modern narrative prose based on oral diction, addressing both children and adults. In the latter decades of romanticism, when popular and realistic tendencies made themselves felt together with an incipient political and social liberation from absolutist rule, prose writing came to the forefront in Danish as in European literature of the 1830s. 1827 was an epoch-making year in the history of literature: the year when Goethe proclaimed the existence of a new world literature in a letter to his assistant and close associate Johann Peter Eckermann, when Hugo signed the preface to his romantic play *Cromwell* and Scott published his article on the supernatural in *Foreign Quarterly*

Review.[67] A taste for the supernatural and the realistic at the same time demanded a new kind of prose. People with an extensive knowledge of folklore, such as Ingemann and Andersen in Denmark and the Grimm brothers in Germany, were able to draw on a large stock of popular legends and superstitions. That Andersen, within the compass of his literary work, had participated in a general development from eighteenth-century classicism to early nineteenth-century romanticism is clearly seen already in his first major work *A Walking Tour*, and in his first tale, "Dødningen, et fyensk Folke-Eventyr" (The Dead Man: A Folktale from Funen), which concludes his volume of *Poems* from 1830 and constitutes the first version of the tale "Reisekammeraten" (1835; The Traveling Companion). The witty and affected style Andersen used in his early, immature attempts was criticized by Ingemann and his wife, who encouraged him to continue writing tales, but also to opt for a style with greater simplicity and seriousness. The rediscovery of a childlike universe in which also ordinary people take part would, according to Ingemann, be the true basis for a revival of story telling.

Andersen took notice of this bit of advice, but by preserving an adult undertone of irony and humor he managed to create his personal mode of double articulation. He felt himself naturally attracted to a childlike sphere and to the nearby world of children. He addressed himself directly to the child in the adult person by taking a short-cut to a world of fellowship and frankness shared by the storyteller and his public. A new interest in childhood with all its implications regarding faith and ideology was a characteristic of romantic literature in the 1830s. The child conceived as an ideological factor symbolized the true source of optimism and belief in the future, and this became an effective argument in polemics against the defenders of pure enlightenment and reason.[68] This fight against the hegemony of reason had begun with Jean-Jacques Rousseau, and had also appeared in Bernardin de Saint-Pierre's novel *Paul et Virginie* (1787), which in a dramatized version was the first play Andersen ever attended at the Royal Theater one of the first days in September 1819 after his arrival in Copenhagen. The notion of the child playing the part of an intermediary of imagination and feeling in literature was also accentuated by Novalis in Germany and Oehlenschläger and Grundtvig in Denmark.

By presenting children in literature as adults in disguise, the classicists of the enlightenment had kept any interest in childhood within narrow limits. To the rationalists of the eighteenth century, childhood seemed a period of waiting; to the romantics the world of children became the very center and culmination of life. It was not until the emergence of a new fairy tale literature that the child found a place in adult literature, and the tension between the manners of the highly educated, adult person and the spontaneity of the child as a representative of unconscious life is certainly at work in a sophisticated manner in many of Andersen's tales and stories. Tieck, who had been the first to renew the writing of short prose as a transitional form, was a master of the fairy tale. His *Volksmärchen von Peter Lebrecht* appeared already in 1795. Tieck had also given his fairy-tale play *Der gestiefelte Kater* (1797) the significant subtitle: "Ein Kindermärchen," and another fairy-tale play *Ritter Blaubart* (1797) he called "Ammenmärchen." Even a number of Hoffmann's and Chamisso's tales were told for children. On the whole the fairy tale seemed to constitute a genre *per se*, expressing the quintessence of imagination, the very canon of poetry. Hoffmann was strongly influenced by Carlo Gozzi, the Venetian playwright, who masterfully exploited folktale motifs in his comedies. The subjects of these tales have been handed down orally as well as in print and are frequently related to those in legends, myths and medieval ballads as well.

The romantics took over the themes and the material from the folktales in the same way as they used medieval ballads and epics as sources. The literary tale of German classicism and early romanticism as we know it from Goethe and Novalis, however, never seems to have been very popular in its mode and narrative technique. On the contrary, these tales were symbolic, complex and far from the simple folktale. It was not until the Grimm brothers began to reshape the folktale with their edition of *Kinderund Hausmärchen* (1812–15) that an oral narrative art came into fashion. It was by merging the folktale and the literary tale that Andersen succeeded in creating his works of excellence.[69]

The folktale is characterized by oral transmission, anonymous origin, formulaic structure and a general lack of style. The literary tale on the other hand is expressed in a sophisticated form in which the individual style of the author is apparent. Characters, setting and detailed descriptions of nature and surroundings play an important part. It is often allegorical and symbolic, as it reflects both a childlike universe and an adult world. It contains a considerable portion of realism, but preferably in a compound of the real and the imaginative.

The romantic literary tale developed in many directions. It was made up of motifs borrowed from comedies, anecdotes, short stories, symbolic stories, fables, and arabesques, among others, and thus it became a supple instrument for expressing the writer's personal philosophy of life. In the 1830s and during the later phases of the romantic movement, where popular and realistic tendencies took over the lead, this kind of short prose reached its height with writers such as Nicolay Gogol, Gottfried Keller, Berthold Auerbach, Charles Baudelaire, and Edgar Allan Poe. In Denmark Oehlenschläger had tried already in 1805 to introduce the genre with *Vaulundurs Saga* (The Saga of Vaulundur), and in 1816 he had published two volumes of fairy tales, *Eventyr of forskiellige Digtere* (Fairy Tales by Various Authors), in which translations from Tieck, Motte Fouqué, Heinrich von Kleist, and Johann Musäus were represented. In 1820 Ingemann had published a volume of *Fairy Tales and Stories*, which had not aroused any attention. The reading public was not familiar with short prose of that kind and fairy tales were generally considered to belong in the nursery.

Only when Andersen at Ingemann's suggestion abandoned the sentimental and high-flown style of contemporary prose and replaced it with a colloquial language in which the narrator's own voice is heard and the presentation comes close to drama, did a real renewal take place. Andersen had read both Hoffmann, Tieck, Jean Paul, and Brentano since his early years. On his way back from Italy in 1834 he attended performances given by the children's ballet in Vienna, in which he may have found inspiration for two of his very first tales not based on folktales, "Little Ida's Flowers" and "Hyrdinden og Skorstensfeieren" (1845; The Shepherdess and the Chimney Sweep). Novalis' fragmentary novel *Heinrich von Ofterdingen* (1802) contains an allegory about Arcturus and Ginnistan telling how the realm of prose and reason is overthrown and poetry is set free. Arcturus's crystal palace reappears in Andersen's tale "The Snow Queen." Other lines can be drawn back to Goethe's *Die Leiden des jungen Werthers* (1774; The Sufferings of Young Werther) and *Faust* (1808), the poems of Schiller, and the comedies of Holberg. Numerous loans, parallels and traces of reading in European literature have already been pointed to in Andersen scholarship, for instance Andersen's dependence both on Motte Fouqué's *Undine* (1811)[70] and August Bournonville's ballet *Sylfiden* (1836; The Sylphide) for his own tale of "The Little Mermaid."

A certain shortness and clarity, a brisk action, a natural dialogue, humor and irony are essential ingredients in Andersen's narrative prose. However, his poetics of double articulation implies that a discourse that is childlike in the positive meaning of the word by appealing to the world of children and telling about it in their own words, has to be counterbalanced by some humor and irony in order to make another interpretation possible than the one based on lack of sophistication. This double articulation is not only part of a specific poetics, it is a new strategy as well, because it enables the writer to give a full expression of a world of experience resulting from a split in the adult mind.[71]

The literary fairy tale was a demanding genre revealing its possibilities only to a writer who in his personal development would measure up to its requirements. All indications point to the fact that Andersen in the years just before his literary breakthrough in 1835 underwent a serious crisis that brought him maturity as a story teller. His social background, his strange vegetating as a young man in the Copenhagen slum, his moral strength and his first agonizing experiences as a writer had awakened a tremendous energy in him. His tales were not just a trio of folktales, romantic literary tales, and his autobiography. In fact, one can point to only about nine of his tales as being reproduced folktales. Andersen felt an urge to delve deeper into the anonymous layers of the history of civilization, which make up the common heritage of all humanity. It is easy to demonstrate that Andersen on the surface knew how to imitate the nuances, gestures and the diction of the Copenhagen bourgeoisie so masterly depicted in his tales and stories. But beneath this local and often humorous level there is a region taking us back to a prehistoric world.

As a storyteller Andersen was original, because he more or less deliberately kept in touch with the unconscious aspects of his soul. Beneath the personal experiences, which to a large extent reflect his own life story, we find the general and elementary conditions and conflicts that belong to all humanity. There is a common stock of experience and belief shared by all people, and if the solutions to the problems that arise cannot be explained in term of providence or fate, they tend to become meaningless. This tension between the belief in the wisdom of the people, a simple conviction of the possibility of being selected by fate, and a modern and adult knowledge about the absurdity of human existence, makes up the true high-voltage field in Andersen's writing. His strength does not lie as much in the delineation of the hero's individual character as in the description of his fate. It is the simple and strong emotions he depicts, the passions carrying life and death in them. Therefore the struggle for life and the pursuit of happiness are the main themes of his tales and stories. He never hesitates to pass beyond the borders of life and death in his desire to let his characters fulfill their lot. He even permits a few of them to ascend directly into Heaven.

Whether Andersen is treating his subject with a profound seriousness or a brilliant sense of humor, any human being regardless of race, sex, social class or religion will nod in recognition to the incidents or situations being described. Poverty, social struggle, childhood, love, human betrayal, and death constitute the central themes of Andersen's tales and stories. Without the rich harvest of German literary tales and the Grimm brothers' achievements these tales and stories would never have come into existence.

However, Andersen's realism seems much more comprehensive than theirs, his humor more evident and his irony present everywhere as a double exposure of the motifs.

The folktale is unequivocal in its view of fate, because it is rooted in popular belief. It deals with the way fate does justice to the repudiated and the disowned. It elevates the humble hero and rewards the humiliated person. By bravely defying the way of the world, it creates a reality in which poetry and devoutness are crucial. But it is not the values and ideas of the folktales that permeate Andersen's creative work. A great many of his tales and stories approach the eighteenth-century rationalist approach to telling fairy tales, such as that proclaimed by Christoph Martin Wieland. According to Wieland the fairy tale should approach an expression of knowledge of the way of the world, should contain wit, satire and allegory expressed in any possible form. This definition, which has the fable as a literary model, suffices to explain the character of a large number of Andersen's tales and stories. In fact they have many sources. There is a romantic-religious group conveying the tradition of the folktale and the German literary tale, such as "The Little Mermaid" and "De vilde Svaner" (1838; The Wild Swans). There is also a second group of satires and allegories related to the classical fables, such as "Keiserens nye Klæder" (1837; The Emperor's New Clothes) with a motif borrowed from a Spanish collection of anecdotes from the fourteenth century, Juan Manuel's, *El Conde Lucanor*, or "Den uartige Dreng" (1835; The Naughty Boy) which is based on the Greek poet Anacreon. Finally there are examples of realistic short stories devoid of any supernatural element, such as "En Historie fra Klitterne" (1860; A Story from the Sand Dunes) and "Hvad Fatter gjør, det er altid det Rigtige" (1861; What the Old Man Does Is Always Right).

Generally speaking, the complex and highly sophisticated forms did not appeal to Andersen. He aimed deliberately at creating works of simplicity, truth and nature by conveying an atmosphere of intimacy. As a storyteller he acts like a phenomenalist philosopher grasping the characteristic details and trying to let the truth appear by glimpses of intuition. In accordance with the program of the earliest romantics, Andersen tried to develop his own mythology based on tradition. The essential characteristic of a great writer is that he has created types and characters more alive to the tradition than real human beings. Andersen not only succeeded in creating imperishable characters, he also invented creatures of a pure imaginative character like the heroes and heroines of the sagas and the myths; such are the title figures of "The Snow Queen" and "The Ice Maiden." It is a remarkable feature about Andersen's tales that the supernatural settings—populated with all kinds of fanciful figures—border directly on the bourgeois world of everyday life. Andersen's skill in linking the sphere of normal life to a supernatural or fabulous world by making these separate worlds function together with imperceptible transitions between them, is quite unique.

More and more Andersen felt the urge to specialize in writing short prose. The retold folktales and the fictitious fairy tales were after 1850 replaced by various kinds of tales and stories with the German author Berthold Auerbach's *Schwarzwälder Dorfgeschichten* (1843–54) as a model. Andersen tried to extend his small genre in all possible directions. One way of experimenting was by writing new tales and stories upon request. In 1846 he was asked by Thorvaldsen to write "Stoppenaalen" (1847; The Darning Needle), and several years later, following a suggestion by Dickens, he finished "Skarnbassen" (1861; The Dung Beetle). Just as some of Andersen's narratives are connected with European colleagues of his time—such as "Det gamle Huus" (1848; The Old House), which he wrote after a visit to the German author Julius Mosen, whose little son had presented him with a tin soldier at his departure, and "Vanddraaben" (1848; A Drop of Water), which he wrote for his close friend Ørsted—others are closely attached to definite geographic localities, such as "The Ice Maiden," which is a genuine Swiss tale, "Psychen" (1861; The Psyche), which is set in Rome, "Metalsvinet" (1862; The Metallic Pig) in Florence and "Venskabs-Pagten" (1862; The Treaty of Friendship) in Greece.

In Andersen's writing a trend toward popular and realistic storytelling dominated the 1850s and 1860s. He seemed restless in his attempts at fording new modes of expression and went over his manuscripts again and again. His texts tended to increase in length and complexity. At the same time he came under the influence of the Swedish singer Jenny Lind (see Chapter 1) and went through a crisis of religious and philosophical scruples. Only about one-sixth of his 156 tales and stories are without any reference to death. In twenty-four of them death is the main theme and in another twenty-five death is part of the conclusion. Whereas Andersen avoids all descriptions of sexuality, since this topic found no place in the literature of the time, he confined himself to telling about illegitimate children and their life stories. He kept turning death over in his mind, because as a lifelong bachelor he had repressed his own sexuality. When all his attention turned on death, his descriptions approached the macabre. He liked to describe skulls, skeletons, burials, and cemeteries; however he could also spare the details and simply let death appear as an old man wrapped in a horse cloth as in "Historien om en Moder" (1847; The Story of a Mother).

Besides death described as the universal lot of all humans, we find Andersen's concept of immortality as a transcendental phenomenon. He held the view that man has a right to immortality because of all the injustice and sufferings the majority of people are subject to during their lifetime, and he proportioned this concept to his aesthetics, as expressed in his tale of "Ærens Tornevei" (1863; The Thorny Path of Honor): "Fairy tale and reality are so close to one another, but the fairy tale has a harmonious resolution on this earth. Reality removes it from our life on earth by relating it to time and eternity." Andersen's later writings reveal a brooding and sometimes even overly scrupulous man occupied with new experiments. By taking his point of departure in the folktale and the romantic concepts of the child and the people as the main objectives of all poetry, Andersen deliberately tried to go beyond national borders and place himself as a poet for all humanity. He built his world from below, using the prose sketch and the child as simple models, letting the arabesque unify poetry and visual art, as proposed by Friedrich Schlegel (see above), and combining in his own way the idea of a fanciful imagination and a light irony with an exuberant abundance of details. Precisely by insisting on the origin of the arabesque in pictorial art did Andersen succeed in creating a prose richly endowed with the colors and contours of a visual world. Reality and dream did not exist apart from each other as incompatible extremes.

ANDERSEN'S POETIC MESSAGE AND HIS HERITAGE

The romantic writers shared a concept of the folktale as a genre that contained all the topics of the collective human mind. In the light of this concept Andersen wrote his tales and stories as the result of a kind of comprehensive impact of influences. Motifs and form came from the folktale, but the ideas were modern and the style sophisticated. In the course of time he continued with new experiments: exploiting and reproducing myths, sagas, legends, parables, and fables in order to create works of great artistic value for the general reader. It was his deliberate intention to make his prose capable of expressing all ideas and sentiments imaginable.

As Andersen wished to bring about a fusion of literature and religion, he also wrote texts which approach the prose hymn, such as the concluding chapter of *In Sweden*, "Poesiens Californien" (The California of Poetry) and "Det ny Aarhundredes Musa" (1861; The Muse of the New Century), in which he tried to convey his poetic message to his readers. His liberal humanism and democratic ideas had in fact more to do with the revival of enlightenment than with the revival of nationalism, which took place in his own time. Being a cosmopolitan and a loyal patriot at the same time, Andersen ran a great risk of being accused of vacillation, but he remained firm in his conviction that every nation was only a single letter in the large alphabet of cultural development toward a global civilization, in which human rights, rationality, and democracy would compensate for national selfishness and the irrationality of power. Sometimes he even tried to prophesy about the future role of literature as a vehicle for this global and religious humanism as in "The Muse of the New Century":

> We, the elders of today, would tremble at hearing the powerful notes, perceiving in them a Ragnarok, the fall of the old gods, forgetting that down here ages and races disappear and only a small picture of each, encapsulated in the word, swims on the river of eternity like a lotus flower, telling us that all of them are and were flesh of our flesh in different garb.

Andersen's dreams about a reconciliation between faith and knowledge, religion and natural science, were made more specific and turned into a cultural vision of the future. The foundation of a global civilization could possibly be realized by means of the fairy tale, because it was expressed in a form which joined two contradictory and conflicting urges in human nature: a desire for the supernatural and a love of truth. The motifs in Andersen's tales and stories, novels and plays are generally problems shared by all human beings irrespective of sex, race, and ideology. These problems are related to childhood, poverty, nature, love, career, death, and literature itself. He wanted to describe the triumph and humiliation of humanity brought into focus through the magical power of fantasy.

Still it seems obvious that in spite of his moral and religious idealism with all its belief in the immortality of the soul, Andersen was incapable of reaching an agreement between the light and the darkness of his own melancholy mind. He dreamed of a new world order based upon the leadership of the best men and women. The nobility of talent and heart should replace the aristocracy of birth, but Andersen nevertheless did not want to make himself too clear on political and moral issues. As an artist he wished to address everyone who would listen to him, and wherever he read aloud to an audience at a royal court or in the Copenhagen Workers' Union, he made a supreme effort to do his very best.

When Denmark had lost the war with Prussia in 1864 and surrendered Schleswig-Holstein, Germany had suddenly turned into a serious threat to the existence of small neighboring countries. For Andersen, the noble German nation, which before any other country had bestowed upon him a spiritual citizenship, suddenly turned into an enemy. Time and again Andersen was accused of being a bad patriot. He experienced the classical conflict of being a European as well as a Dane, and as a man of honor he paid the full price for the defeat of his nation. The words of Talleyrand: "C'est la plume qui est devenue l'épée" had certainly been pronounced too early.

Andersen gave vent to his feelings quite openly. When Grand Duke Carl Alexander in the 1850s made him his personal friend and in Weimar offered him a position (see above), he had declined. When Andersen went to see the world exhibition in Paris in the spring of 1867, he returned by train through Germany. "At Giessen I learned that the Grand Duke of Weimar was in the same train," Andersen wrote in his diary on June 1:

> I even knew his escort without remembering his name, it was embarrassing for me not to be able to rush out and shake his hands. I didn't know how he would greet me, how I myself would later feel if I had followed my instinct; therefore I drew the window curtain all the way every time he walked by.[72]

The world had become smaller and a harder place to live in. About ten years earlier, in 1855, Andersen had written the following introductory passage in his autobiography:

> My life is a beautiful fairy tale, rich and happy! If as a boy, when I went out into the world, poor and alone, I had met a mighty fairy and she had said: Choose your own course and career, and then according to the development of your mind and as it obviously has to happen in this world, I will guide and protect you, my destiny could never have been happier, wiser and better than it is. The story of my life will say to the world what it says to me: there is a loving God, who directs all things for the best.[73]

Meanwhile doubt was lying as a snake in the grass around the root of the fairy tale tree. Since the war of 1864 Andersen's creative power had been handcuffed. In "Loppen og Professoren" (1872; The Flea and the Professor), a hybrid of an arabesque based on Léon Gambetta's escape in a balloon from a besieged Paris on October 7, 1871, during the Franco-Prussian War, he also lets his modern hero escape all private and political worries through a flight. This attempt from Andersen's last years as a storyteller at fording a refuge in the grotesque points ahead to twentieth-century modernism and back to his own youth as well.

If the character of a certain kind of literature could possibly be defined by the number of essential contrasts expressed in it, Andersen's works rank among the first. The last tale he wrote, "Tante Tandpine" (1872; Auntie Toothache)—an arabesque of fantasy in the style of Hoffmann—is a complex allegory dealing with original sin as the true stimulus of civilization and with his own increasingly ambiguous relationship to his vocation as an artist.

When Andersen stopped going abroad toward the end of the 1860s, his tales and stories continued to travel on their own. There were indeed countries in Europe he never managed to visit. He never undertook any travel through Eastern Europe, but still the greatest critical acclaim came to him from Russia. "Long ago he found his adopted country with us," wrote the Russian author S. J. Marsak. It was not until the 1830s that Russians became acquainted with any Scandinavian literature beside Holberg.[74] Already at that time the critic Vissarion Belinsky had reviewed *The Improvisatore* favorably, and in 1838 a Russian translation of Marmier's article about Andersen, "Une vie de poète" in *Revue de Paris* (see above), was published. On the whole, Andersen's novels did not attract much attention, but in the 1850s the revolutionary democrats began to take an interest in Andersen's tales and stories, resulting in an official ban of "The Emperor's New Clothes" by the imperial censor. In A. Lavrent'ev's memoirs *Sutkiv Kopengagene* (n.d. available) the following graceful portrait of Andersen occurs:

> In front of me stood a very tall, thin figure dressed in an old-fashioned, black frock coat. Above the long, aquiline nose there were a pair of eyes probably without peer on this earth. They were blue and exceedingly deep, sensitive, good and also naive as only the eyes of children can be. They contained so much goodness and tenderness, so much fantasy and poetry as can only be recognized in his works, not least in his marvelous fairy tales for children.[75]

Toward the end of the nineteenth century Peter Emanuel Hansen, a Dane who had settled in Saint Petersburg, and his Russian-born wife Anna Vasiljevna Vasiljeva, issued a brilliant translation of Andersen's selected works in four volumes (1894–95). The two translators concluded their task with a translation of the tales and stories, and so it becomes quite obvious that the reception of Andersen's works in Russia clearly distinguishes itself from that in English-speaking countries. In the East European countries Andersen has always been regarded the way he himself wanted to be viewed: as a serious writer, addressing all people, children, women, and men, and one of the very few writers knowing how to communicate works of great artistic value to common people. This general appeal is addressed in the preface to the above-mentioned the fairy tale-edition: "The fairy tales are interesting by the way in which they nourish intellect, emotions, and imagination in all age groups." To renowned Russian writers such as Anton Chekhov and Leo Tolstoy, Andersen's tales and stories became a permanent source of wonder and joy. Tolstoy often discussed Andersen with Maksim Gorky, advising him to write a simple and truthful prose using the Danish storyteller as his model.

Although Andersen was not a philosopher by profession, he was capable of advocating ideas deeply rooted in a liberal and social humanism of common European extraction. He held the view that pagan self-assertion is as valuable as Christian self-denial and he had a clear concept of individual freedom as a necessary condition for all creative work. Sometimes his social instincts and his demand for public recognition made him submit to his critics, and he was generally looked upon as a clumsy fool and a hypochondriac by many of his Danish contemporaries. To ridicule others and to be ridiculed himself was part of his destiny as a first-rank writer. As a writer of his age he not only behaved like an isolated atom in society but also as an ingredient in a social pattern. Any kind of shyness was unknown to him. He left all his writings to posterity making no attempts to conceal any intimacies or secrets of his heart. In spite of all his infirmities he never lost his credibility either as an artist or as a human being.

It is possible to define civilization as a condition in which a great number of extremes and contrasts have been balanced and expressed as a whole. Good writing also testifies to this assumption. Andersen's artistic message is a belief in the victory of light over darkness and the temporary triumph of goodness over the evil powers of the world. The fundamental oppositions between life and death, good and evil, true and false, rich and poor, and faith and doubt are the only themes worthy of the artist's concern, and they can never be exhausted. In his endless striving toward immortality Andersen felt committed to the ideas of his time, the evolutionary and progressive thoughts of the early romantic writers and philosophers. He conceived of himself as an adventurer from the bottom of society climbing up the ladder of fortune. Only the swamp can produce a white lotus. Like all the other great Europeans of the 1830s and 1840s he was a child of the French Revolution and the social and political unrest of the Napoleonic Wars, attracted or repelled by the new opportunities for social progress and political conflict. By not taking sides either in political matters or in religious disputes he remained free in his creative work, preserving his ability to address the greatest possible number of readers. Andersen was a contemporary of Nikolay Gogol, Hoffmann, Stendhal, Scott, and Dickens, a generation which succeeded in following up on Napoleon's military adventures with cultural conquests. As a citizen of an old monarchy that had lost its wars, he had the greatest possibilities of turning a defeat on the political level into new victories by conquering not only the national scene but the European stage as well. This point of view has definitely a great bearing on Andersen's life story. His father had worshipped Napoleon and died as a soldier who had never taken part in a battle (see Chapter 1). Out of his father's frustrated mind came the son's commitment to the dreams of greatness they had shared together in his early childhood. Andersen's literary achievements were deeply rooted in a social heritage and in the political decline of a former European power. At a time when the larger European nations cherished their national pride and colonized the rest of the world, the smaller nations could only make their influence felt by achievements in art, literature, and science. Andersen not only succeeded in renewing an insignificant, yet internationally recognized genre and in becoming the most conspicuous Dane in the Europe of his time, he actually ended up as the most widespread and the most frequently translated writer in all history. As a man without prejudice he tried to disregard the national self-sufficiency he had met in his own country, because he wanted to play his part as an intermediary between nations and their creeds.

Andersen managed to create tales and stories in which realism and modernity participate in a way that Hoffmann had dreamt of, and he realized the most daring dreams in his own career. Still Andersen reluctantly had to admit that the apple of immortality was a hard one to bite and that his success might have been bought too dearly. He had been very well aware of the price he had had to pay for his victories, making his way with difficulty through a life full of disappointments and defeat. As a man of a swelling self-confidence he had tasted the sweetness of fame, but he could not avoid his lot of hardship. There was first of all his renunciation of love between man and woman. That was indeed a deliberate sacrifice due to his physical and mental constitution. He seems to have been healthy, strong and persevering, yet he was delicate and had a sensitive skin in more ways than one, an irritable and edgy man bordering on insanity. Then there was a worm gnawing at him from within. Anxiety and loneliness, the affliction of modern man, were Andersen's loyal traveling companions throughout his life. This nervous hypochondria brought about a somber frame of mind in which his best works have been tuned. Among the notes left after his death was found a slip of paper on which he had written: "I have often heard about the English that they suffer from spleen; I only know about this illness that it is an eccentricity, but still a kind of sadness in which they often take their own lives; I suffer from something like that."[76]

In so saying, Andersen has confirmed the myth that all true greatness is enclosed within a frame of mortal weakness. He realized that, if one may use Danton's words, truth is not only bitter, but that in the long run it is the only remainder of any human being. And as Andersen believed that the voice of the heart is also *vox Dei*, he received all the acclaim and all the homage paid to him without any false modesty. According to Johanne Luise Heiberg (see above) Andersen was, after all, not a masculine person. He therefore had his largest audience among women and children, and since they make up the majority of all mankind, he could feel assured in his hopes for immortality. "If you want to make yourself understood by us, you will have to talk to us in a simple language," another expert on the tales of reality and mankind, Antoine de Saint-Exupéry once said. It was this plain speech that Andersen used at the royal and princely courts in Germany, Austria, England, and France, but even though he wrote the tale called "Klods-Hans" (1855; Clod-Hans), he was never a bungler himself. As a person of great diplomacy and shrewdness he wanted to contribute to a solution of one the major problems of art and literature: to be popular without being banal, simple without being silly.

Andersen has had many imitators, but only a few lawful successors. To those who have adopted his narrative technique and style belongs August Strindberg, whose concise short stories and fairy tales bear the impress of Andersen's oral diction and brevity; but Strindberg as a writer is far more passionate than Andersen and much less humorous. The same is true of another Swedish writer, Selma Lagerlöf, who as a representative of the popular tradition of narrative art has also been influenced by Andersen. On the other hand, even though comparisons have been made, it seems quite obvious that the tales by Karen Blixen (1885–1962) (pseudonym Isak Dinesen), in spite of the fact that to a certain extent she has also benefited from the folktale, rest on a literary foundation quite different from Andersen. Blixen and Andersen both exploit the huge literary tradition of Europe and the Near East. They also have a common metaphysical basis for their narrative art, but whereas Andersen believed in democracy and concentrates on the contrast between heart and spirit, Blixen is an aristocrat dealing with a split between fate and freedom.

When the heart gets the better of the story, Andersen tends to become sentimental, and when his spirit lets his fantasy go its own way, his fables become empty pretense, but as a master of the tale he is unrivaled, when most in earnest, as in "The Story of a Mother", and most satirical as in

"Nattergalen" (1843; The Nightingale). It is a general characteristic of Andersen's art that he had a keen sense of literary delicacy and balance, which his imitators have too often lacked.

NOTES

1. J.C. Brandes. *Ariadne auf Naxos*. Duodrama in one act, 1778. G.B. Sporon, tr. Music by Georg Benda; Fr. W. von Gotter. *Medea*. Melodrama in one act, 1781. Fr. Schwarz, tr. Music by Georg Benda. Both plays had been performed at the Royal Theater in Copenhagen in 1778 and 1788.

2. See Christian Svanholm. *H.C. Andersens ungdomstro*. Trondheim: Bruns bogh., 1952.

3. Letter from Ingemann to Andersen from October 29, 1853. See Niels Kofoed. *H.C. Andersen og B.S. Ingemann. Et livsvarigt venskab*. Copenhagen: C.A. Reitzel, 1992, p. 180.

4. See Andersen's autobiography *Mit Livs Eventyr*. Copenhagen: C.A. Reitzel, 1855, pp. 48–49 and 55–59.

5. *H.C. Andersen Levnedsbog 1805–1831*. 2nd. ed. H. Topsøe-Jensen, ed. Copenhagen: Schonberg, 1971, p. 96.

6. Ibid., p. 135.

7. Ibid., p. 143.

8. H.C. Andersen. *Mit eget Eventyr uden Digtning*. Copenhagen: Lademann, 1986, p. 41.

9. *H.C. Andersens Dagbøger 1825–1875*. Kåre Olsen and H. Topsøe-Jensen, eds. Copenhagen: Det danske Sprog-og Litteraturselskab/G.E.C. Gad, 1971, 1, p. 45.

10. H. Topsøe-Jensen. *Omkring Levnedsbogen. En Studie over H.C. Andersen som Selvbiograf 1820–1845*. Copenhagen: Gyldendal, 1943, pp. 55–57. Manuscript in the Royal Library of Copenhagen, NKS 643, 8.

11. H.C. Andersen. *Fodreise fra Homens Canal til Østpynten af Amager i Aarene 1828 og 1829*. Johan de Mylius, ed. Copenhagen: Det danske Sprog- og Litteraturselskab/Borgen, 1986, p. 55.

12. The arabesque played an important role in Schlegel's concept of poetry. As a term dealing with literature it appears for the first time in *Athenäum* (Fr. 418) in 1798, where Schlegel talks of Tieck's "Märchen" as poetic arabesques, the second time in *Athenäum* (Fr. 421) about Jean Paul. It is also treated in *Gespräch über die Poesie*, 1800. See Friedrich Schlegel. *Literary Notebooks, 1797–1801*. Hans Eichner, ed. London: Athlone Press, 1957.

13. See Niels Kofoed. "Genreproblemet i H.C. Andersens Billedbog uden Billeder. Prosaskitse og Arabesk." *Anderseniana*, III, 4, 1982, p. 23.

14. Heiberg in *Maanedskrift for Litteratur*, 1, 1829. Quoted from *Fodreise*, p. 131; see note 11.

15. Heinrich Teschner. *Hans Christian Andersen und Heinrich Heine*. Münster: Westfäl. Vereindruck, 1914.

16. Elias Bredsdorfff. *Hans Christian Andersen og England*. Copenhagen: Rosenkilde og Bagger, 1954.

17. See note 10.

18. *Breve fra Hans Christian Andersen*, 1. C. St. A. Bille and Nicolai Bøgh, eds. Copenhagen: Gyldendal, 1878, p. 59.

19. *Mit eget Eventyr uden Digtning*, p. 65.

20. Breve til og fra Bernh. Sev. Ingemann. V. Heise, ed. Copenhagen: C.A. Reitzel, 1879, pp. 86 and 120.

21. Goethe in a letter to Zelter. See Albert Sergel. *Oehlenschläger in seinen persönlichen Beziehungen zu Goethe, Tieck and Hebbel*. Rostock: C.J.E. Volckmann, 1907, p. 40.

22. *Breve fra Hans Christian Andersen*, 1, p. 111.

23. Kofoed. *Et livsvarigt venskab*, pp. 45–46.

24. *Mit Livs Eventyr*, p. 313. See also Mogens Brøndsted. "Livsrejsen. Omkring H.C. Andersens 'I Sverrig'." *Danske Studier* (1967), 5–45.

25. *Breve fra Hans Christian Andersen*, 1, p. 113.

26. See *Breve fra Hans Christian Andersen*, 1, p. 125.

27. See Paul Johnson. *The Birth of the Modern World Society 1815–1830*. London: Weidenfeld and Nicholson, 1991, pp. 146–47.

28. *H.C. Andersens Dagbøger 1825–1875*, 1, pp. 270–71.

29. *Breve fra Hans Christian Andersen*, 1, p. 275.

30. *Breve fra Hans Christian Andersen*, 1, p. 228.

31. *Breve fra Hans Christian Andersen*, 1, p. 268.

32. See Niels Kofoed. "Goethes indflydelse på den unge H.C. Andersen." *Anderseniana*, 2, V, 4, 1965, p. 324.

33. See Gérard Lehmann. *Improvisatoren og H.C. Andersens første Itahensrejse*. Odense: Odense University Press, 1976, pp. 192–93.

34. *H.C. Andersens dagbøger 1825–1875*, 1, p. 467.

35. See Lotte Eskelund.... *sah ich zum erstenmal die Donau. Hans Christian Andersen in Österreich*. Vienna and Munich: Jugend und Volk, 1979, p. 12 and *Da Andersen var i Wien*. Copenhagen: Spektrum, 1991.

36. *Breve fra Hans Christian Andersen*, 1, p. 251.

37. See F. Baldensberger. "La grande communion romantique de 1827 sous le signe de Walter Scott." *Revue de Littérature Comparée*, 7, 1926–27.

38. *Romaner og Rejseskildringer*, 2. Copenhagen: Gyldendal, 1943, p. 133.

39. *H.C. Andersens Dagbøger 1825–1875*, 1, p. 263.

40. *Romaner og Rejseskildringer*, 2, p. 143.

41. Letter to Ingemann on Feb. 10, 1835. *Breve fra Hans Christian Andersen*, 1, p. 292.

42. Letter to Frederik Læssøe on March 9, 1838. *Breve fra Hans Christian Andersen*, 1, pp. 410–11.

43. *Breve fra Hans Christian Andersen*, 1, p. 301.

44. *Mit eget Eventyr uden Digtning*, p. 84.

45. *Breve fra Hans Christian Andersen*, 1, pp. 332–33.

46. Letter to Kirstine Marie Iversen on Jan. 4, 1837. *Breve fra Hans Christian Andersen*, 1, p. 365.

47. See *Mit eget Eventyr uden Digtning*, p. 87.

48. *Breve nil Hans Christian Andersen*. C. St. A. Bille and Nicolai Bøgh, eds. Copenhagen: C.A. Reitzel, 1877, p. 285.

49. Ibid., p. 285.

50. *Breve fra Hans Christian Andersen*, 1, pp. 425–26.

51. Kofoed: *Et livsvarigt venskab*, p. 103.

52. See *H.C. Andersens Dagbøger 1825–1875*, 1, p. 429.

53. About Marmier, see Helge Topsøe-Jensen. *Omkring Levnedsbogen*, p. 155; Xavier

Marmier. "Une vie de poète." *Revue de Paris*, Oct. 1837; Kofoed. *Et livsvarigt venskab*, p. 108. Marmier's article was later included in his book *Histoire de la littérature en Danemark et en Suède*, 1839.

    54. *H.C. Andersens Dagbøger 1825–1875*, 2, pp. 324–25.

    55. *Breve fra Hans Christian Andersen*, 1, p. 384.

    56. Ibid., p. 132.

    57. *H.C. Andersens Dagbøger 1825–1875*, 2, p. 325.

    58. Ibid., p. 352.

    59. Ibid., p. 333.

    60. Andersen's epic was inspired by Julius Mosen's poem *Ahasver* (1838) and to some extent by Lamartine's epic poem *La chute d'un ange* (1838) and travelogue *Souvenirs d'un voyage en Orient* (1835).

    61. *Romaner og Rejseskildringer*, 6, p. xi.

    62. See Brøndsted. Note 24.

    63. *Breve fra Hans Christian Andersen*, 2, pp. 81–82; see also *H.C. Andersens Dagbøger 1825–1875*, 2, pp. 356–58.

    64. Elias Bredsdorf, *Hans Christian Andersen 1805–75*. London: Phaidon, 1975, p. 183.

    65. *H.C. Andersens Dagbøger 1825–1875*, 4, p. 213.

    66. *Romaner og Rejseskildringer*, 5, p. ix.

    67. See F. Baldensberger. See note 37.

    68. See H. Kind. *Das Kind in der Ideologie und der Dichtung der deutschen Romantik*. Dresden: Dittert, 1936.

    69. Niels Kofoed. *Studier i H.C. Andersens Fortællekunst*. Copenhagen: Munksgaard, 1967, p. 96. See also Richard Benz. *Märchendichtung der Romantiker*. Gotha: Perthes, 1908.

    70. See, for instance, Sven H. Rossel, "Undine-motivet hos Friedrich de la Motte Fouqué, H.C. Andersen og Jean Giraudoux." *Edda*, 70 (1970), 151–61.

    71. Søren Baggesen. "Dobbeltartikulationen i H.C. Andersens eventyr." *Andersen og Verden*. Odense: Odense University Press, 1993, pp. 26–27.

    72. *H.C. Andersens Dagbøger 1825–1875*, 7, pp. 297–98. Bredsdorff. *Hans Christian Andersen 1805–75*, pp. 224–25.

    73. *Mit Livs Eventyr*, p. 1.

    74. Cynthia Dillard. "Ludvig Holberg in the Russian Literary Landscape." *Ludvig Holberg: A European Writer*. Sven H. Rossel, ed. *Internationale Forschungen zur Allgemeinen und Vergleichenden Literaturwissenschaft*, 8. Amsterdam/Atlanta: Rodopi, 1993, pp. 162–90.

    75. About Andersen and Russia, see L.J. Braude. "H.C. Andersen i Rusland." *Anderseniana*, 1987, pp. 5–24.

    76. Edvard Collin. *H.C. Andersen og Det Collinske Huus*. Copenhagen: C.A. Reitzel, 1882, pp. 456–57.

SELECTED BIBLIOGRAPHY

Editions

H.C. Andersens Samlede Skrifter, 1–15. 2nd ed. Copenhagen: C.A. Reitzel, 1876–80.

———. *Romaner og Rejseskildringer*, 1–7. H. Topsøe-Jensen, ed. Copenhagen: Det danske Sprog- og Litteraturselskab/Gyldendal, 1943–44.

———. *Eventyr*, 1–7. Erik Dal, Erling Nielsen, and Flemming Hovmann, eds. Copenhagen: Det danske Sprog- og Litteraturselskab/Hans Reitzel, 1963–90.

Ungdoms-Forsøg af William Christian Walter. Cai M. Woel, ed. Copenhagen: Christtreus Bogtrykkeri, 1956.

———. *Fodreise fra Holmens Canal til Østpynten of Amager i Aarene 1828 og 1829*. Johan de Mylius, ed. *Danske Klassikere*. Det danske Sprog- og Litteraturselskab/Borgen, 1986.

Correspondence

Breve til Hans Christian Andersen. C. St. A. Bille and Nicolai Bøgh, eds. Copenhagen: Gyldendal, 1877.
Breve fra Hans Christian Andersen, 1–2. C. St. A. Bille and Nicolai Bøgh, eds. Copenhagen: Gyldendal, 1878.

Diaries

H.C. Andersens Dagbøger 1825–1875, 1–12. Kåre Olsen and H. Topsøe-Jensen, eds. Copenhagen: Det danske Sprog- og Litteraturselskab/G.E.C. Gad, 1971–76.
H.C. Andersens Almanakker 1833–1873. Helga Vang Lauridsen and Kirsten Weber, eds. Copenhagen: Det danske Sprog- og Litteraturselskab/G.E.C. Gad, 1990.

SECONDARY LITERATURE

Anderseniana. First Series, 1–13 (1933–46); Second Series, 1–6 (1947–69); Third Series, 1–4 (1970–86). Annually since 1987.
Andersen og Verden/Hans Christian Andersen and the World. Johan de Mylius, Aage Jørgensen and Viggo Hjørnager Pedersen, eds. Odense: Odense University Press, 1993.
Behler, Ernst, Heinrich Fauteck, et al. *Die europäische Romantik*. Frankfurt/M.: Athenäum, 1972.
Bredsdorff, Elias. *H.C. Andersen and Charles Dickens: A Friendship and Its Dissolution*. *Anglistica*, 7. Copenhagen: Rosenkilde and Bagger, 1956.
Bredsdorff, Elias. *H.C. Andersen og England*. Copenhagen: Rosenkilde og Bagger, 1954.
Bredsdorff, Elias. *Hans Christian Andersen: The Story of His Life and Work 1805–75*. London: Phaidon, 1975. New York: Charles Scribner's Sons, 1975.
Brix, Hans. *H.C. Andersen Eventyr*. Copenhagen: Schubotheske, 1907.
Collin, Edvard. *H.C. Andersen og det Collinske Huus*. Copenhagen: C.A. Reitzel, 1882.
Eskelund, Lotte. *... sah ich zum erstenmal die Donau. H.C. Andersen in Österreich*. Vienna and Munich: Jugend und Volk, 1979.
Eskelund, Lotte. *Da Andersen var i Wien. H.C. Andersens rejser i Østrig i årene 1834–1872*. Copenhagen: Spektrum, 1991.
Grønbech, Bo. *H.C. Andersens Eventyrverden*. Copenhagen: Povl Branner, 1945.
Johnson, Paul. *The Birth of the Modern World Society 1815–1830*. London: Weidenfeld and Nicholson, 1991.
Kofoed, Niels. *Studier i H.C. Andersens Fortællekunst*. Copenhagen: Munksgaard, 1967.
Kofoed, Niels. *H.C. Andersen*. Copenhagen: G.E.C. Gad, 1967.
Kofoed, Niels. *H.C. Andersen og B.S. Ingemann. Et livvarigt venskab*. C.A. Reitzel, 1992.
Lehmann, Gérard. *Improvisatoren og H.C. Andersens første Italiensrejse*. Odense: Odense University Press, 1976.

Mylius, Johan de. *Myte og Roman. H.C. Andersens romaner mellem romantik og realisme.* Copenhagen: Gyldendal, 1981.

Möller-Christensen, Ivy York. *Den gyldne trekant. H.C. Andersens gennembrud i Tyskland 1831–1850. Odense University Studies in Scandinavian Languages and Literatures*, 24. Odense: Odense Universitetsforlag, 1992.

Nielsen, Erling. *H.C. Andersen.* Stockholm: Natur och Kultur, 1960.

Nørregaard-Nielsen, Hans Edvard. *Jeg saae det Land. H.C. Andersens rejseskitser fra Italien.* Copenhagen: Gyldendal, 1990.

Rubow, Paul V. *H.C. Andersens Eventyr.* Copenhagen: Levin and Munksgaard, 1927.

Westergaard, E. Koed. *Omkring H.C. Andersens første eventyr.* Copenhagen: Hans Reitzel, 1985.

AAGE JØRGENSEN

Heroes in Hans Christian Andersen's Writings

A SON OF THE PEOPLE

Let us begin in medias res: with a fabulous main character nicknamed Clod-Hans by his brothers,—which doesn't exactly suggest anything heroic. On the other hand, Clod-Hans gives his name to the text, a conventional fairy tale (from 1855) not particularly influenced by Romanticism, but clearly rooted in the art of popular storytelling.[1] As you will recall, the brothers want to ask the princess's hand in marriage. She will marry the man who has "the most to say for himself", and since the brothers are "so witty that they thought themselves too clever for words", and beyond that have impressive, supposedly useful abilities, the father willingly provides them with horses. When Clod-Hans realizes what is happening, he immediately has "a yen to get married": "If she takes me, she takes me; and if she doesn't take me, I'll take her, anyway." That's how simple Clod-Hans's life is and that's how spontaneously he tackles things. That his father refuses to lend him a horse is no problem, for Clod-Hans has his own billy-goat and is therefore mobile. So it's easy sailing for him, "halloo, here I come!" Along the way, he makes his matchless discoveries: a dead crow, an old wooden shoe with no leather top, a pocketful of the finest mud. On the back of his goat and in possession of these wonderful finds, he rides, as it is written, "right into the hall", where his brothers have just had a terrible setback, despite their abilities. They start

From *Hans Christian Andersen: A Poet in Time* (1999). © 1999 by Odense University Press and the authors.

175

out well enough by finding it "terribly hot" and "dreadfully warm" respectively, but when the princess explains that it is due to the fact that "my father" and "we" respectively are in the process of broiling chickens, that shuts them up. Clod-Hans also notices "a scorcher", but when she answers, "I'm roasting young chickens", he immediately scores points with clever conversation and fancy contributions to the royal cuisine. Not even the prospect of seeing the entire story verbatim in the newspaper can stop him; on the contrary, he throws what is left of his mud right in the alderman's face, to the utter delight of the princess.

In recent years, Mikhail Bakhtin's carnival concept has often proved an effective instrument in the context of literary analysis. It deals with situations in which things are stood on their heads, so to speak. Where the bottom rung of society is momentarily on the top, and where the refined and distinguished, the respectable and ideal are subjected to ridicule. Where room is given to bodily functions, to digestion and reproduction, where sexuality is for once both spoken of and allowed to speak, where bad table manners and belching undercut the show of proper etiquette, and so on. A burlesque and grotesque world of the belly unfolds itself and challenges the intellect's ability to maintain control.

Clod-Hans is in all modesty a text of that kind.[2] Its language is not exactly the most refined. It opens onto the perishable and the putrefying. The hero rides his goat right into the castle's fancy room with mirrored-ceiling (which in turning things upside down, contributes to the brothers' breakdown). And not only does he use mud in the food, but with what he has left, he also dirties the alderman's ruling-class face.

As can be seen in connection with the title, *Clod-Hans* is "an old story retold". Here, as a 50-year-old writer, Andersen returns to his popular or rather folktale point of departure. The retold folktale is found in several variants, and we do not know precisely which one Andersen knew. But in the Danish Folklore Archives, there is a transcript of a tale told by Black Grethe to her daughter, in the village Kjøng, southwest of Odense, and "given to Jens Kamp before 1904". This variant, *Klotte-Hans*, was undoubtedly in circulation in Funen in the early 19th Century.[3]

This well-turned and somewhat coarse tale, whose young lad rides a ram for the simple reason that the father only has two horses, clearly satisfies a social wish-fulfillment dream. What was not possible in the reality of the feudal social system, could be fulfilled in fiction. Not to put too fine a point on it, the hero gives the princess a turd and gets a kingdom in return.

But *Klotte-Hans* was not suitable for the fashionable urban bourgeois nursery. It differs from the literary tale in striking ways. The refined modern teller of tales—Andersen, that is—spins his story in such a way that without losing any vigour, it remains fully presentable in cultivated circles. He manages this by using several strategies. First of all, it is evident that *Clod-Hans* is invested with a powerful artistic mastery of language. The story is also expanded, refined and removed from the specifically folktale milieu and in a way transferred to "modern times". For example, in Andersen's version there aren't three brothers, but rather two and then one more, whom no one takes into account. And why not? Because the brothers have been ascribed abilities of a kind that had never been seen in a folktale, and which turn out to be utterly useless after all. To know the guild articles and the city newspaper by heart corresponds in large measure to knowing the telephone directory by heart today. The tale opposes two kinds of education: the brothers' sterile memorization which has no relation to the real world, and Clod-Hans's highly effective cunning, which brings him the fulfillment of his desires.

Clod-Hans is, in short, a popular hero. He uses his resources masterfully and achieves his goal, he is the princess's equal and indifferent to public opinion. He gets a wife, crown and throne, and the alderman gets mud in his face. The fiction rewards him and could have been rounded off in the traditional folktale manner: they lived happily ever after. However, the narrator moderates the simplicity with some ironic distance: in a story this sort of thing can happen, in the reality outside of the story is it hardly possible. So instead, Andersen sends a little greeting to the expanding bourgeois press: "we had this story straight from the alderman's newspaper—but that is one you can't always depend upon".

A MAN OF ACTION

There are few examples of this kind of folktale-retold in Hans Christian Andersen's stories, but that was what he began with,—with *The Tinder Box* at the beginning of the very first of the little booklets (1835).[4] Here, he takes up the same Oriental Aladdin story that Oehlenschläger had dramatised in the year of Andersen's birth. Oehlenschläger's Aladdin gets hold of the magic lamp because Noureddin sees at the palace square how he gets the orange in his turban by a stroke of luck, as it were. In the same manner, Andersen's Soldier gets hold of the tinder box because the old witch is in need of a helper. By means of their sources of light both get whatever their heart desires, including of course a princess. And both stand to lose her again. But Andersen turns the Soldier's story around in fairy-tale fashion, so that it ends with a wedding,—during which the dogs have a good time throwing the courtiers up in the air. Here we see a carnival element which was not present in Oehlenschläger's universal, romantic drama. On the other hand Andersen's tale omits the long hard battle through which Aladdin wins back the palace and Gulnare. The Soldier gets his tinder box back through cunning and then, with the help of the dogs, can obtain the princess and the kingdom. While Oehlenschläger tells a story of sublimation, Andersen tells one of the unfolding of drives and of self-realization. The Soldier cannot resist kissing the girl, for he is after all "a real soldier" and can apparently see that she is "a true princess". A real soldier doesn't care for nonsense, without any scruples he cuts off the witch's head,—to which his critics and the public objected, even though she obviously represents psychological states that must be overcome.

I will defy that criticism and designate the Soldier as one of Andersen's popular heroes. And not because he cuts the witch's head off, but because after he does so, which amounts to freeing himself from mother fixation, he shows that he can master his magical lamp and thereby also his drives. And note that this is mastery, not repression. Here in any event, the princess leaves the copper palace, that is liberates herself from father fixation, and becomes queen, which appeals to her. And, as written: "The wedding lasted all of a week, and the three dogs sat at the table, with their eyes opened wider than ever before."—No one need doubt that the new royal couple, acclaimed by the people, will live happily ever after.

A CHILD OF HAPPINESS

Late in his life (1870), Hans Christian Andersen wrote a little novel whose title—and the fact that the Aladdin theme is once again played out in it— makes it far more relevant than was the case with *Clod-Hans* to draw on it in an effort to clarify what might be meant by the word "hero" in the context of the author's work. *Lykke-Peer* (*Lucky Peer*) is a novel about an artist and in this respect marks a return to Andersen's first great international effort as a novelist, *Improvisatoren* (*The Improvisatore*, 1835).[5]

At precisely the same moment, two boys are born in one and the same house. The merchant's son is christened Felix, while the warehouse worker's boy is called Peer. He acquires his nickname when, while playing, he finds the merchant's wife's engagement ring in the gutter. The lucky child chooses a life in the theater, first ballet, then singing, but as an adolescent, he loses his voice. An anonymous benefactor (the theater's singing teacher, we later learn) ensures that he is sent to a provincial city and taken in as a boarder by the schoolmaster, Mr. Gabriel, whose wife—we note en passant—bids him welcome with the line: "Good heavens, how grown-up you are!" (and orders that a communicating door be nailed shut for the sake of propriety) (334).[6] She arranges for him to play Romeo in the local theater's performance of Shakespeare's tragedy, with the pharmacist's daughter as Juliet, which results in his falling in love with her. But at a ball given by the local deacon, Felix gets in the way and conquers the beauty. After two years of diligent study, Peer must return to the capital and at the final moment, during a scary dream in which the pharmacist's daughter appears as another elfmaid and tempts him to perdition, he gets his voice back. The singing teacher is still his mentor and oracle of wisdom, and Peer advances from one success to another,—while Felix enjoys life's more material pleasures and is promoted to gentleman-in-waiting. Together at a painting exhibition, they meet a young baroness, "in her sixteenth year, an innocent, beautiful child" (372), whose maternal home becomes Peer's gateway to "the great world" (373). He was "happy in his art and with the talents he possessed" (375), though with a touch of sadness at the thought of the transitory nature of all things, including the performing arts. Until the day when he marvelously improvises on the piano and brings the baroness to make a declaration, whereupon she thinks: "Aladdin!" He now writes an opera with that title, composing both lyrics and music, and rehearses it with the orchestra—and has it performed with himself in the lead role. The sounds and tones of the work "subdued all listeners and seized them with a rapture that could not rise higher when he [Aladdin] reached for the lamp of fortune that was embraced by the song of the spirits" (383). The cheering at this finale pours down upon Peer, and in this moment of triumph, he collapses, dead to the world.

We can understand that Peer is positioned between two women: the pharmacist's daughter, who plays Juliet in the provincial Shakespeare performance, and the baroness, who inspires the Aladdin opera. The pharmacist's daughter represents the petite bourgeoisie as temptation with the prospect of perdition. In Peer's feverish dream, she reveals herself to him as hollow in her back, profligate. The baroness, on the other hand, representing the aristocracy, is the one who throws him the laurel wreath, is the one who "like a spirit of beauty" leads the cheering at his triumph.

But the moment of triumph is also the moment of death. At the end Peer is called "more fortunate than millions" (384). He is spared the struggle to hold on to his luck, and possibly also for running his head into a wall in an attempt to transform the platonic relationship to a life together. Artistic fortune has its price: it doesn't simply allow itself by magic to be reconciled with a bourgeois married life. This is Andersen's version of what Georg Brandes a few decades later was to call aristocratic radicalism. The great artist is his era's seeing-eye dog.

Hans Christian Andersen's novel, as well as the main character's opera, are situated in the wake of Oehlenschläger's famous drama, in the cultural tradition established by that work. As is known, *Aladdin* appeared in the second volume of *Poetiske Skrifter* (*Poetic Writings*), as an Oriental-sanguine counterpart to the Nordic-melancholy saga pastiche, *Vaulundurs Saga*. That piece became the unavoidable lifelong assignment for the golden era's writers and artists. It taught that nature's cheerful son is as a matter of course granted happiness, but must achieve an awareness of "the ethical dimension of his task" in order to hold on to or recover it, should it be lost. "Not until after manly fight / is its full value appreciated by the owner", is it written of the lamp.[7]

Within the Aladdin figure, we can find the very core of the romantic conceptual structure, which ingeniously and organically combines philosophies of nature, personality, and aesthetics. This is brought about through the recognition that one and the same force—or spirit, as it was called at the time—flows through all of creation, though with different strengths. Schelling's well-known formulation—spirit in nature sleeps in the stone, dreams in the plant, awakens in the animal, becomes conscious in man and reaches fulfilment in the artist—beautifully illustrates this organic thinking. Its dynamic quality is also significant: everything strives for a *higher* consciousness. Man does so insofar as a seed is planted within him, which his lifelong duty is to bring to full fruition, just as an acorn is invested with the potential that can guide its growth toward becoming the most magnificent oak tree. It is called culture,—becoming cultivated and unfolding one's inherent possibilities in their pathway toward the idea. The artist, the genius, differs from ordinary people in that he consciously aims for the very source of the divine power which flows through nature and human life. When taken to its logical conclusion, Romantic philosophy is a philosophy of identity. "To embrace everything, that is love", wrote Oehlenschläger in *Sanct Hansaften-Spil* (*Midsummer Night's Play*). And in *Jesu Christi gientagne Liv i den aarlige Natur* (*The Life of Jesus Christ Symbolized in the Seasons*) Simon Peter comes to the realization that "taken in itself everything is nothing, but taken as a whole everything is everything". The mystical raises itself up to and dissolves itself into the mythic.

In the framework of a philosophy of identity, the hero can be recognized by his purposeful, exuberant growth. He is like a tree that grows up into the sky without losing connection to its roots. The ultimate hero is the great artist.

In the moment of triumph and of death, Lucky Peer undoubtedly experiences identity with the divine, with the world of the idea. But it is worth noticing that his opera does not follow Aladdin's story to the very end. It breaks off at exactly that point where he takes hold of the lamp in the underground cave. The story continues. With the lamp, Aladdin acquires the power to create a palace and win the princess, Gulnare. But it should also be noted that he becomes careless with the lamp, so that Noureddin gets hold of it,—after which he loses everything again. At one point, his spirits are so low that suicide appears to him as the only possibility. But at that very moment, there emerges within him another and higher nature, and he gets the strength to take up the battle, first with Hindbad, and later with his true counterpart, the brooding Noureddin. Out of that development, there emerges a ripened hero with his luck intact, but in a purified and ennobled form, as though spirit were added to it. Ripeness is all, as Shakespeare said.

THE CHILDLIKE HERO

Materially, *Lucky Peer* draws in several ways upon Hans Christian Andersen's so-called *Levnedsbog* (*Life Book*), his first autobiography, covering the period 1805–31, and written in 1832, that is before the great journey he undertook in 1833–34, a freer, fresher, more ingenuous and less elaborate work than the subsequent autobiographies.[8] The explicit purpose of the project is to seek clarity about himself. Although he finds his own personality or character "quite inexplicable", he nevertheless feels "that an invisible, loving hand guides all things", and "that life itself is a grand and wonderful poem" (6). Is it a hero we now see extricating himself from his infant state? And if so: a hero on the stage of life? The *Life Book* contains formulations which in fact suggest just that. As a child, he reads biographies: "[...] my imagination for adventure was awakened, I thought of life itself as an adventure and looked forward to appearing in it myself as a hero" (42). More and more, he relates his own life to the portrayals of heroic life in the books he reads. He decides, "just like the heroes in the many adventure stories I had read to get out—all alone—into the world" (49), that is, to the capital. Once again, however, specifically mentioning that the good Lord will see to it that things go as they should. Also when Weyse raises money and Siboni promises singing lessons, it is God who gets the credit, but Andersen is in no way surprised: "that's the way I had imagined it, and in all novels and stories the hero succeeded in the end" (62). In the end! But the year is 1819 and Andersen has just barely arrived in Copenhagen. Subsequently, and especially after his deportation to Slagelse, "heroic places" will be few and far between, while those places where he will need comforting by God and motherly ladyfriends, come one after another. He was given comfort, for example, during his visits to the

Wulff family at Amalienborg. He cites from his own journal: "Oh God, this is just like Aladdin, I am also sitting in the castle and looking down. God Almighty! No, you will not abandon me" (135). The reference here is to the *final* monologue in Oehlenschläger's work; Andersen would gladly have skipped over the difficult balance sheets of existence. Later, when Meisling's lessons as well as Ludvig Müller's preparatory training for the degree examination were well behind him, he made the acquaintance of the Læssøe family.

> On many an evening, I could completely become as a child in their home. I became natural just because I did not feel shy and knew that my errors and spontaneous remarks would never be weighed without their letting the good tip the scale in my favour. While other people tried to turn me into a man of the world, they appreciated my curious, childlike character. (198f)

One can wonder why Hans Christian Andersen develops this autobiographical description at such an early point in his life. Probably above all for the purpose of legitimizing himself in relation to culture and its purveyors within the Copenhagen elite, whom he had approached, and who had in a sense invested in him,—for the purpose of giving an impression of his inner riddle, which could explain that the goal of becoming cultivated had not fully been achieved because his gift was of a most unusual nature. For that reason, the autobiography's central and most moving section becomes the one on the five accursed years—Meisling's compulsory lessons in Slagelse and finally in Helsingør.

THE LIFE'S FAIRY TALE HERO

The Fairy Tale of My Life is next on the program![9] What has been said up to this point about the artist hero and about the way the 19th Century's idea of the hero was shaped by the entire Romantic philosophy of personality and focus on culture, leads us to the question: isn't the fairy tale of life essentially Hans Christian Andersen's proposal of a contemporary hagiography? In the history of literary genres, that word refers to portrayals designed to present a person's life and deeds in so convincing a manner, that the Pope will be moved to declare the person a saint. It was not of course up to the budding saint himself—of whom it was also required that he be dead—to write the hagiography. The point is that hagiographic portrayals are written with a specific purpose in mind, and this in turn accounts for the genre's significant influence on the biographical and thereby also the autobiographical tradition in European literature. Johannes Jørgensen writes about the holy Francis of Assisi and Georg Brandes of the unholy François de Voltaire, because they want to unfold an ideal of personality,—and both are, by the way, also writers of *auto*biographies, in which they model themselves on their heroes. In the same way, Hans Christian Andersen has a task to accomplish with his autobiographical works, especially with *The Fairy Tale of My Life*, which begins with the well-known passage:

> My life is a beautiful fairy-tale, so eventful has it been and wondrous happy. Even if, when I was a boy and went forth into the world poor and friendless, a good fairy had met me and said, "Choose thy own course through life and the object for which thou wilt strive, and then, according to the development of thy mind, and as reason requires, I will guide and defend thee," my fate could not have been more wisely and happily directed. The story of my life will tell the world what it tells me:—There is a loving God who directs all things for the best. (A, 13)

At its conclusion, the work circles back upon itself in the following way:

> The fairy-tale of my life right up to the present hour is thus laid before me so eventful, so beautiful and so full of comfort. There came good even out of evil and joy out of pain; it is a poem more full of profound thoughts than I could possibly have written. I feel that I am a child of good fortune. So many of the noblest and best men and women of my day have dealt with me kindly and openly, and it is but seldom that my confidence in Man has been disappointed. Even the heavy days of bitterness contain the germs of blessings. All the injustice I thought I suffered and every hand which was heavy in the way in which it influenced my development brought good results after all. / As we progress towards God all pain and bitterness are dispersed, and what is beautiful is left behind. We see it like a rainbow against dark clouds. May men be mild in their judgement of me as I am in my judgement of them; and I am sure they will be. The story of a life has something of the sacredness of a confession for all noble and good men. I have told the fairy-tale of my life here openly and full of confidence as though I were sitting among cherished friends. (A, 346)

These concluding words are dated April 2, 1855. "Right up to the present hour" means therefore quite literally: 'in the first 50 years of my life'. Here Andersen is taking stock of his life. It is thanks to the good Lord, who guides everything for the best, together with a strongly purposeful personal commitment, that the 50th birthday does not appear to be a random pause,— for immediately before that, Andersen places a kind of acknowledgment for Grímur Thomsen's review of his collected writings. In his eyes, this discussion of his work becomes the proof that the long and arduous battle on his home grounds against every kind of small-mindedness is now finally bearing fruit. The period of rejection is over, the recognition and victories throughout Europe—which peaked in 1847—now finally makes an impact on the attitude of Danish critics. Listen carefully and notice the points that are so deftly emphasized:

> Just at this present time, as I am about to complete my fiftieth year and as my "Collected Works" are being published, the "Danish Monthly Review of Literature" has published a review of it by Mr. Grímur Thomsen. [..] It seems almost that Heaven wished me to end this chapter of my life by seeing the fulfilment of H.C. Ørsted's words to me in those heavy days when no one appreciated me. My native land has given me the cherished bouquet of recognition and encouragement. (A, 346)

It is in this way that Hans Christian Andersen organizes his life for posterity,—as a divinely guided path, along which hardships purify him in his journey toward the stars. The trials have a meaning, when viewed in retrospect from the present summit. Olympus makes a good blotting-pad, when the days of rejection are enumerated and forgiveness dispensed.

Taking stock of one's life has for all good and noble souls something of the power and sanctity of confession, as Andersen sees it; in this way he himself justifies our inscribing of this life's fairy tale in a sacred context. Glory be to God!

Andersen also makes a claim concerning cultivation. In our progress toward God beauty arises, while bitterness melts away.

It is however something of a problem that what is most decisive comes to Andersen from without. That Thomsen writes in warm and friendly tones about the fairy tales and virtually fulfills the prophecy with which H.C. Ørsted comforted the poet when he was criticized for his first fairy tales, cannot really be compared to what Aladdin experiences when a higher nature emerges from deep within him and prevents him from taking his own life in the Persian river. Aladdin is formed from within, Andersen gains recognition from without. It is the surrounding world that changes, not his own personality. It is the people who increasingly come to him in an open and loving way, not he who makes peace with existence.

He repeats this manoeuvre in 1869, when he completes the continuation of the fairy tale of his life, which he penned for the American edition of his writings. This time, the obvious culmination was the festivity at which he was proclaimed honorary citizen of Odense in December 1867. When he was approached, Andersen had proposed that they wait until September 4, 1869, the fiftieth anniversary of his departure for Copenhagen. In this case, he did not however get his way, but the proposal was presumably nothing more than an off-hand remark. After the celebration itself, but before his departure, he took part in the Lahn Foundation's annual festival. Some fuss was made over Andersen on that occasion as well. "It was as if one sunbeam after another shone into my heart, it was more than I could bear! In such a moment one clings to God as in the bitterest hour of sorrow" (B, 569). And once outside of the city, Andersen finally realized what honor, joy and delight "God had endowed upon me through my native town". And further on, in conclusion:

> The greatest, the highest blessing I could attain was now mine.
> Now for the first time could I fully and devoutly thank my God
> and pray: "Leave me not when the days of trial come!" (B, 569)

This final remark is essentially concerned with the future. Although allegedly his heart could not contain so much happiness, there was no occurrence of what Andersen allowed to happen to Lucky Peer a few years later:

> A fire rushed through him; his heart swelled as never before [..].
> Dead in the moment of triumph, like Sophocles at the Olympian
> games, like Thorvaldsen in the theater during Beethoven's
> symphony. An artery in his heart had burst, and as by a flash of
> lightning his days here were ended, ended without pain, ended in
> an earthly triumph, in the fulfilment of his mission on earth.
> Lucky Peer! More fortunate than millions! (383f)

Andersen spared his hero all tribulations. His own heart sighed but didn't burst when he left the scene of his triumph (which marked the fulfilment of the prophecy that Odense would some day be lit up in his honor)—on the way to awaiting trials.

If the truth be told, and it can be if the journals and letters are allowed to supplement the autobiography, then trials were an integral part of the poet's life. Some years ago, in *Flugten i sproget* (*Flight into Language*), Torben Brøstrom and Jørn Lund argued that it was precisely there, in language, that the poet occasionally overcame the experience of loneliness and coldness that came increasingly with fame. They write somewhere[10] about

> the realization that came in the final years of his life, that artistic growth was won at the expense of human development, that fame had not only cost blood, sweat and tears, but had left him with a disheartening sense of coldness, which his analytical acuity prevented him from repressing, and which he had to face head on—just before the end came.

It is Klaus P. Mortensen who sharpened the two writers'—and our—grasp of this in *Svanen og Skyggen* (*The Swan and the Shadow*), which as the title also indicates, tells "the story of young Andersen".[11] The evidence suggests that as his literary achievement was eventually honored by general European and Danish recognition, the poet understood with ever increasing clarity that success had cost a terrible price: emotional coldness.

The final chapter in Brostrøm and Lund's book is entitled "Language and poetry. The unfulfilled dream". Here, the obvious connection between *The Improvisatore* and *Lucky Peer* is drawn, in the following way:[12]

> [Andersen's] drive for poetic unfolding was also a dream of personal unfolding. He wanted both to create art and to redeem it. The improvisatore at the gateway to the literary production and Lucky Peer at the close of it, can accomplish anything, reach everyone around them, interpret shared experiences as well as individual, bound impulses and memories, see poetic possibilities and create in the here and now a kind of expression which is in harmony with eternity, with the universal poetic primitive force.

The Improvisatore was written by Hans Christian Andersen in continuation of the journey he undertook to become cultivated, during which he paradoxically and fortunately liberated himself from (or at least kept a certain distance from) the imposed and hard won cultivation. In the novel, he goes so far as to let the hero, Antonio, prevail both artistically and matrimonially. That was just before he wrote *The Tinder Box*, which he brought off with improvisational ease.

THE REALIZATION AND THE PRICE

Hans Christian Andersen produced essentially two sets of heroes: the popular (represented here by Clod-Hans and the Soldier) and the literary (represented by Lucky Peer and Hans Christian himself). His popular heroes pass their tests and win their princesses and live happily ever after. The literary heroes attune their spiritual powers to an exalted level, but have to pay dearly for that. As will be recalled, it isn't the learned man who marries the princess in the fairy tale, *The Shadow*, but precisely those shadowy properties he represses, and which ultimately kill him.

Though with social and cultural odds against him, Hans Christian Andersen achieves happiness, but specifically in the form of success: being cheered by the public, outer appearances. What he loses along the way is the popular hero's drive, and what he ultimately can only rave about is Lucky Peer's uncompromising spiritual aristocraticism. It is in the interval that, with our Lord as his guide, and thanks to an inherent stubborn tenacity, he achieves the coveted goal, *recognition*.[13]

NOTES

1. "Clod-Hans", quoted from *The Complete Andersen*, translated by Jean Hersholt, illustrated by Fritz Kredel. New York 1952, Section II, pp. 175–79 [entitled "Clumsy Hans"]. (Original Danish version: "Klods-Hans", *Historier*, illustrated by Vilhelm Pedersen, 1855, pp. 114–19; cf. *H.C. Andersens Eventyr*, ed. by Erik Dal, et al., Vol. 2: *1843–55*, 1964, pp. 291–94, and Vol. 7: *Kommentar*, 1990, pp. 162–63.)

2. Cf. Jens Aage Doctor, "H.C. Andersens karneval", in *Andersen og Verden*, ed. by Johan de Mylius, et al., 1993, pp. 410–19. (The author's doctoral thesis: *Shakespeares karneval*, 1994.)

3. The version in question can be found in *Fortællerstil*, ed. by Kristian Kjær and Henrik Schovsbo, 1975, pp. 85–86. Jens Kamp was a Danish folklorist (1845–1900).

4. "The Tinder Box", quoted from *The Complete Andersen*, Section I, pp. 1–7. (Original Danish version: "Fyrtøiet", *Eventyr, fortalte for Børn*, Vol. I:1, 1835, pp. 1–16; cf. *H.C. Andersens Eventyr*, Vol. I: *1835–42*, 1963, pp. 23–29, and Vol. 7: *Kommentar*, 1990, pp. 19–23.)

5. *Lucky Peer* is quoted from *The Complete Andersen*, Section III, pp. 316–84. (Original Danish version: *Lykke-Peer*, 1870, 1870, 183 pp.; cf. *Romaner og Rejseskildringer*, Vol. 5, 1944, pp. 241–317.) The American edition is, despite the title, complete only as far as the fairy tales are concerned, but Hersholt may have considered Andersen's shortest novel to be rather like a fairy tale. (An English translation prior to Hersholt's appeared in *Scribner's Monthly*, Vol. 1, 1871.)—Cf. Johan de Mylius's doctoral thesis, *Myte og roman. H.C. Andersens romaner mellem romantik og realisme*, 1981, pp. 210–25 (chapter entitled "Kunst som myte").

6. The portrayal of Peer's stay with the Gabriel family can be compared with the portrayal in the so-called *Levnedsbog* (see note 8) of Hans Christian Andersen's stay with

the Meisling family. Mrs. Meisling is cited in that work—as a prelude to the description of her seduction attempt—for her exclamation: "This is no real he-man" (131).

7. *Aladdin eller Den forunderlige Lampe*, ed. by Jens Kr. Andersen, 1978, p. 281 (and preface p. 7). (Cf. *Aladdin or The Wonderful Lamp*, translated by Henry Meyer, 1968, p. 222: "To grasp it dauntlessly it is your part / to fight courageously. First then you are / able to hold its value in regard".)

8. The page references in this section are to *H.C. Andersens Levnedsbog*, ed. by H. Topsøe-Jensen, 1962 (3rd impr., 1988).

9. The page references in this section are to [A] *The Fairy Tale of My Life*, translated by W. Glyn Jones, illustrated by Niels Larsen Stevens, 1954, and [B] *The Story of My Life*, translated by Horace E. Scudder, New York 1871 (= Author's Edition, Vol. 7); Scudder's translation has been slightly revised. (Cf. the Danish standard edition: *Mit Livs Eventyr*, Vols. 1–2, ed. by H. Topsøe-Jensen and H.G. Olrik, 1951 (2nd impr., 1975).)

10. Torben Brostrøm & Jørn Lund, *Flugten i sproget. H.C. Andersens udtryk*, 1991, p. 138 (in the chapter entitled "Norgesturen", by Jørn Lund).

11. Klaus P. Mortensen, *Svanen og Skyggen—historien om unge Andersen*, 1989.

12. *Flugten i sproget*, p. 155. (The chapter was written by Jørn Lund.)

13. This article was presented as a paper on two occasions: first at a Hans Christian Andersen symposium held at the university in St. Petersburg on May 17, 1996, as part of the Danish-Russian festival of children's culture organized by the Danish Literature Information Center (DLIC); and subsequently at The Second International Hans Christian Andersen Conference, held at the H.C. Andersen Center, Odense University, from July 28 to August 3, 1996. The Danish version appeared in *BUM/Børne-og ungdoms-litteratur magasinet*, Vol. 14: 1–2, 1996, pp. 32–38; *H.C. Andersen i Rusland*, ed. Aage Jørgensen, et al., 1997, pp. 37–48; and Aage Jørgensen, <u>Børgens Fædreland-og andre guldalderstudier</u>, 1999, pp. 109–29.

JACKIE WULLSCHLAGER

Kiss of the Muse:
1860–1865

You are a lucky man. When you look in the gutters, you find pearls.
—B.S. INGEMANN, letter to
Hans Christian Andersen, 10 April 1858

Andersen called Harald Scharff "a butterfly who flits around sympathetically." They first met in Paris in 1857; Andersen was on his way home from his visit to Dickens, and Scharff was staying in the French capital with the Danish actor Lauritz Eckhardt. Scharff was then twenty-one, lean and lithe, a flamboyant dancer at the Royal Theatre in Copenhagen. In his memoirs Auguste Bournonville wrote that Scharff "is full of life and imagination, and is unquestionably the finest leading man [of Danish ballet]." Photographs of him starring in Bournonville's productions, as Gennaro in *Napoli* and as the Norse hero Helge in *The Valkyrie*, show a very handsome young man with dark eyes and long lashes, black curly hair and thick sensuous lips; he sometimes wore a curling moustache. Like Stampe, there is something irresolute and uncertain in his expression and bearing which is apparent even when he is acting out the forceful role of a warrior, but his face has nevertheless a magnetism which suggests why he was so compelling a performer.

In Paris, Scharff and Andersen visited Notre-Dame together, but their

From *Hans Christian Andersen: The Life of a Storyteller* (2001): 373–98. © 2000 by Jackie Wullschlager.

paths did not cross again until July 1860, when Andersen was travelling in southern Germany and made a detour to the Bavarian village of Oberammergau to see the famous Passion Play, performed there every ten years. Eckhardt and Scharff, who shared a house in Copenhagen, were there to see it too, and the three Danes teamed up and travelled back to Munich together, where they were in each other's company ceaselessly for the next week.

By 1860, southern Germany was beginning to replace Weimar in Andersen's affections. "Munich has an immense attraction for me," he wrote to Carl Alexander. "In the *Bazaar* I have compared it to a rose-bush, which is now in full bloom. The Au-Kirche is a veritable passion-flower, as if sprung up in a moment; the Basilica a golden pink with exquisite perfume and organ tones." Tainted less by the war than the northern states, touched by the warmth and sensuality of Italy across the Alps, spectacular in its landscapes of high mountains plunging down to crystal clear lakes and its colourful baroque architecture, and presided over by sentimental King Max, who fussed over Andersen like a favourite pet, Bavaria drew him back continually. By the time he reached Oberammergau and put up with the pastor, he was excited, and in a receptive mood. Few places could have been more conducive a setting in which to fall in love than this picturesque Alpine village where the outsides of the chalets were painted with brightly coloured religious scenes and the villagers, like Andersen's grandfather, made their living by wood carving.

That such a place should host a theatrical spectacle of rare magnificence and spiritual grandeur was for Andersen overwhelming. "I had always feared that the representation of Christ on the stage must have something sacrilegious about it, but, as it was given here, it was elevating and noble," he told Carl Alexander. The open-air theatre, built of beams and boards on the green plain outside the village, embodied the convergence of nature and religion; the folk elements of the Passion Play's tradition also attracted Andersen. The play lasted from eight in the morning until five in the afternoon; "we sat under the open sky; the wind sighed above us, the birds came and flew out again. I thought of the old Indian play in the open air where the Sakuntala was given; I thought of the Greek theatre ... There was an ease and a beauty about it that must impress everyone," Andersen wrote. And everything was more exhilarating because he was falling in love with Scharff.

The pleasure continued in Munich. "Scharff and Eckhardt came to me, we talked together until after 11 p.m. ... went with Eckhardt and Scharff to the Basilica ... now I am going with Scharff and Eckhardt to Kaulbach's studio ... to the Residenz Theatre with Scharff and Eckhardt ... came home at 10 p.m. and had a visit from Scharff and Eckhardt," he jotted down in his diary over a week in the city; then, on 9 July 1860, "don't feel at all well; Eckhardt and Scharff travelling to Salzburg at 8 o'clock today." The next day, Andersen, who had been photographed very little since the early days of the daguerreotype in the 1840s, went to the studio of the photographer Franz Hanfstaengel, and came away with a splendid photograph of himself.

In a full-length, sitting portrait in profile, with sunlight streaming in behind, Hanfstaengel captured a look which is at once serene, serious and full of movement and excitement; the dignity and humanity of a man on the brink of old age, and the radiance and warmth that lit up Andersen's face as he stood on the verge of a new love affair. Early pictures show that Andersen's eyes were unnaturally small; here they are open, wide, eager, illuminating his powerful, intelligent features. Wrapped up, as he always was, even in midsummer, in layers of long coats and waistcoats, with a thick tie around his neck, there is something self-protective about the elegant pose, yet it is eased out of stiffness by the expressive, big, bony hands, and by a playfulness about the sensual lips, which seem about to burst into talk. Andersen, who was generally convinced that he was ugly, was ebullient about the result. "I've never seen such a lovely and yet life-like portrait of myself. I was completely surprised, astonished, that the sunlight could make such a beautiful figure of my face. I feel unbelievably flattered, yet it is only a photograph. You'll get to see it, it is the only portrait which my vanity allows me to leave to those coming after me. How the young ladies will exclaim 'And he never got married!'" he wrote home to Henriette Collin.

Unlike some more handsome young men, Andersen aged well; at fifty-five a lifetime of thought and concentration was etched into his features, and Scharff's attentions at this time perhaps made him believe in himself more strongly. While early accounts of his appearance all emphasize his gaucheness and peculiarity, after 1860 the accent is always on his distinguished and animated features. "Andersen's personal appearance is prepossessing," wrote the American consul George Griffin, who visited him in the early 1860s.

> He would not however be called a handsome man in the popular acceptance of the term. He is tall and slender. While standing or sitting, he holds his body erect, but when walking he stoops a little. His nose is large but well-proportioned and his hair, which curls around his temples, is sprinkled with gray. His forehead is high, but not broad, still it is a noble-looking forehead, and not

altogether unlike that of one of Titian's heads. His eyes are of a dark grey and literally beam with intelligence.

Another admirer, J.R. Brown, visiting around the same time, remembered:

> Before me stood a big bony figure, a man who had his best years behind him, but still wasn't quite old. He had lively eyes in a fine, wrinkled face, which was vivacious, and in the middle of this face a big protruding nose which by some quirk of fate was a bit crooked and was flanked by two protruding cheek bones below which were deep wrinkles. Numerous folds and grooves lay round the corners of a large mouth which was like a deep, irregular opening; one could easily have taken it for the mouth of a monster who ate children—if it were not for the kind and sunny smile round the corners of his lips and the humanity which shone from every fold and groove.

A liaison with a figure of such gravitas and fame may have been one of Andersen's attractions to the flighty Scharff, who was over thirty years younger and still had his name to make at the Royal Theatre; certainly letters flew between the two for the rest of the year, and Andersen sent Scharff his photograph.

Andersen moved on to Switzerland, but the joy of his foreign trip was extinguished by Scharff's departure and, alone abroad, he soon grew despondent. His diaries from Geneva, where he spent the beginning of September, show how rapidly he descended into depression:

> *1 September*: Want to go home ... my blood in a wild turmoil.

> *2 September*: My spirits are down; want to go home and yet don't want to ... I have a morbid feeling, a strange fear about going crazy.

> *3 September*: It's as if there's a demon riding my spirit. Where does it come from? Why? I'm unusually tired of everything! ... Took a walk by the rushing Rhone; a demonic urge to throw myself in ... I made cut-outs, which were greatly admired, for two nice little boys, Emile and Ernest. People were very attentive to me, and at 9 o'clock I was driven home. If only I could curb the demon

riders that oppress my spirit. It reminds me of a dream I had about a bat that was grappling with me and almost choked me.

4 September: Upset. My spirit demon-ridden. Wished for sudden death; a frequent thought.

5 September: Nervous, in a morbid mood and got to feeling worse and worse ... My legs were shaking; I didn't feel well.

6 September: My mood depressed.

7 September: Was in a foul mood ... At home I found a couple of books ... in one I was mentioned in favourable terms. I read aloud in French ... I really am having an incredibly good time; only I myself can ruin my enjoyment ...

But not even flattery satisfied him for long, and although he had intended to spend Christmas in Italy, he turned back at Geneva, and in a black, confused mood began the journey north to Denmark. "I'm drifting like a bird in a storm, a bird that cannot fly but also cannot quite fall. O Lord! My God! have mercy on me!" he wrote in his diary on 27 October. He reached Copenhagen in November ("went to bed as usual in a bad mood, godless") and fled to Basnæs for the Christmas holiday.

Here, as often happened, his spirits lifted and his creative energy returned. His diary is full of close, acerbic observations on those at the Basnæs house party ("Nelly is a strange, cold person who stands as if her hands were wet and she were saying: 'Don't touch me!'"), and on New Year's Eve he wrote the short tale "The Snowman," whose setting recalls the woods on the estate: "all the trees and bushes were covered with hoar frost. It was like a forest of white coral, as though all the branches were studded with silvery blossom ... It was like lace, and as dazzling white as though a brilliant white light streamed from every branch. The silver birch stirred in the wind and seemed to be as much alive as trees in the summertime. How lovely it all was!"

Here lives a snowman, who ought to have been in his element but can get no peace because he falls in love with a stove which he has glimpsed in the kitchen. "It's the exact opposite of you! It's as black as soot, and has a long neck with a brass front! It eats wood till the fire comes out of its mouth," a watchdog tells him, but all day the snowman gazes in:

"I must get in; I must lean my head against hers, if it means breaking the window."

"You'll never get in there," said the watchdog. "And if you did get to the stove, you'd be off! Off!"

"I'm as good as off now," said the snowman. "I'm breaking in two, I think." ...

Whenever the stove door was opened the flames would leap out in the way they had, shining bright red on the snowman's white face and throwing a red glow all over his chest.

"I can't bear it," he said. "How it suits her to put her tongue out!"

The frost crunches and crackles, and like Andersen in the months before he wrote the story, the snowman "could have felt happy, and he ought to have felt happy, but he wasn't happy; he was pining for a stove." The weather changes, as the watchdog has threateningly predicted, and the snowman melts—at which point the dog sees that he has been built around a stove-scraper, which explains his lovesickness, but "'it's all over now! Off! Off!' And soon the winter, too, was over ... And then no one ever thinks of the snowman any more."

Lyrical and poignant, "The Snowman" is another veiled, self-mocking autobiography which expresses Andersen's view of love as a burning, unreciprocated pain, his bitter acceptance that he would end life alone and a comic awareness that, as he wrote in his diary, "only I myself can ruin my enjoyment." The Snowman is a light-hearted cousin of the tragic Fir Tree; in this story Andersen returns to his earlier, tragi-comic mode of sketching the fleeting autobiography of an everyday object which seems to have caught his eye at random and yet whose life story has an uncanny appropriateness to its physical form. Just after "The Snowman" Andersen wrote "The Silver Penny," after he was cheated by a false coin; with the story, he joked, he got his money back. To tell such tales was almost a compulsion, like relating his own life story. Sometimes such ideas stayed in his mind for years before coalescing with some event or mood in Andersen's own life. Although it is told with the lightest touch, "The Snowman" sprang to life at least partly out of Andersen's discontent and pining over Harald Scharff.

He saw Scharff again during the winter of 1860–1861, and began a long, slow campaign to fix his interest. In January 1861 he had his photograph taken by the Copenhagen photographer Rudolph Striegler; in contrast to the upright, rigid poses he adopts in all other photographs, this one is languid and seductive, and he sent it to Scharff with an inscription, using the familiar "Du" form, "Dear Scharff, here you have again Hans Christian Andersen." On 20 February, Scharff's twenty-fifth birthday, he gave the dancer five volumes of his "Fairy Tales and Stories," and four days later Scharff came to see him; for his birthday in April Scharff gave him a reproduction of the Danish sculptor Herman Bissen's "Minerva." Nevertheless, Copenhagen left him restless and ill-tempered, and on 4 April 1861, just after publication of a new volume of tales including "The Snowman," and only four months after his return from his last foreign trip, he set off again, this time determined to reach Rome.

He was in a febrile and nervous state, which his choice of travelling companion, Edvard's son Jonas, only made worse. By now Andersen felt too old to travel far alone, and the Collin grandsons were becoming a necessity to him, to jolly him along and look after him. Jonas, at twenty-one, was a clever, moody, strong-minded and taciturn young man with a passion for zoology; as Edvard's son, he caused Andersen more agony than any of his cousins, because Andersen was so desperate for the relationship to be successful, while Jonas inevitably picked up something of the manoeuvrings between his father and Andersen, and knew that, although Andersen was his host and was paying his entire expenses, he could treat him badly. Edvard predicted problems, but was extremely grateful: "At this moment I only feel capable of telling you, my dear Andersen, that I more and more appreciate what you are doing for Jonas ... I hope you will always get pleasure from what you are doing; that Jonas is grateful to you, you can be sure of it, even if he doesn't express it in so many words; this is hardly his skill, as surely as it is not mine."

It took Andersen and Jonas nearly a month to reach Rome, travelling by train to Marseilles, by stagecoach to Nice and Genoa, and then by boat to Civitavecchia. By the time they arrived, suffering from over-exposure to one another in train carriages and closed coaches, from exhaustion and frayed nerves, their relationship was in tatters. Jonas was red-faced with anger and silent; "I asked him if I had done anything to incur his displeasure; he said no, he wanted to go home to do some writing. I became dispirited—I live for him, do everything for him; and he said the other day that I have only 'my egoism'—I'm feeling despondent, unwell. Sat in tears on my bed," Andersen wrote in his diary on 5 May. A few days later: "I explained how ill I felt. He told me to pull myself together and then went off ... I had the feeling and the hope that he would be concerned enough about me to stay, but he went ... Jonas had as refrain, 'You must pull yourself together!'" Towards the end of the month, there was little improvement: "Jonas went around always brooding ... He has no consideration for me, just like Drewsen's sons [his cousins Viggo and Harald]; I was grieved and offended ... I did ... without supper, terribly depressed, spiteful and in tears, jumping out of bed and ranting, beside myself... Got up early and went out. Came home just as unhappy, brooding, was irritable and upset."

Another evening, after they had quarrelled about Viggo Drewsen, whom Jonas praised over artists and writers because "he worked on his own development and had nothing to do with other people," Andersen wrote his tale "The Snail and the Rosebush" in revenge. Andersen, or the creative artist, is the rose bush, who cannot help giving beautiful, blooming roses to the world; Jonas is the snail—the image is wonderfully apt, because as a budding zoologist he collected snails locked inside his own house who snarls, "The world doesn't concern me. What have I to do with the world? I have enough of myself, and enough in myself ... What am I giving? I spit at it! It's of no use. It doesn't concern me." The tale has often been taken as Andersen's view of the creative life versus the intellectual one, with the snail an embodiment of Kierkegaard; it is in fact a shrewd comment on the narrow-minded impetuosity of youth versus the tolerance and generosity towards the wider world that comes with middle age. This was the core of the conflict between Jonas and Andersen. A wise and loving parent would perhaps have accepted Jonas's youth and found him less of an irritant than Andersen did; Andersen remained too much a child, anxious to be indulged and to be in the right himself, to be able to do so.

Once again, Rome had turned sour on Andersen; it also, as usual, made him feel sensual and sexually frustrated, and he was probably no easier to live with than was Jonas. He poured out his discomfort in another Roman tale, "The Psyche," begun in the theatre during a badly danced ballet days after his arrival, and continued on and off throughout the trip. The germ of the story had been in his mind since he began *The Improvisatore* in Rome thirty years earlier. He began it, he said, when he remembered an incident that occurred there in 1833–1834: a young nun was to be buried, and when her grave came to be dug there was found a beautiful statue of Bacchus. The story also owes much to his own early experiences in Rome, to the life of the Danish artist-monk Küchler, who had intrigued him since Küchler painted the first, puritanical portrait of him in 1834, and something, too, to Andersen's continuing obsession with Scharff.

It turns on a gifted sculptor with "warm blood" and "a strong imagination" who is consumed by sexual longing as his friends taunt him to use a prostitute, which he cannot bring himself to do—Andersen had endured similar teasing in Rome in 1833–1834. The sculptor devotes himself to his art, preferring the cold marble of his statues to female flesh and blood, but he is such a perfectionist that he destroys most of what he makes. His best work is a figure of a noble young woman, his "Psyche," and in fashioning it he falls in love with her. When she rejects him, he gives up his resistance and listens to a friend telling him, "Be a man, as all the others are, and don't go on living in ideals, for that is what drives men crazy ... Come with me: be a man!" They find a pair of girls, but sex is described in terms of repulsion. The sculptor cries:

> "I feel as if the blossom of life were unfolding itself in my veins at this moment!"
> Yes, the blossom unfolded itself, and then burst and fell, and an evil vapour arose from it, blinding the sight, leading astray the fancy—the firework of the senses went out, and it became dark.

His decision is to bury his beautiful statue of Psyche, to give up art and, as Küchler did, become a monk. Andersen visited Küchler at his monastery while he was writing the tale and was much taken by another monk there, Brother Ignatius ("He was a young man, kind and happy in Christ; remarked that there was religious feeling in the North and that each approached God in his own way ... We all were in search of truth. He found he had so much in common with me"), who appears by name in the story as a model of the spiritual life. But the sculptor finds no peace:

> What flames arose up in him at times! What a source of evil, of that which he would not, welled up continually! He mortified his body, but the evil came from within ... The more deeply he looked into his own heart the blacker did the darkness seem. "Nothing within, nothing without—this life squandered and cast away!" And this thought rolled and grew like a snowball, until it seemed to crush him.
> "I can confide my griefs to none. I may speak to none of the gnawing worm within. My secret is my prisoner; if I let the captive escape, I shall be his!"

Aware that he has wasted his gifts, he dies. Centuries later the white marble statue of Psyche is discovered when a young nun is buried, and although the artist is unknown, his art, as well as "the Psyche—the soul—will still live on!"

How much of Andersen's own sexual uncertainty went into this sultry, guilt-ridden tale? He recognized it as one of his most erotic works, and was furious when Bentley dedicated the English translation without his permission to the Princess of Wales ("I'm not at all pleased to have a story like 'The Psyche' dedicated to a young woman"). It is remarkable how close "The Psyche" is to the pent-up emotional tone and lurid Italian setting of *The Improvisatore*, and to the tales of sexual revulsion or denial, such as "The Travelling Companion" and "The Little Mermaid," which he wrote in the 1830s. Like his other tales of the same period, "The Psyche" questions the value of art, but, though more acrid in mood and contorted in style, its final message is that of "The Little Mermaid"—that immortality can be won through art not sex. "The Little Mermaid" was written twenty-five years earlier at the height of Andersen's obsession with and renunciation of Edvard Collin. Did he feel any bitterness that he was now travelling with Edvard's grown-up son, yet emotionally he had himself barely moved on, and was caught in the throes of a similar fixation on another young man, Harald Scharff? Certainly the tale, followed weeks later by a greater work of brooding eroticism, "The Ice Maiden," suggests that "the gnawing worm of sexuality gave him no peace.

Publicly, however, a quite different persona was at work in Rome. This was the occasion, for example, when Andersen met Robert Browning at the Palazzo Barberini, the home of the wealthy American sculptor William Wentmore Story; Henry James was there and recalled Andersen as the quintessential Pied Piper, charming a group of children:

> The small people with whom he played enjoyed, under his spell, the luxury of believing that he kept and treasured—in every case and as a rule—the old tin soldiers and broken toys received by him, in acknowledgement of favours, from impulsive infant hands. Beautiful the queer image of the great benefactor moving about Europe with his accumulations of these relics. Wonderful too our echo of a certain occasion—that of a children's party, later on, when, after he had read out to his young friends "The Ugly Duckling," Browning struck up with the "Pied Piper"; which led to the formation of a grand march through the spacious Barberini apartment, with Story doing his best on a flute in default of bagpipes.

The dying Elizabeth Barrett Browning made Andersen the hero of her last poem, "The North and the South," in which the South yearns for a poet to express its beauty. The poem ends:

> The North sent therefore a man of men
>> As a grace to the South;
> And thus to Rome came Andersen.
>> —*"Alas, but must you take him again?"*
> Said the South to the North.

In a letter, she left another record: "Andersen (the Dane) came to see me yesterday," she wrote, "kissed my hand, and seemed in a general *verve* for embracing. He is very earnest, very simple, very child-like. I like him. Pen [her twelve-year-old son] says of him, 'He is not really pretty. He is rather like his own ugly duck, but his mind has developed into a swan'—That wasn't bad of Pen, was it?" Andersen knew he was perceived as something of a curiosity; in a short comic tale of self-acceptance, "The Butterfly," written just after he left Rome, he painted himself as a butterfly who flits about indecisively between girlfriends only to find he has become too old to be married, ending "a crusty old bachelor ... stuck on a pin in a box of curios."

Another well-known writer charmed by Andersen in Rome was the Norwegian poet Bjørnstjerne Bjørnson, who soon got the measure of Andersen's crankiness and minor upsets, and unlike Jonas was willing to indulge them. When Andersen complained about the draughts and the crowds, Bjørnson suggested good-humouredly that the moment Andersen entered heaven he would turn round and ask Peter to close the door against the draught—unless of course he demanded to go back the minute he was in the doorway because he was being pushed by the crowds. He was, he said, very fond of Andersen, both for the glories and the weakness of his character.

After Rome, Andersen and Jonas went on to Switzerland, staying at the resort of Montreux on Lake Geneva, with its magnificent Alpine backdrop, where, Andersen wrote, "was wrought my Wonder Story 'The Ice Maiden' ... in which I would show the Swiss nature as it had lain in my thoughts after many visits to that glorious land." "The Ice Maiden," more a novella than a tale, is the tragic love story of two Swiss peasants, Rudy and Babette, told in fifteen parts. Its emphasis on setting, on letting the story almost emerge by itself through the ice and snow, the use of dreams, the brooding psychological unease, the images of destruction that ring out from the start—all these link it with the recent works of 1858–1859, but with the figure of the Ice Maiden, Andersen returns to the dramatic mythic creations of his middle years.

The story opens with a light touch and with Andersen's reassertion of the romantic belief in the child as visionary, as young Rudy chatters to his pet cats and dogs—"for you see, children who cannot talk yet, can understand the language of fowls and ducks right well, and cats and dogs speak to them quite as plainly as father and mother can do ... with some children this period ends later than with others, and of such we are accustomed to say that they are very backward, and that they have remained children a long time. People are in the habit of saying many strange things." The cats and dogs remain commentators throughout, telling us of the progression of the love affair ("Rudy and Babette were treading on each other's paws under the table all evening. They trod on me twice, but I would not mew for fear of exciting attention"), but the tragic impulse of the story is overriding, its fatalism hanging heavy and thundering as the glaciers and streams of melted ice that rush down the valleys. Andersen's mountain scenery is spectacularly drawn; here Rudy's mother is killed, and the Ice Maiden, "the Glacier Queen," who rules this "wondrous glass palace," feels cheated that she has not captured Rudy too. She is one of Andersen's femmes fatales:

> She, the death-dealing, the crushing one, is partly a child of the air, partly the mighty ruler of the river ... she sails on the slender fir twig down the rushing stream, and springs from one block to another, with her long snow-white hair and her blue-green garment fluttering around her and glittering like the water in the deep Swiss lakes.
> "To crush and to hold, mine is the power!" she says. "They have stolen a beautiful boy from me, a boy whom I have kissed, but not kissed to death. He is mine, and I will have him!"

Rudy goes to live with his grandfather, a woodcarver like Andersen's, and becomes the embodiment of nature, climbing and hunting in the mountains like an animal, repeatedly depriving the Ice Maiden of her prize. In this cinematic story, she looms in and out of dark icy snowscapes, sometimes as a hallucination, sometimes as a real, terrifying presence. Once Rudy nearly falls, and "below, in the black yawning gulf, on the rushing waters, sat the Ice Maiden herself, with her long whitish-green hair, and stared at him with cold death-like eyes." But his undoing is to fall in love with Babette, who represents culture and worldly sophistication, and to become jealous when a cultivated Englishman gives her a book of Byron's poems. He swaps Babette's betrothal ring for a kiss from a phantom woman on the mountains, and as in "The Psyche," this instant of pure eroticism spells darkness and death:

> In that moment ... he sank into the deep and deadly ice cleft, lower and lower. He saw the icy walls gleaming like blue-green

glass, fathomless abysses yawned around, the water dropped tinkling down like shining bells, clear as pearls, glowing with pale blue flames. The Ice Maiden had kissed him—a kiss which sent a shudder from neck to brow; a cry of pain escaped from him; he tore himself away, staggered, and—it was night before his eyes.

In "The Snow Queen," when Kai is seduced by the icy *femme fatale*, he is rescued by the purity of Gerda's childish love, but here there is no redemption. Rudy is saved, briefly reunited with Babette and then snatched from her on the eve of their wedding day, as they celebrate the flowering of adult love by sailing at sunset under a mountain that "gleamed like red lava"—as in *The Improvisatore* and "The Little Mermaid," the signal colours of "The Ice Maiden" are those Andersen used to symbolize passion, fiery red and deathly blue. Rudy is dragged under the water where he sees crowds of the drowned who have sunk into the crevasses among the glaciers, and

beneath all the Ice Maiden sat on the clear transparent ground. She raised herself towards Rudy and kissed his feet; then a cold, death-like numbness poured through his limbs, and an electric shock—ice and fire mingled! ... "Mine, mine!" sounded around him and within him. "I kissed you when you were little, kissed you on your mouth. Now I kiss your feet, and you are mine altogether!" And he disappeared beneath the clear blue water.

Babette realizes "The Ice Maiden has got him"—the words spoken almost half a century earlier by Andersen's mother when his father died.

Now this deep-seated memory merged with the fatalism of a lifetime, with his idea of sex as death—forbidden, frightening—and with intimations too of the price the artist pays for his gift. In his ballet version of the tale *Le Baiser de la Fée* Stravinsky interpreted the early kiss of the Ice Maiden as the kiss of the muse, marking out the hero Tchaikowsky for suffering brilliance;[1] Andersen's use of the symbolic kiss may in turn have derived from the fatal kiss planted on the brow of the hero by the fairy-woman in Bournonville's ballet *La Sylphide*, which opened in Copenhagen in 1836. "The Ice Maiden" is one of Andersen's most powerful tales; the heroine is one of the three demonic women in his stories—the others are the Snow Queen and his late creation Auntie Toothache—who are archetypes as memorable as those from myth or legend. Bjørnson, to whom the story was dedicated, thought it exceptionally bold:

"The Ice Maiden" begins as if it were rejoicing and singing in the free air, by the pine trees, and the blue water, and the Swiss cottages. The thought that fashions the last portion has something divine in it—so it impresses me, the thought that two people should be separated at the very highest point of their happiness; still more that you showed clearly how as when a sudden breeze ruffles the still water, so there dwelt in the souls of both that which could overthrow their happiness; but that you should have the courage to do this with these two of all people!

Bjørnson was one of the earliest critics fully to appreciate Andersen's widening range; he wrote to Jonas Collin junior that all the other forms from which Andersen had been discouraged—the novel, drama, even philosophy—now turned up in his fairy stories, which were no longer traditional tales but freewheeling narratives embracing tragedy, comedy, the epic and the lyric; their lack of restraint made one tremble to think what he might do next.

Andersen was still working on "The Ice Maiden" as he travelled home to Denmark in August, staying *en route* in Sorø with Ingemann, to whom he read it as he was revising the ending and changing the title from first "The Mountain Hunter" and then "The Eagle's Nest." At the last moment his relations with Jonas improved, and Andersen suggested that Jonas call him "Du": "he was surprised but said Yes in a firm voice, and thanked me. Later, when I was in bed he came in to me before lying down in his own room, took my hand and repeated once more such a heartfelt 'Thank you!' that tears came into my eyes; he gave me a kiss on my forehead and I felt so happy." This was the best compensation he could have had for Edvard's refusal to accept "Du" terms thirty years earlier; its symbolism as a healing of Collin wounds was magnified when Jonas senior, aged seventy-five, died just days after this *rapprochement* with his grandson.

Although the old man had been declining for months, Andersen was shocked at how intensely he felt the loss of his father-figure and first patron. "Toward evening I had a physical reaction ... felt faint and went to bed," he wrote; he returned to Copenhagen for the funeral, after which he "ate at a restaurant and felt very alone." Heiberg, who had died the year before, had written that as civil servant, patron of the arts and director of the Royal Theatre, Jonas had been "an active participant and often instigator of almost everything produced in this country of any lasting significance." Jonas had always been instinctively more in sympathy with Heiberg's art than with Andersen's, and in his final year he was much cheered by twilight visits from the widowed Johanne Luise Heiberg, his favourite protégée, who described in her memoirs how she tiptoed along to the house standing behind the iron gates and rang the doorbell which had once sounded constantly as "the high and the lowly, the young and the old, all sought out this mighty man." Now the house was silent, a dozy servant peered out curiously from "a half-opened door ... as though he did not really believe in the unwonted sound of the bell," and the pair sat by the firelight and reminisced about the heyday of the theatre. Jonas Collin haunted Andersen's dreams until his death; in 1865, four years after the old man's death, Andersen had a nightmare in which "mighty Collin" was pitted against "poor Andersen," dependent on him as in adolescence for his survival in the intellectual classes.

It often happens, however, that the death of a parent or parental figure both galvanizes and liberates an individual towards a new sexual relationship, and so it was with Andersen. In the winter of 1861–1862 his friendship with Scharff finally turned into a love affair, about which he was too excited to be discreet. Through the autumn he read aloud his erotic tales "The Psyche" and "The Ice Maiden" to Scharff as he was preparing them for publication in November 1861, then on 2 January 1862 he noted in his diary, "Scharff bounded up to me; threw himself round my neck and kissed me! ... Nervous in the evening." Five days later he received "a visit from Scharff, who was very intimate and nice." In the following weeks, there was "dinner at Scharff's, who was ardent and loving," on 16 January; "a visit from Scharff, who is intimate and deeply devoted to me," on 23 January; and several more visits during the rest of the month. He saw Scharff, now promoted to a solo dancer, perform at the Royal Theatre several times in January and February; on 12 February he recorded a visit to the theatre which simply ends "Scharff," and on 13 February he wrote, "Yesterday Scharff was at my house, talked a lot about himself with the greatest familiarity."

By 17 February the relationship had been noticed and Andersen's doctor, Edvard's brother Theodor Collin, was warning him to be careful. "The odor put me in a very bad mood," he wrote, "he emphasized how strongly I showed my love for S, which people noticed and found ridiculous." He was so upset by Theodor that he fled home from a lunch at Louise Lind's—his old love Louise Collin, Theodor's sister—but nothing could now stop the flow of the affair. On 20 February Andersen was celebrating his 26-year-old lover's birthday at a dinner at Eckhardt's house; he sent Scharff a bouquet, a teacup and saucer and a book of Paludan-Müller's poems. Next day Scharff was again at Nyhavn, "intimate and communicative," gossiping about Madame Heiberg and the Royal Theatre—their chief shared interest.

Through March the two saw each other every few days and Andersen often saw Scharff dance at the theatre; the diary for 6 March records, for example, "visit from Scharff ... exchanged with him all the little secrets of the heart; I long for him daily," and on is March, "Scharff very loving, gave him my picture." Andersen was utterly absorbed in him; he spent an evening at the house of the young banker Einar Drewsen, another Collin grandson (Ingeborg's son), in whom he confided—"I told all about my erotic time"— and on 2 April the highlight of his fifty-seventh birthday was Scharff's present, a silver toothbrush engraved with his name and the date.

The happiest photographs we have of Andersen, taken by Georg Hansen in Copenhagen to be mounted on visiting cards, date from these months. Leaning on the back of a chair, his elbows on a table and his head leaning against his hands, his expression smiling and his face shining with pleasure, they show Andersen in a relaxed and sunny mood. Elizabeth Jerichau-Baumann's portrait of Andersen reading to children was also painted at this time; though sentimental, it catches a luminous grace and contentment about Andersen, absorbed in his imaginative world, that is rare. We can only guess at the physical details of his relationship with Scharff, but there is no doubt that here was an affair, which brought him joy, some kind of sexual fulfilment and a temporary end to loneliness. As important, Scharff was Andersen's link to youth at a time he felt himself getting old; his enthusiasms, his flighty, high-pitched personality, his youthful beauty and his lithe dancing were all restorative for the ageing writer.

His new fairy tales sold out rapidly and were well-received, he had 8,200 rixdollars in the bank at New Year 1862 and a few weeks later Theodor Reitzel offered him an astonishing 3,000 rixdollars for a reissue of the illustrated edition of his collected tales and stories—the first payment on which he had to pay income tax, introduced in 1862 at a rate of two per cent, which Andersen considered outrageously high. When the theatre season ended in June and Scharff departed with Eckhardt for Vienna, Andersen did not languish long in Copenhagen; he used the money from Reitzel to fund an exotic trip he had long wanted to make, to Spain, and in July 1862 he set out, again taking Jonas Collin with him. The journey was not a success. Andersen was unknown in Spain and received none of the gratifying recognition that usually bolstered him up on foreign trips; indeed the reverse happened, and several times he was laughed at in the street for his long lanky figure. It was the primitive and medieval aspect of Spain that most appealed to him, such as his visit to the Alhambra to see the Moorish halls in the sunlit air, where he was driven in a diligence drawn by ten mules with jingling bells; crossing to Tangier, where he took tea with the Pasha, was, he said, the highlight of the entire journey. These experiences poured into notes for his travel book, *A Visit to Spain*, finished on his return in 1863. But the account has none of the enthusiasm and beneath-the-skin knowledge of the country of his best travel books, such as *Pictures of Sweden*, and the muted tones of his diary too show that this was a lacklustre trip. His heart was not in it, and how much he was still preoccupied with Scharff is suggested from the diary entry for 15 September in which a dramatic description of a flood in Barcelona is interrupted by the underlined sentence "Sent letter to Eckhardt and Scharff" and then continued, with an account of those who had drowned.

The desperation for new experiences and inspiration which had marked his journeys as a young man was gone; he was weary, irritable and often bored. Jonas, who travelled with an increasing collection of small animals such as snails, provided a focus for his complaints and some moments of farce, as when the Spanish customs confiscated his menagerie and its supply of poisonous food, and he and Andersen had to wait for a chemist to inspect it. A photograph of the pair of travellers in Bordeaux *en route* for Denmark in January 1863 shows the strain: Jonas, square-faced, tight-lipped and cold, the very image of his father, stands erect and unhesitating, staring straight ahead; Andersen, sitting at right angles to him, is taken in profile, looking tired, tense and old. By the time they arrived home, Jonas was recorded as "an insolent fool on whom I have wasted the kindness of my heart."

But Copenhagen in 1863 gave Andersen no peace. The clouds of war were gathering, and the relationship with Scharff that had brought such pleasure was clearly on the wane. In June Scharff was still loving, and at a party he boldly proposed a toast "to his two dearest friends, Eckhardt and Hans Christian Andersen," but on 27 August Andersen wrote in his diary: "Scharff's passion for me is now over; he has transferred his attentions completely to someone else fascinating. I am not as upset about it as over earlier, similar disappointments." So the world-weary older man contrasted his resignation with the intense feelings of youth. He may have been remembering his agony at what he considered Henrik Stampe's betrayal back in 1844, or even the blow to his youthful desire for Ludvig Müller in 1832— or there may have been other romances with men in the intervening years, too secret even to be mentioned in the diary.[2]

But Scharff's attentions had kept him young, and as soon as he realized they were over Andersen felt like an old man. He guessed that he would never have another love affair, although his sexual interest in women would still revive. "I am not satisfied with myself. I cannot live in my loneliness, am weary of life," he wrote on 16 September. "Felt old, downhill, sad," he noted on 5 October; the next day, "visited Scharff, who gave me his photograph and was a good child ... Poor young love, I can achieve nothing there." Through the autumn of 1863 his spirits fell; "Scharff has not visited me in eight days; with him it is over," he wrote on 13 November; in December he saw Scharff at Eckhardt's house—Eckhardt was by now married—where he read some fairy tales and noted, with the infallible instinct of the spurned lover, that a dancer called Petersen was there. A few years later Scharff and Camilla Petersen were engaged, though they never married. Andersen now had to recognize that, like all the young men with whom he had toyed, Scharff would move on from homosexual flings to a stable heterosexual relationship; he married another ballet dancer, Elvida Møller, in 1874, when he was thirty-eight.

There was no apparent bitterness; Andersen and Scharff continued to move in overlapping social circles, saw each other from time to time, and Andersen remembered Scharff's birthday almost every year until his death. There was a poignant coda to the relationship in 1871, when Scharff was due to dance the lead in Bournonville's ballet version of "The Steadfast Tin Soldier," one of Andersen's most memorable characterizations of resignation and disappointment in love. Shortly before the ballet opened, Scharff, while performing a dance in a divertissement for *The Troubadour*, ruptured a kneecap, "an accident which," said Bournonville, "in all my years of experience, has not happened to any dancer, either here or abroad." Scharff had given his parts a highly individual stamp, and he was severely missed as the star of the Copenhagen ballet. "This tragedy," Bournonville wrote, "was greeted with universal sympathy, for while there was certainly hope of a cure which would make it possible for him to move about unhindered in private life, and maybe even on the dramatic stage, he had to be considered lost to the Ballet."

The end of Andersen's affair with Scharff combined with two national events, the death of King Frederik VII on 15 November, and the signing of a new constitution for Denmark and just one of the duchies, Schleswig, to make Andersen look towards the new year of 1864 with horror. The new constitution, separating Schleswig and Holstein, provoked Prussia, and by the end of 1863 Danish troops were being called up for war. "The year is over; the outlook is pitchblack, sorrowful, bloody—the New Year," he noted in his diary; in his autobiography he wrote:

> The bloody waves of war were again to wash over our fatherland.
> A kingdom and an empire stood united against our little country.

A poet's way is not by politics ... but when the ground trembles beneath him so that all threatens to fall at once, then he has only thought for this which is a matter of life and death ... He is planted in his fatherland as a tree; there he brings forth his flowers and his fruit; and if they are sent widely through the world, the roots of the tree are in the home soil.

During the 1864 war he was much harsher on Germany than in 1848–1851, refusing to speak German: "it was against my heart of hearts to speak that language, found it unpatriotic." Meeting Robert Lytton, he said, "at present there is for me in that language the sound of cannon and of the shouts of enemies. I would rather speak bad English." Two days later he wrote that "Today I've been really tormented by the pressure of political events ... I feel each kindness people in Germany have shown me, acknowledge friends there but feel that I, as a Dane, must make a complete break with them all. They have been turned out of my heart: never will we meet again ... My heart is breaking!" New Year's morning 1864 at Basnæs was a tingling, frosty day. Andersen had apple dumplings and spiced red wine, and read aloud to the guests, but the cosiness and luxury could not take his mind off war and the soldiers in their cold barracks, and once again he was unable to write. "Every day soldiers left for the seat of war, young men, singing in their youthful gaiety, going as to a lively feast. For weeks and months I felt myself unfitted to do anything; all my thoughts were with the men."

He returned to Copenhagen on 5 January. "Mrs. Anholm's eldest son was there to welcome me. My room was toasty warm. A cup of tea was my dinner. Walked over to Edvard Collin's." War brought financial problems to Copenhagen, and that year Andersen lent money both to Edvard (2,500 rixdollars) and to Henrik Stampe (1,000 rixdollars); his own savings exceeded 10,000 rixdollars. He tried to absorb himself in the city's social life, visiting the same group of people almost every day, and depending, as he had since his student days, on the weekly rota of dinners with leading Copenhagen families. Though early patrons like Jonas Collin and Ørsted were dead and the children of Andersen's contemporaries had mostly left home, the dramatis personae were remarkably unchanged. On Mondays he dined with Edvard and Henriette Collin; on Tuesdays with Ingeborg Drewsen and her husband; on Wednesdays with Ørsted's widow and his daughter Mathilde; on Thursdays—the evening formerly devoted to Jonas Collin—with the merchant Moritz Melchior; on Fridays with Ida Koch, the widowed daughter of Admiral Wulff and sister of Henriette; on Saturdays with an aristocratic friend, Madame Neergaard; and on Sundays with another merchant family, the Henriques. Andersen was just beginning now to know the Henriques and the Melchiors, wealthy Jewish families related by marriage; they were to be of paramount importance to him in his last decade. In 1864, however, his greatest support was Edvard's sympathetic wife Henriette, whom he now felt closest to within the Collin family. In his extended autobiography, he paid her tribute: "I lost for a moment my hold on God, and felt myself as wretched as a man can be. Days followed in which I cared for nobody, and I believed nobody cared for me. I had no relief in speaking to anyone. One however, more faithful and kind, came to me, Edvard Collin's excellent wife who spoke compassionate words and bade me give thought to my work."

But he could not work. His muse dried up as wholly as it had done during the first Danish–German conflict; as before, he could not dislodge thoughts and nightmares of war from his head. "I feel gloomy and depressed. Can't get anything done. Wish for an end to everything," he noted in January 1864, then a few days later, "overwhelmed and bitterly aware of my forsakenness" and "Now I'm sitting at home all alone. The African cactus gets shifted every evening away from the cold windows, but I'm not expecting any flowers, not even that it will survive." On the eve of his fifty-ninth birthday on a April, Andersen looked back: "the past year of my life has been full of trials and tribulations ... The king died. The war is threatening Denmark with destruction. I've aged. I have false teeth that torment me. I'm not in good health. I'm heading for death and the grave." Andersen signed a petition to the Swiss people to stir up international sympathy for the Danes; after it was published he began to suffer nightmares that the Germans would attack him. "What a night I've spent in self-torture, in rehearsing fixed ideas, in half madness, envisioning myself at the bottom of a ship, cast into a dark cell, tortured and abused—I'm making a fool of myself by recording my fixed idea. I lay bathed in sweat, unsleeping in the early morning hours," he wrote on 18 April. Two hours later came word of a Danish defeat, along with the news that Viggo Drewsen, Ingeborg's dark, curly haired, rebellious son, of whom Andersen was fond despite their difficult travelling days together, was wounded and taken prisoner.

Another Danish defeat followed in June; "Godless and therefore unhappy," Andersen noted on 30 June. A ceasefire was declared on 20 July, and a peace treaty drawn up on 30 October, by which Denmark lost both Schleswig and Holstein. "I am disgruntled and depressed, angry with so many people. Only disaster, violation, oblivion and death are waiting for me," Andersen wrote in his diary the next day. That night, he recorded his recurrent nightmare: "Last night I again dreamed my usual, hideous dream about a living child that I press up against my warm breast—this time, though, it was just in my sleeve; it breathed its last, and I was left with only the wet skin."

The dream, so close to the images of dead children in his tales, may have had many subconscious meanings, but it seems linked to his awareness both of his public image and of his own creativity. At some level, he had been exploiting the child in himself as a persona since his teens—the image he liked to cultivate of innocent but gifted *naïf*. This recurring dream may have been an acknowledgement that by doing so he had in a sense killed it, thus forcing himself always to act a part. Yet childhood memories and echoes of folk tales remained the well-spring of his creativity; this dream was symbolic too at a time when he was mourning the loss of his creative powers. A few weeks after recording it, he was complaining about a tumour in his hand, which he thought he would die from, adding that he believed it was time for him to die as he hadn't enjoyed life, nor accepted the gifts God had given him.

Yet almost as soon as war was behind Denmark, and "the darkest, gloomiest year" of Andersen's life was over, inspiration flooded back. At Basnæs on New Year's Day 1865, he began "The Will o' the Wisps are in Town," which summed up his desperate feelings about the war, his doubts about art as devilish as well as redemptive, his fears about the end of civilized values.

> For more than a year and a day I had written no wonder-story; my soul was so burdened; but now, as soon as I came out into the country to friendly Basnæs, to the fresh woods and the open sea, I wrote "The Will o' the Wisps are in Town" in which was told why it was that the wonder stories had been so long unwritten; because without was war, and within sorrow and want that war brought with it.

Set in a hazy, chiaroscuro world reminiscent of *A Walking Tour*, the story tells of "a man who once knew many stories, but they had slipped away from him—so he said; the Story that used to visit him of its own accord no longer came and knocked at his door." He sets out to seek the story, in the woods, on the seashore, and finds it at the home of the Moor-woman, a grotesque parody of the poet's muse.

> And the man asked about the Story, and inquired if the Moor-woman had met it in her journeyings ... "I don't care about it

either way," cried the woman. "Let the rest write, those who can, and those who cannot likewise. I'll give you an old bung from my cask that will open the cupboard where poetry is kept in bottles, and you may take from that whatever may be wanting. But you, my good man, seem to have blotted your hands sufficiently with ink, and to have come to that age of satiety, that you need not be running about every year for stories, especially as there are more important things to be done."

But as she mocks him, she tells him a story about the will o' the wisps who live on the marsh and go "dancing like little lights across the moor." Once a year, those born at "that minute of time" when the wind blows a certain way and the moon stands at a certain size, have the power to enter the soul of a mortal for 365 days, during which time they must lead 365 people to destruction; they then "attain to the honour of being a runner before the devil's state coach." But of course these devilish will o' the wisps are as insubstantial and fleeting as the moment when they are born. They are emblems of the insubstantiality of art, yet paradoxically they make up the authenticity and solidity of the story that Andersen is narrating. "One could tell quite a romance about the Will o' the Wisps, in twelve parts," says the man who tells stories, but "I should be thrashed if I were to go to people and say, 'Look, yonder goes a Will o' the Wisp in his best clothes.'" In the end he concludes that it does not matter if he dares to speak the truth, as no one will believe him; "for they will all think I am only telling them a story." Thus, in this satirical story-within-a-story, the value of fairy tales is demolished and Andersen's own worth as a writer rejected—except that through its comedy and the vitality of its characters, wisps and Moor-woman, "The Will o' the Wisps" reaffirms the very power of the art it appears to doubt. Here Andersen returned to the questioning, innovative mode of the late 1850s, as he turned reinvigorated to those aspects of his life he thought he had put behind him.

"Especially cheerful and well," he wrote in his diary in February 1865. Not even three evictions from his Nyhavn apartment of sixteen years—first rain flooded the bedroom, then snow burst into the living room and finally the landlady declared she needed more space—quenched his spirits. At sixty, he still had no furniture; he simply packed his bags, stayed first with Edvard and next at Basnæs, where he wrote more tales, and in the autumn toured Sweden. In between, he stayed at the new, exclusive Hotel d'Angleterre on Kongens Nytorv; in the winter he was briefly given rooms on the King's estate, where Bournonville was a neighbour. A new volume of tales—

including "The Will o' the Wisps"—was published in November 1865. Andersen was himself more of a will o' the wisp than ever; at the end of 1865 he was planning another exotic trip, to Portugal. He had a decade to live, and was bursting with energy for new experiences of travel, love, friendship and the continual redefining of the genre he had made his own.

FOOTNOTES

1. Later commentators have suggested that the kiss also suggests the stigma of homosexuality.

2. The silence of Danish commentators, from Andersen's own time until the present day, on the subject of his homosexual relationships, is remarkable. Andersen's diaries leave no doubt that he was attracted to both sexes; that at times he longed for a physical relationship with a woman and that at other times he was involved in physical liaisons with men. Danish scholars from Hjalmar Helweg (*H.C. Andersen: En psykiatrisk Studie*) in 1927 to Elias Bredsdorff today have consistently denied Andersen's involvement in homosexual relationships, pinning much on the argument that the Collin family would have known had Andersen had homosexual tendencies, and would not have allowed him to take their young sons and grandsons on foreign holidays. But we know from the diaries that at least two of the Collins, Edvard's brother Theodor and Ingeborg's son Einar Drewsen, discussed Andersen's homosexuality with him at precisely the time when he was travelling abroad with members of the family—not to mention Andersen's confidential relationship with his favourite Collin grandchild, Ingeborg's daughter Jonna, whom Andersen once asked, "do not judge me by ordinary standards," and who was married to Andersen's former lover Henrik Stampe.

Much definitive Andersen scholarship—the editing of the diaries and letters—was completed by the 1960s, when discretion about sexual matters was still considered appropriate in many academic circles, but even recent Danish scholarship has swerved away from it. Patricia L. Conroy and Sven H. Rossel, editors of the English edition of Andersen's diaries (1990), for example, include none of the erotic references to either Stampe or Scharff, leaving only the tantalizing hint that "at Oberammergau he saw two familiar faces from home—the actor Lauritz Eckhardt and the ballet dancer Harald Scharff—which he got to know much better in the coming years." Only two scholarly papers in recent years have discussed Andersen's homo-erotic attachments: Wilhelm von Rosen in "Venskabets Mysterier" in 1980, and the German critic Heinrich Detering in *Intellectual Amphibia* in 1991.

NOTES

The notes refer back to the original publication

373.   "You are a lucky man..."Bernhard Ingemann to HCA, 10 April 1858, quoted in Edvard Collin, *H.C. Andersen og det Collinske Hus*, Copenhagen 1929 (second edition), p. 311.
"a butterfly..." diary, 13 November 1865, *Dagbøger*, vol. VI, p. 322.
"is full of life..." Auguste Bournonville, *My Theatre Life*, translated by Patricia N. McAndrew, London 1979, p. 169.

374.   "Munich has an immense attraction ..." HCA to Carl Alexander, 23 June 1852, *Crawford*, p. 293.
         "I had always feared ..." HCA to Carl Alexander, 24 July 1860, ibid. p. 417.
         "we sat ..." *Fairy Tale*, p. 454.
         "Scharff and Eckhardt came ... etc." diary, 3, 4, 5, 7 and 8 July 1860, *Dagbøger*, vol. VI, pp. 394–6.
         "don't feel at all well..." diary, 9 July 1860, ibid. p. 396.
376.   "I've never seen ..." HCA to Henriette Collin, 3 August 1860, *E. Collin*, vol. II, p. 243.
         "Andersen's personal appearance ..." G.W. Griffin, *My Danish Days*, Philadelphia 1875, pp. 207–8.
         "Before me stood..." John Ross Brown, quoted in "Der Dichter Als Mensch," in Bente Kjolbe, *Hans Christian Andersens Kopenhagen*, Copenhagen 1992, p. 64.
377.   "Want to go home ... etc." diary, 1–7 September 1860, *Diaries*, pp. 269–72.
         "I'm drifting ..." diary, 27 October 1860, *Dagbøger*, vol. IV, p. 455.
378   "went to bed ..." diary, 14 November 1860, ibid. p. 465.
         "Nelly is a strange, cold person ..." diary, 30 December 1860, *Diaries*, p. 272.
379.   "only I myself..." diary, 7 September 1860, ibid.
         "Dear Scharff...." note on back of photograph taken by Rudolph Striegler in Copenhagen, 21–22 January 1861, in the Hans Christian Andersen Hus, Odense, reproduced in Henrik C. Poulsen, *Det Rette Udseende. Fotografernes H.C. Andersen*, Copenhagen 1996, p. 62.
380.   At this moment..." Edvard Collin to HCA, 9 May 1861, *E. Collin*, vol. III, p. 15.
         "I asked him ..." diary, 5 May 1861, *Diaries*, p. 273.
         "I explained how ill ..." diary, 9 May 1861, ibid. p. 275.
         Jonas went around ..." diary, 18 and 19 May 1861, ibid. pp. 282–3.
         "he worked on his own development..." diary, 14 May 1861, ibid. pp. 279–80.
382.   "He was a young man ..." diary, 8 May 1861, ibid. p. 274.
         "I'm not at all pleased ..." diary, 18 October 1863, ibid. p. 299.
383.   "The small people ..." Henry James, *William Wentmore Story and his Friends*, Edinburgh and London 1903, vol. I, pp. 285–6.
         "The North sent therefore ..." Elizabeth Barrett Browning, "The North and the South," in *Last Poems*, London 1861.
         "Andersen (the Dane) ..." Elizabeth Barrett Browning to Isa Blagden, 17 May 1861, *The Letters of Elizabeth Barrett Browning*, edited by F.G. Kenyon, London 1897, vol. II, p. 448.
384.   "was wrought..." *Fairy Tale*, p. 464.
386   "'The Ice Maiden' begins ..." quoted in ibid. p. 470.
387.   "he was surprised ..." diary, 20 August 1861, *Dagbøger*, vol. V, p. 112.
         "Toward evening ..." diary, 29 August 1861, *Diaries*, p. 284.
         "ate at a restaurant ..." diary, 2 September 1861, ibid. p. 285.
387.   "an active participant..." quoted in Niels Birger Wamberg, "A Born Achiever: Jonas Collin—Potentate and Philanthropist," in *The Golden Age of Denmark: Art and Culture 1800–1850*, edited by Bente Scavenius, Copenhagen 1994, p. 65.
         "the high and the lowly ... a half-opened door ..." quoted in ibid.
         "mighty Collin ... poor Andersen" Niels Birger Wamberg, A Born Achiever," in *The Golden Age of Denmark*, edited by Bente Scavenius, Copenhagen 1994, p. 60.

388. "Scharff bounded up ..." diary, 2 January 1862, *Dagbøger*, vol. v, p. 141.
"a visit from Scharff ..." diary, 7 January 1862, ibid. p. 142.
"dinner at Scharff's ..." diary, 16 January 1862, ibid. p. 143.
"a visit from Scharff ..." diary, 23 January 1862, ibid. p. 144.
"Scharff" diary, 12 February 1862, ibid. p. 147.
"Yesterday Scharff ..." diary, 13 February 1862, ibid.
"Theodor put me in a very bad mood ..." diary, 17 February 1862, ibid. p. 148.
389. "intimate and communicative ..." diary, 21 February 1862, ibid. p. 149.
"visit from Scharff ... exchanged ..." diary, 6 March 1862, ibid. p. 154.
"Scharff very loving..." diary, 12 March 1862, ibid. p. 155.
"I told all about my erotic time ..." diary, 5 March 1862, ibid. p. 154.
391. "Sent letter ..." diary, 15 September 1862, *Diaries*, p. 290.
"an insolent fool ..." diary, 15 October 1863, ibid. p. 298.
"to his two dearest friends ..." diary, 17 June 1863, *Dagbøger*, vol. v, p. 397
"Scharff's passion for me ..." diary, 27 August 1863, ibid. p. 413.
392. "I am not satisfied ..." diary, 16 September 1863, ibid. p. 418.
"Felt old ..." diary, 5 October 1863, ibid.
"visited Scharff, who gave me ..." diary, 6 October 1863, ibid.
"Scharff has not ..." diary, 13 November 1863, ibid. p. 426.
393. an accident which ..." Augusta Bournonville, *My Theatre Life*, translated by Patricia N. McAndrew, London 1979) p. 371.
"This tragedy..." ibid.
"The year is over..." diary, 31 December 1863, *Diaries*, p. 301.
"The bloody waves of war ..." *Fairy Tale*, p. 495.
394. "it was against my heart ... at present..." diary, 14 April 1864, *Diaries*, p. 307.
"Today I've been really..." diary, 16 April 1864, ibid. p. 308.
"Every day soldiers left..." *Fairy Tale*, p. 498.
"Mrs. Anholm's eldest son ..." diary, 5 January 1864, *Diaries*, p. 303.
395. "I lost for a moment ..." *Fairy Tale*, p. 501.
"I feel gloomy..." diary, 24 January 1864, *Diaries*, p. 305.
"overwhelmed and bitterly aware ..." diary, 29 January 1864, ibid. p. 306.
"Now I'm sitting at home ..." diary, 31 January 1864, ibid.
"the past year..." diary, 1 April 1864, ibid. p. 307.
"What a night ..." diary; 18 April 1864, ibid. p. 309.
"Godless ..." diary, 30 June 1864, *Dagbøger*, vol. vi, p. 81.
"I am disgruntled..." diary, 31 October 1864, ibid. p. 146.
"Last night I again dreamed..." diary, 31 October 1864, *Diaries*, p. 310.
396. "the darkest, gloomiest ..." *Fairy Tale*, p. 503.
"For more than a year ..." ibid. p. 504.
397. "Especially cheerful ..." diary, 4 February 1865, *Diaries*, p. 312.

JØRGEN DINES JOHANSEN

Counteracting the Fall
"Sneedronningen" and "Iisjomfruen":
The Problem of Adult Sexuality in Fairytale and Story

In Andersen's works, a barrier exists that more often than not prevents the protagonists from experiencing adult sexual fulfillment. Indeed, even if this barrier is overcome by the denouement on the level of plot, somehow the reader doubts the authenticity of the putative sexual happiness because the resistance to growing up and enjoying the physical side of adult life seem to be entrenched in the texts. This is well known and serves only as my point of departure. What I want to look at here are the techniques of avoidance in two texts in which the barrier that prevents mature sexuality is openly explored: "Sneedronningen" ["The Snow Queen"] and "Iisjomfruen" ["The Ice Maiden"].

"Sneedronningen" begins with a cosmic prologue staging the opposition between God and the Devil and the latter's ability to harm the original goodness of man with the splinters of the enchanted mirror. The setting then shifts to a small idyllic ambience created by poor bourgeois parents in order to preserve benign nature within an urban milieu. Here the two children, Gerda and Kai, grow up in a humble earthly paradise. The advent of male puberty and the splinters of the mirror mean a fall/Fall and a break up of both the happy and innocent relationship between male and female children and the trust and love between the grandmother and the boy. Instead, little Kai is spellbound by the Snow Queen, a beautiful, mature woman incapable of caring and loving. Little Kai is, thus, not only kissed half

From *Scandinavian Studies*, vol. 74, no. 2 (Summer 2002). © 2002 by the Society for the Advancement of Scandinavian Study.

to death by the Snow Queen, but her kisses also erase his memory of childhood, making it easy to hold him prisoner in the ice castle at the North Pole in Lapland. In Kai's case, the transformation is swift and irreparable as far as he is concerned since he cannot himself escape his confinement in eternal winter.

The story of Gerda's quest and rescue of Kai, on the other hand, is divided into a series of adventures. Her quest begins with the sacrifice of her red shoes, which Kai never saw, to the river, a sacrifice that in Andersen's system of images means giving up selfishness, vanity, and sexual desire. The next stop in Gerda's quest is at the old woman's house. Here the old woman tries all manner of ploys to make Gerda forget her mission, such as combing her hair with the comb of oblivion and by making the roses—the symbols of true love—disappear. She wants to hold Gerda prisoner as a child in eternal summer (all the flowers are blossoming simultaneously). However, the tears of pity that Gerda sheds make this attempt vain. Interestingly, the stories that the flowers tell her at the old woman's house are all but one—the buttercup's story about love between grandmother and grandchild—about the transitory nature of happiness, the wrong way of loving, or the damning effects of erotic desire and longing. Three of these embedded stories are, notably, blatantly erotic: the tiger lily's about a sexual desire that burns hotter than the consuming fire of a funeral pyre. But Gerda answers the lily: "Det forstaaer jeg slet ikke!" (2:58) ["I don't understand that at all" (61)]. The hyacinth's story describes the fragrance that grows even stronger; and the account of the three sisters who vanish and die in the forest is laden with erotic overtones as well. In the last story, the protagonist, the narcissus-ballerina, is described as follows: "see hvor hun kneiser paa een Stilk! jeg kan se mig selv! jeg kan se mig slev!" (2:61) ["See how she stretches out her legs, as if she were showing off on a stem. I can see myself, I can see myself' (62)]. It does not take much effort to infer what is also implied in this self-mirroring.

At this point, then, Kai is imprisoned within the eternal winter of male pride and pubescent sexuality whereas Gerda barely escapes the imprisonment in eternal female childhood, a childhood, however, beset with erotic fantasies: to wit the curious passage: "da fik hun en deilig Seng med røde Silkedyner, de vare stoppede med blaae Violer, og hun sov og drømte der saa deiligt, som nogen Dronning paa sin Bryllupsdag" (2:57) ["then she slept in an elegant bed with red silk pillows, embroidered with colored violets; and then she dreamed as pleasantly as a queen on her wedding day" (60).]

Her pure love for Kai, however, leads to escape from the entrapment of unfulfilled, pubescent longings. Her next stop at the prince and princess's castle shows two kinds of relationships that should be avoided: the stale idyll of the crows and the puerile, unconsummated relationship between prince and princess.

Her imprisonment in the robbers' castle in the woods addresses the unresolvable link between sexuality and destruction. On the one hand, there is the murder of coachman and footmen, the threat that Gerda herself is going to slaughtered and eaten, and the robber girl's sadistic treatment of animals. On the other, there is the unsavory sexuality of the robber witch and the robber girl's threats and sexual advances toward Gerda. Like the prince and princess, however, the robber girl takes pity on Gerda and facilitates her pursuit. She keeps Gerda's muff, though, as token of Gerda's continuing sacrifice.

Whereas the robber witch may be seen as a representation of the bad mother, Gerda next enters the realm of the good mothers (the Finnish woman and the Lapp woman) whose dwellings are reminiscent of wombs. By her faith, fidelity, and non-sexual love, Gerda defeats the demonic powers with the help of the angels. Gerda's tears make Kai remember, as her tears earlier made love blossom, and her love frees him of his imprisonment in intellectual pride and longing for the Snow Queen. Indeed, the pieces of ice dance and spell out the word "Eternity," which the answer to the riddle of life.

In the present context, Gerda's and Kai's journey back to their point of departure, however is of greatest interest. First they meet or hear about some of the significant characters whom Gerda had met on her way out. Notably, both the little robber girl as well as the prince and princess have left their homes, i.e. have severed childhood ties. Second, their journey begins during the winter and continues through the spring; at the moment they enter the grandmother's drawing room though, the wholesome summer sun is shining. During the course of these events, they have matured into responsible adults but, nevertheless, sit on and fit into their little stools. They have grown up but remained children at heart.

As is well-known, an important structural homology links the fairy tale and the *Bildungsroman*: both have three sequences, often dubbed home, abroad, and at home. The name of the last phase may be a slightly misleading because the protagonists most often do not return to the home of their parents, but rather establish their own home with a spouse. "Sneedronningen" is a significant departure from this pattern in the literal return to the parental home. Read in conjunction with Andersen's claim that Kai and Gerda are simultaneously children and adults, it indicates that the concept of time is central to this fairy tale.

Before discussing this point, however, let us turn to "Iisjomfruen," in the plot of which realism and fantasy are intertwined. A traditional realistic story, it presents a young man's maturation and efforts to qualify himself as a provider for his family, his falling in love, his overcoming of the resistance of the young woman's father, and the young couple's happiness after quarrels and misunderstandings. The end of Andersen's story is less traditional in that the protagonist drowns the day before his wedding. He, however, had become an excellent hunter and guide with the help of a talking cat that taught him to climb without becoming dizzy and afraid of heights. Hence, his upbringing had included the supernatural.

Simultaneously, the tale is about the malignant and beneficent forces of nature represented by the Ice Maiden and the daughters of the sun. The story presents a cosmic dualism juxtaposing destructive and restorative powers wherein death—in the story the Ice Maiden—takes the body but the human soul is saved by the heavenly powers. However, already as an infant Rudy had been consecrated to the Ice Maiden because she kissed him when as mere baby he barely escaped the death on the glacier that killed his mother. Throughout the story, she longs for her son, but recovers him only when his sexuality awakens. Thus Andersen here as in "Sneedronningen" merges the cosmic struggle and human sexuality. Nevertheless, there are important differences between the fairy tale and the story: Kai and Rudy are different ages. Whereas Kai has just reached puberty, Rudy is an adult. Kai's imprisonment in the Snow Queen's castle occurs when he as a boy is just on the verge of becoming a young adult and adoring a highly ambiguous female whom he perceives as half mother and half beloved. Rudy, however, had already experienced sexual feelings before he met Babette, and he knows that sexuality is something that has a disturbing autonomy and that it is not inextricably bound to the beloved. Babette, moreover, is not like Gerda, she is not giving up sexuality: on the contrary, she is flirtatious, she enjoys the advances of her rich cousin, and she delights in Rudy's jealousy. Whereas Kai falls and is immediately immobilized by the destructive forces and Gerda's quest means the overcoming of various hazards by virtue of her almost angelic nature Rudy and Babette's road to union and final separation is filled with temptations that they must resist, which begin, though, before they meet. Although Rudy is in love with Babette, he kisses Annette (even the names indicate that the great leveler—lust—to a certain extent makes them interchangeable). In addition to this initial mistake, Rudy is further tempted by the Ice Maiden's maids. It is difficult not to read the second scene in which he thinks he is with the schoolmaster's Annette—whom he, by "mistake" kissed earlier—as a fall where he succumbs to the spell of the maid and to his own desire.

*Derstrømmede Livsens Glæde ind i hans Blod, den hele Verden var
hans, syntes han, hvorfor plage sig! Alt er til for at nyde og lyksaliggjøre
os! Livsens Strøm er Gladens Strøm, rives med af den, lade sig bare af
den, det er Lyksalighed. Han saae paa den unge Pige, det var Annette
og dog ikke Annette, endnu mindre Troldphantomet, som han havde
kaldt hende, han modte ved Grindelwald; Pigen her paa Bjerget var
frisk som den nysfaldne Snee, svulmende som Alperosen og let som et
Kid; dog altid skabt af Adams Ribbeen, Menneske som Rudy. Og han
slyngede sine Arme om hende, saae ind i hendes forunderlige klare
Øine, kun et Secund var det og i dette, ja forklar, fortæl, giv os det i
Ord—var det Aandens eller Dødens Liv der fyldte ham, blev han loftet
eller sank han ned i det dybe, dræbende Iissvæg, dybere, altid dybere,
han saae Iisvæggene som et blaargrønt Glas; uendelige Kløfter gabede
rundt om, og Vandet dryppede klingende som et Klokkespil og dertil saa
perleklart, lysende i blaahvide Flammer, Iisjomfruen gav ham et Kys,
der iisnede ham igjennem hans Ryghvirvler ind i hans Pande, han gav
et Smertens Skrig, rev sig los, tumlede og faldt, det blev Natfor hans
Øine, men han aabnede dem igjen. Onde Magter havde ovet deres Spil.*
(4:154–5)

(A living joy streamed through every vein.
"The whole world is mine, why therefore should I grieve?"
thought he. "Everything is created for our enjoyment and
happiness. The stream of life is a stream of happiness; let us flow
on with it to joy and felicity."

Rudy gazed on the young maiden; it was Annette, and yet it
was not Annette; still less did he suppose it was the spectral
phantom, whom he had met near Grindelwald. The maiden up
here on the mountain was fresh as the new fallen snow, blooming
as an Alpine rose, and as nimble-footed as a young kid. Still, she
was one of Adam's race, like Rudy. He flung his arms round the
beautiful being, and gazed into her wonderfully clear eyes,—only
for a moment; but in that moment words cannot express the
effect of his gaze. Was it the spirit of life or of death that
overpowered him? Was he rising higher, or sinking lower and
lower into the deep, deadly abyss? He knew not; but the walls of
ice shone like blue-green glass; innumerable clefts yawned
around him, and the water-drops tinkled like the chiming of
church bells, and shone clearly as pearls in the light of a pale-blue
flame. The Ice Maiden, for she it was, kissed him, and her kiss

sent a chill as of ice through his whole frame. A cry of agony
escaped from him; he struggled to get free, and tottered from her.
For a moment all was dark before his eyes, but when he opened
them again it was light, and the Alpine maiden had vanished. The
powers of evil had played their game. [407–8])

This situation, so similar to and yet so different from the passage in which
Kai is kissed by the Snow Queen, describes Rudy's temptation and fall. The
narrator—and Andersen I presume—are giving two reasons for this fall.
First, it is, according to the norms of the story, a grave sin to presume that
"alt er til for at nyde og lyksaliggjøre os!" ["everything is created for our
enjoyment and happiness"]. Second, the woman is first and foremost defined
by her sex and her sexual nature. He is uncertain of her identity: she may be
the woman he once kissed "by mistake," but she is definitely not Babette.

Likewise, her cousin's advances first tempt Babette although she resists
them. Two days before her wedding, though, she has the ghastly dream of
her own future adultery and of losing Rudy. In the dream, she even prays to
God that she will die on her wedding day. However, it is not she who dies,
but Rudy. In the attempt to seize the boat, Rudy dives into the lake—the
element of the Ice Maiden—where she finally kills him.

A twofold explanation of Rudy's death and the final separation of the
young couple suggests itself. First, Rudy's death is fated because he somehow
already belongs to the Ice Maiden, i.e. he is swayed by a sexuality that is
linked not only to mortality, but also to active destruction. Second, however,
death and the resulting sexual abstinence are explicitly conceived as a gift
sent from God. There are two reasons for this interpretation: first, death is a
blessing because it prevents future sins. Second, the narrator deems it a
blessing to die at the verge of fulfillment, i.e. in the enjoyment of expectation
in the moment when lasting happiness seems assured. Their virginal love not
yet consummated is untouched by experience. Sudden death in the bloom of
youth is, thus, constructed as a blessing because of its disruption of human
erotic happiness: it both prevents future sinning, and the ensuing sorrow
purifies Babette and leads to a quiet life in God instead of a life spent in the
tribulations of desire.

In addition to ideological trends of the Danish Golden Age that might
support this line of thinking, Andersen's configuration of the plot emerges
from personal psychological considerations that precluded his portraying an
authentic union between men and woman in erotic happiness. However, this
is not the subject of this article. Here attention must remain focused on the
literary reasons why Kai and Gerda both survive while Rudy and Babette are

separated by his death. In order to attempt an answer, let us return to the time–space relations of the two texts and to their understanding of causality.

The question of genre—whether there is a difference between *eventyr* (fairytale) and *historie* (story)—is complicated. In one of his own observations from 1874 regarding the tales, Andersen comments on the change in their title that took place in 1852. Prior to that year, the titles of the collections of tales had been either *Eventyr fortalt for Børn* (Fairy Tales told for Children) or *Nye Eventyr* (New Fairy Tales), as in the case of the 1849 deluxe edition with 125 illustrations of his collected fairy tales published by C.A. Reitzel. Concerning this edition, Andersen goes on to say:

> *Med dette Pragtbind var Eventyr-Samlingen afsluttet, men ikke min Virksomhed i denne Digtart; et nyt betegnende Navn maatte derfor tages til den nye Samling, og den kaldtes "Historier"—det Navn, jeg i vort Sprog anseer at være det bedst valgte for mine Eventyr i al deres Udetrækning og Natur. Folkesproget stiller den simple Fortælling og den meest dristige Phantasie-Skildring ind under denne Benævnelse; Ammestuehistorien, Fabelen og Fortællingen, betegnes af Barnet, Bonden og Almuen, ved det forte Navn "Historier".* (SS 1880:15:302–3)

(This edition *de luxe* concluded the collection of fairy tales, but not my work within this kind of literature. Consequently, a new name had to be given to the new collection, and it was called Stories [*Historier*] in our language, the name that I find most fitting for the nature and size of my tales. Vernacular language reduces the simple story and the most daring representation of fantasy to this common denominator; the child, the peasant, and common people call the cock-and-bull story the fable, and the tale "stories.")

It is difficult to see the logic of Andersen's distinction other than perhaps the wish to separate works imitating the simple folk tale from other kinds of writing. Furthermore, Andersen himself was not very consistent in applying these labels. For instance, Flemming Hovmann's commentary to the critical edition of the tales, *H.C. Andersens Eventyr I–VII 1963–1990*, shows that Andersen referred to "Iisjomfruen" both as a story and as a fairy tale. The reception of the collection, *Nye Eventyr og Historier* (1862) was favorable, and one of the dailies, *Fædrelandet*, calls "Iisjomfruen" "a kind of fantastic novelle," but, like Andersen, the critics were not consistent in their use of generic labels. Nevertheless, at that time, it seems that few critics and colleagues perceived a difference between a psychological and in some respects "realistic" work such as "Iisjomfruen" (which in spite of Andersen's own vacillation should be called a story) and tales modeled on the folk tale. Andersen, however, frequently altered the genre framework within which he was working. In our context, his shifting perspective is illustrated by the subtitle of "Sneedronningen" which is "Et Eventyr i syv Historier" (2:49) [A fairy tale told in seven stories]. And, with regard to "Sneedronningen," the difficulty is not only a question of the added complexity occasioned by the sequence of stories, but also involves a radical change of theme. The folk tale has little concern for the salvation of the protagonists' souls, but is preoccupied with the obstructions to achieving maturity—including sexual maturity—with making illegitimate relations between the sexes legitimate, and with social advancement. These themes are found throughout Andersen's work but always with a twist and very often turned upside down as in "Sneedronningen" itself. Hence, this fairy tale is very far from the folk tale. What, though, is the difference between "Sneedronningen" and "Iisjomfruen," and is the difference responsible for the very different solution to the problem of development and maturation? My answer is that the decisive difference has to do with the different handling of time and space in the two texts.

In "Sneedronningen" geographic references are not totally absent; there are references to Finland, Italy, and Lapland. However, this part of the world is basically treated as a mythic location of the Snow Queen's castle. As for time, it is not represented as chronology, as calendar time. It is, rather, presented cyclically, i.e. the changing and returning of the seasons and with summer and winter absolutely dominant. These two contrary seasons are strongly thematized in the fairy tale: summer is linked not only to the regenerative forces of nature, but also to innocence, faith, piety, and the love and redeeming power of Jesus and God. Winter is linked with sexuality, intellectual pride, and calculation and with destruction, the demonic powers, and damnation.

Cyclical time is, of course, a basic way of conceiving of the changes and recurrences of outward nature. Furthermore, fundamental differences between the cyclical time of outward nature and the linear time of human existence arise. Whereas nature's cyclical time is conceived as repetition, human time is seen as transitory with every moment unique and unrepeatable. The consequence of this deplorable fact is that the past cannot be changed; the most we can do is to edit its narration.

In "Sneedronningen," however, the time of outward nature is molded to serve the protagonists, while human time is made flexible to the extent that not only prior states of mind but even prior relationships can be restored. The basic paradox of he fairy tale is, of course, contained in the last paragraphs. As Kai and Gerda walk homewards it is spring; as they arrive in grandmother's drawing room, they realize that they have grown up. Nevertheless, they sit down hand in hand on the small chairs remaining from their childhood. In the warmth of summer, the grandmother reads the passage from Matthew 18:3, "except ye be converted, and become as little children, ye shall not enter into the kingdom of heaven." In "Sneedronningen" Andersen offers a literalist reading and exemplification of this passage. Hence, the formative influence of physical growth on the mind is both recognized and denied. Kai's physical and intellectual growth and the advent of puberty occasion the end of the infantile paradise. The point of Gerda's entire quest, however, has been to rescue Kai by lifting the spell of the Snow Queen and, thus, to restore him to what he was before his abduction. The flexibility of the time–space coordinates of the fairy tale universe and the necessary suspension of causal relationships render the retroaction and the consequent the literalist exemplification of the sacred text, i.e. Matthew, possible.

In "Iisjomfruen" things are different. Despite the fourfold presence of the supernatural (as fairy tale lore, as folklore, as reminiscences of gothic tales, and as a more or less Christian allegory of opposed cosmic forces), this story has less narrative latitude to determine the level upon which the denouement will take place. The reason is its precision with regard to the space–time coordinates. It takes place in various Swiss cantons in the years before and after 1856. And according to the narrator, what is narrated ends up in the guidebooks. In fact, his reading the Baedecker for Switzerland inspired the part of the story about the drowning of the groom. He made one significant change though: in the Baedecker, the couple had just been married whereas Rudy and Babette are going to be married the next day.

Its precise setting in the immediate past of a part of a Europe known to very many people, its reference to a past event, and the realistic psychology of the protagonists make a denouement like that of "Sneedronningen" impossible. It would be too implausible and offend against the logic of both characters and plot. Even though there are both supernatural helpers and a powerful supernatural enemy, undoing the protagonists' realistically conceived psychosexual development would be impossible because it has been the engine of the story. In "Sneedronningen," Kai suddenly falls and Gerda immediately sacrifices her own development into a maiden to save him. In "Iisjomfruen," both Rudy and Babette grow, and they experience

repeatedly the tribulations and temptations of desire. Furthermore, in the
central passage describing Rudy's temptation and fall, he has a vision, i.e. he
is endowed with an inner life, whereas this is not the case in
"Sneedronningen." Hence, despite the fantastic elements, "Iisjomfruen" is a
story (*historie*) not a fairy tale.

Differences of genre, then, seem to determine the different endings of the
two texts. In some important respects, however, they still tell the same story: the
story of the impossibility of erotic love between adults, and the story about how
God's ways may be mysterious to man but nevertheless lead to salvation and
true happiness. The narrator of "Iisjomfruen" even becomes a little insistent,
quarrelsome, and didactic at the end. He first challenges the reader with the
question, "Kalder Du det en sørgelig Historie?" (4:161) ["Do you think this a
sad story?" (412)]. And he ends with "'Gud lader det Bedste skee for os!' men
det bliver os ikke altid aabenbaret, saaledes som det blev for *Babette* i hendes
Drøm" (4:162) ["'God permits nothing to happen, which is not the best for us.'
But this is not often revealed to all, as it is revealed to Babette in her wonderful
dream" (413)]. In "Sneedronningen," we witness a miracle, the co-presence of
child-like innocence and adulthood; in "Iisjomfruen," it is claimed and
somehow demonstrated that the wages of sin is death, but we are told that such
punishment is for our own good. In "Iisjomfruen" too, however, time is in a
sense manipulated because even if the stern necessity of linear time and
individual death is not denied, it is made unimportant, almost negligible. At the
moment of Rudy's death, the narrator concludes:

> "*Min er Du!*" *klang det i det Dybe;* "*min er Du!*" *klang det i det Høie,
> fra det Uendelige.*
>   *Deiligt at flyve fra Kjærlighed til Kjærlighed, fra Jorden ind i
> Himlen.*
>   *Der brast en Stræng, der klang en Sørgetone, Dodens Iiskys beseirede
> det Forkrænkelige; Forpillet endte for at Livs-Dramaet kunde begynde,
> Misklangen opløses i Harmonie.* (4:161)

("Thou art mine," sounded from the depths below; but from the
heights above, from the eternal world, also sounded the words,
"Thou art mine!" Happy was he thus to pass from life to life,
from earth to heaven. A chord was loosened, and tones of sorrow
burst forth. The icy kiss of death had overcome the perishable
body; it was but the prelude before life's real drama could begin,
the discord which was quickly lost in harmony. [412])

There, in accordance with a central tenet of Christianity, the moment of death becomes a cosmic struggle for man's soul and in Andersen, the soul's homecoming. In his review of Andersen's collection of fairy tales and stories from 1858, the Danish author Meïr Goldschmidt wrote that Andersen revealed a bent to move from a piety of nature to ecclesiastic piety, and says: "Dette Sidste kan være snare godt og gavnligt, men næppe i Længden for Eventyrpoesien. Thi det specifikt Religiøse vil være Eneherre" (*Eventyr* 6:174) [This (i.e. ecclesiastic piety)—may be very good and beneficial, but just barely in the long run for fairy tales because the specifically religious wants to be autocratic].

Even if the end of "Sneedronningen" is in a sense flawed as well, it abides by the logic of the tale and the unity of its universe. The universe of "Iisjomfruen," however, does not possess any unity. It is fundamentally split, and its parts seem to contradict each other. Andersen, thus, does not trust the force of his own story and he directly intervenes to set things straight. Accordingly, I think Goldschmidt is right. Andersen stops narrating and starts preaching, and the sermon he gives is outrageous because one might accuse him of curing the illness by killing the patient. This response is not just the reaction of a twenty-first century reader. Even Ingemann complained that Andersen had the heart kill off Rudy to prevent their union. However, the important question is not one of sympathizing with the detractors of the story or with the young couple; it is also a question of Andersen's inability to find a narrative form congenial to his message. And I should add that I find the denouement of the latter impossible anyway.

WORKS CITED

Andersen, Hans Christian. *H.C. Andersens samlede skrifter.* 15 vols. Copenhagen: C.A. Reitzel, 1876–80.
———. *H.C. Andersens Eventyr.* 7 vols. Copenhagen: Reitzels Forlag, 1963–90.
———. *The Complete Hans Christian Andersen Fairy Tales.* Ed. Lily Owens. New York: Gramercy Books, 1984.

Chronology

1805   Hans Christian Andersen was born in a small cottage in the poorest part of Odense, Denmark, on April 2, to Hans Andersen, a twenty-two year old shoemaker, and Anne Marie Andersdatter, a very kind and hardworking peasant woman approximately eight or so years his senior; due to the high rate of infant mortality during this time, Andersen is christened on that very same day.

1807   In May, the family moves to their first settled home, a small one-room house close to a baker's shop on 3, Munkemøllestræde (Monk's Mill Street); Andersen lives here for the next twelve years with his family who, although poor, are better off than some because they only have one child.

1811   Andersen witnesses the great comet from St. Knud's churchyard, which he later describes as a "frightful and mighty fireball," and which his neighbors interpret as a sign of impending doom.

1816   In April, his father becomes delirious and his mother sends Andersen to Mette Mogensdatter, a "wise woman." Among other things, she places a twig from "the same kind of tree upon which the Savior was crucified," on his chest; he returns home terrified from the experience, but says he has seen nothing; his father dies two days later at the age of thirty-three and is buried in a pauper's grave at St. Knud's Church. His mother is now very poor, working at a variety of jobs; for his part, Andersen begins to cultivate the cultured middle class of Odense, starting with Mrs. Bukenflod, a clergyman's widow; he also begins to read Shakespeare and poetry, and writes plays which he can act out in his puppet theatre.

1818   In June, a troupe from the Royal Copenhagen Theatre arrives in Odense; Andersen is allowed to visit backstage; he is given a walk-on part in the operetta *Cendrillon* and longs to join the group in Copenhagen; in July his mother marries a much younger shoemaker and Andersen becomes further resolved to leave Odense.

1819   In April, just after his confirmation, Andersen's mother and step-father move into a house with a small garden, a picturesque and idyllic place where he can lose himself in singing and daydreaming; he establishes a persona of the naïve talented country boy which he correctly intuits will be an asset in gaining access to a more cultured class; Andersen's talents make him an attraction in Odense; on September 4, he leaves for Copenhagen.

1819–22   On September 6, a very young and naïve Andersen arrives in Frederiksberg; Andersen meets Henrik Hertz, a young Jewish writer, who will eventually become his friend; during the next three years, under extremely difficult financial conditions, Andersen struggles to gain a foothold at The Royal Theatre, as a singer, dancer or actor; at various intervals, he manages to get the support of The Royal Theatre and connects with various members of the Danish aristocracy.

1822   Andersen's makes his debut as a writer, turning in a few plays to The Royal Theatre;   very few copies of *Youthful Attempts* are actually sold, with the remainder used for wrapping paper; the wealthy and philanthropic Jonas Collin, theatre manager and financial deputy at the Royal Theatre, becomes Andersen's guardian, affording him the opportunity to attend the grammar school at Slagelse.

1822–27   Attends school in Slagelse and Elsinore.

1826   When the Slagelse principal, Simon Meisling, is moved to

	Elsinore Grammar School, Andersen follows him, although their relationship is a problematic on; he writes his famous poem, "The Dying Child."
1827	Having complained to Collins about Simon Meisling's mistreatment, Collins removes Andersen. from the school and pays for private tutoring; a number of poems are published in the leading literary journal of the day and "The Dying Child" appears in both Danish and German versions.
1828	Andersen passes the entrance exam at the University of Copenhagen and matriculates there; He takes the examination which entitles him to begin his studies (philologicum) and passes this examination the following year.
1829	Andersen makes his official and successful debut with his first prose work, *A Walking Tour from Holmen's Canal to the Eastern Point of Amager in the Years 1828 and 1829*; and debut as a playwright with *Love in Saint Nicholas Church Tower*.
1830	Publishes *Poems*.
1831	Publishes first important collection of poems; *Fantasies and Sketches*; first journey abroad to Germany where he encounters Ludwig Tieck in Dresden and Adalbert von Chamisso in Berlin; Andersen publishes *Shadow Pictures from a Journey to the Harz Mountains and Saxon Switzerland, etc, etc., in the Summer of 1831*, his first travelogue.
1832	Andersen writes his first autobiography which will remain unpublished and unknown until 1926.
1833	Publishes *Collected Poems*.
1833–34	Using a scholarship to travel, Andersen embarks on a journey to France and Italy via Germany. He meets Heinrich Heine and Victor Hugo in Paris, and Bertel Thorvaldsen, who will become a close friend, in Rome.
1835	*The Improvisatore*, Andersen's first novel and *Fairy Tales, Told for Children*, Andersen's first collection of tales, are published.
1836	Publishes *O.T.*, possibly a reference to Odense Tugthus, the town goal.

1837   *Kun en Spillemand* (*Only a Fiddler*) is published; the novels
            are soon translated into German and, eventually, into
            Swedish, Dutch, English and other languages; Andersen
            makes his first trip to Sweden and meets the author
            Frederika Bremer; the French *home de letters*, Xavier
            Marmier, writes a biographical article on Andersen., "Vie
            d'un poète," and includes a French translation of "The
            Dying Child"; the article is published in *Revue de Paris* and
            has a decisive influence on Andersen becoming a known
            literary figure in Europe.

1838   Søren Kierkegaard attacks Andersen in his review of *Kun en
            Spillemand*. Andersen finally achieves financial stability as
            he is granted the standard royal literary scholarship.

1839   *Picture Book without Pictures* is published.

1840   *The Moorish Maid* and *The Mulatto* are published.
            Andersen's play, *The Mulatto*, is a success at The Royal
            Theatre, and it is also staged in Stockholm and Odense.

1840–41   Andersen travels to Italy, Greece, and Constantinople,
            returning via the Balkans, Vienna, Dresden, and Leipzig,
            where he meets Franz Liszt and Felix Mendelssohn-
            Bartholdy.

1842   *A Poet's Bazaar*, a travel account, is published, which
            includes the famous chapters on the railway and a concert
            with Franz Liszt.

1843   Andersen begins a new series of fairy tale booklets; Meets
            Clara Schumann, a pianist, in Copenhagen; Months later
            Schumann dedicates a musical setting of his poem to
            Andersen; journeys to France and Germany; falls in love
            with the Swedish singer, Jenny Lind; unsure of her own
            talent, Jenny, like Andersen, is temperamental, very
            sensitive and needs to be handled with great delicacy.

1843–48   Andersen publishes five collections of tales.

1844   He journeys to Germany and meets the hereditary Grand
            Duke Carl Alexander of Saxony-Weimar-Eisenach, with
            whom he will become a close friend; receives an invitation
            to visit King Christian VIII on the North Frisian island of
            Föhr.

1845–46	H.C. travels to Germany, Austria, and Italy; his novels begin to appear in English translation.
1846	On January 6, Andersen receives the Knighthood of the Red Eagle from King Friedrich Wilhelm IV of Prussia.
1847	*The True Story of My Life* is published.; Andersen travels to England and Scotland and meets Charles Dickens.
1848	*The Two Baronesses* is published and his first fairy tales are published in French.
1849	Andersen travels to Sweden; Invitation from King Oscar I.
1851–52	Andersen journeys to Germany, Italy, and Switzerland; his travel account, *I Sverrig* (*In Sweden*), containing his poetical manifesto (a blend of poetry, religion and science) is published; Hans Christian is made a titular professor.
1852–53	Two collections of stories.
1853	The Danish edition of *Samlede Skrifter* (*Collected Works*) begins to appear.
1854	Andersen travels to Germany and Italy.
1855	Andersen travels to Germany and Switzerland; meets Richard Wagner in Zurich; *The Fairy Tale of My Life* is published.
1856	Andersen travels to Germany.
1857	Andersen travels to England as the guest of Charles Dickens; *To Be, or Not To Be?* is published.
1858–72	Publishes eleven collections of tales and stories; Andersen reads aloud from his fairy tales for the first time at the newly-established middle-class Workers' Association.
1859	He receives the Maximilian Order of Art and Science from King Maximilian II of Bavaria.
1861	Andersen travels to Italy; he meets with Bjørnstjerne Bjørnson and Robert and Elizabeth Barrett Browning in Rome.
1862–63	Andersen travels to Switzerland, Spain, Morocco, and France.
1863	Travel account *I Spanien* (*In Spain*) is published.
1865	Meets Edvard Grieg; travels to Sweden; receives an Invitation from King Karl XV.

1866	Andersen travels to Portugal via Amsterdam and Paris; his account of this journey, *Et Besøg i Portugal* (*A Visit to Portugal*), is published in 1868.
1867	Andersen makes two visits to the World Exhibition in Paris; he is made honorary citizen of Odense on December 6.
1868	He meets Johannes Brahms in Copenhagen.
1869–70	Andersen travels to Vienna and the Riviera.
1870	*Lucky Peer*, H.C.'s last novel, is published; he meets Henrik Ibsen.
1873	H.C. travels to Switzerland. It is his last journey abroad.
1875	After several years of serious illness, Andersen dies on August 4 at Rolighed, the country seat of the Jewish merchant family Melchior. The Melchior family have taken care of Andersen during his final years; his funeral is held at the Cathedral of Copenhagen on August 11.

Contributors

HAROLD BLOOM is Sterling Professor of the Humanities at Yale University. He is the author of over 20 books, including *Shelley's Mythmaking* (1959), *The Visionary Company* (1961), *Blake's Apocalypse* (1963), *Yeats* (1970), *A Map of Misreading* (1975), *Kabbalah and Criticism* (1975), *Agon: Toward a Theory of Revisionism* (1982), *The American Religion* (1992), *The Western Canon* (1994), and *Omens of Millennium: The Gnosis of Angels, Dreams, and Resurrection* (1996). *The Anxiety of Influence* (1973) sets forth Professor Bloom's provocative theory of the literary relationships between the great writers and their predecessors. His most recent books include *Shakespeare: The Invention of the Human* (1998), a 1998 National Book Award finalist, *How to Read and Why* (2000), *Genius: A Mosaic of One Hundred Exemplary Creative Minds* (2002), and *Hamlet: Poem Unlimited* (2003). In 1999, Professor Bloom received the prestigious American Academy of Arts and Letters Gold Medal for Criticism, and in 2002 he received the Catalonia International Prize.

ELIAS BREDSDORFF (1912–2002) was a Lecturer in Danish at the University of Cambridge, where he became a Fellow of Peterhouse from 1963 until his retirement in 1979. He is the author of "Intentional and Non-Intentional Topicalities in Andersen's Tales" (1999); *Hans Christian Andersen: The Story of his Life and Work 1805–75* (1975); and Hans Andersen and Charles Dickens: A Friendship and its Dissolution (1956).

WOLFGANG LEDERER was a retired professor at the California College of Arts and Crafts and in 1980 became Director Emeritus of the school's division of design. He was also considered a master of book design, working on numerous volumes for University of California Press, and winner of The Book Club of California Oscar Lewis Award. He is the author of *The Fear of Women* (1968) and *African Figures* (2000).

CELIA CATLETT ANDERSON is Emeritus Professor of English at Eastern Connecticut State University. She is an editor of *Nonsense Literature for Children: Aesop to Seuss* (1997).

JON CECH has been Professor of English at the University of Florida and a Review Editor of *Children's Literature*. He is the author of *Charles Olson and Edward Dahlberg: A Portrait of a Friendship* (1982) and editor of *American Writers for Children, 1900–1960* (1983).

KAREN SANDERS is the author of "Ethics and Journalism" (2003); "Staging the Invisible: From the Scene of Theatre to the Scene of Writing" (1993) and "Signatures: Spelling the Father's and Erasing the Mother's in C.J.L. Almqvist's Ramido Marinesco and H.C. Andersen's O.T." (1993).

HANS CHRISTIAN ANDERSEN has taught at the Newcastle Business School at Northumbria University.

ALISON PRINCE is a freelance writer and illustrator of children's books, adult novels, biography, and poetry. She is the author of *Kenneth Grahame: An Innocent in the Wild Wood* (1994) and *The Witching Tree* (1996).

NIELS VILHELM KOFOED is Chairman of the B.S. Ingemann Society and was the Chair of the Department of Scandinavian Languages and Literature at the University of Washington. He is the author of "The Arabesque and the Grotesque: Hans Christian Andersen Decomposing the World of Poetry" (1999) and *H.C. Andersen: den Store europæer* (1996).

AAGE JØRGENSEN has taught at the University of Aarhus and has been a Senior Lecturer at the Langkær Gymnasium. He is the author of *Idyll and Abyss: Essays on Danish Literature and Theater* (1992) and editor of *Isak Dinesen, Storyteller* (1972).

JACKIE WULLSCHLAGER is a literary critic, author, and European arts correspondent for *The Financial Times*. She is the author of *Inventing*

Wonderland: The Lives and Fantasies of Lewis Carroll, Edward Lear, J. M. Barrie, Kenneth Grahame, and A.A. Milne (1995).

JØRGEN DINES JOHANSEN has been Professor of General and Comparative Literature at the University of Southern Denmark. He is the author of *Literary Discourse: A Semiotic-Pragmatic Approach To Literature* (2002) and *Dialogic Semiosis: An Essay on Signs and Meaning* (1993).

Bibliography

Andersen, Hans Christian. *The Diaries of Hans Christian Andersen*. Translated by Patricia L.Conroy and Sven H. Rossel, trans. Seattle: University of Washington Press, 1990.

———. *The Fairy Tale of My Life*. Translated by Horace Scudder. London and New York: Paddington Press, 1975.

———. *Hans Christian Andersen's Fairy Tales*. Reginald Spink, trans. Everyman's Library. London: Dent, 1992.

Böök, Frederik. *Hans Christian Andersen: A Biography*. Norman: University of Oklahoma Press, 1962.

Bredsdorff, Elias. *Hans Christian Andersen: The Story of His Life and Work, 1805–1875*. Phaidon Press, 1975; Charles Scribner's Sons, 1975.

———. *Hans Andersen and Charles Dickens: A Friendship and Its Dissolution*. Copenhagen: Rosenkilde and Bagger, 1956.

———. "Beginnings in Traditional Folk Tales and in H.C. Andersen's *Eventyr*." *Scandinavica* vol. 21, no. 1 (May 1982): 5–15.

Burnett, Constance. *The Shoemaker's Son: The Life of Hans Christian Andersen*. London: George G. Harrap, 1943.

Conroy, Patricia L. and Sven H. Rossel. *The Diaries of Hans Christian Andersen*. Seattle: University of Washington Press, 1990.

Dahl, Svend and H.G. Topsøe-Jensen, eds. *A Book on the Danish Writer Hans Christian Andersen: His Life and Work*. Copenhagen: Berlingske, 1955.

Dahlerup, Pil (coord.). "Splash! Six Views of 'The Little Mermaid.'"

Scandinavian Studies 62, no. 4 (Autumn 1990 Autumn): 403–429.

Dollerup, Cay. "Translation as a Creative Force in Literature: The Birth of the European Bourgeois Fairy-Tale." *The Modern Language Review* 90, no. 1 (January 1995): 94–102.

Godden, Rumer. *Hans Christian Andersen*. London: Hutchinson, 1955.

Gronbech, Bo. *Hans Christian Andersen*. Boston: Twayne Publishers, 1980.

Hugus, Frank. "Opera as Allegory in Hans Christian Andersen's *Improvisatoren* and *LykkePeer*. *Edda* 1(1999): 19–30.

Johansen, Jørgen Dines. "The Merciless Tragedy of Desire: An Interpretation of H.C. Andersen's 'Den lille Havfrue.'" *Scandinavian Studies* 68, no. 2 (Spring 1996): 203-41.

Jørgensen, Aage. "'... A Rag, but of Silk': Some Recent Danish Contributions to Andersen Research." *Norwich Papers* 3 (November 1995 Nov): 31–43.

Jørgensen, Aage. "Hidden Sexuality and Suppressed Passion: A Theme in Danish Golden Age Literature." *Neohelicon* 19, no. 1 (1992): 153–74.

Marker, Frederick J. *Hans Christian Andersen and the Romantic Theatre: A Study of Stage Practices in the Prenaturalistic Scandinavian Theatre.* Toronto: University of Toronto Press, 1971.

Meyer, Priscilla and Jeff Hoffman. "Infinite Reflections in Nabokov's Pale Fire: The Danish Connection, Hans Andersen and Isak Dinesen." *Russian, Croatian and Serbian, Czech and Slovak, Polish Literature* 41, no. 2 (February 15, 1997): 197–222.

Mylius, Johan de, Aage Jørgensen and Viggo Hjørnager Pedersen, editors. *Hans Christian Andersen: A Poet in Time.* Odense, Denmark: Odense University Press, 1999.

Rossel, Sven Hakon, ed. *Hans Christian Andersen: Danish Writer and Citizen of the World.* Amsterdam: Rodopi, 1996.

Sanders, Karin. "Signatures: Spelling the Father's and Erasing the Mother's in C.J.L. Almqvist's *Ramido Marinesco* and H.C. Andersen's *O.T. Scandinavian Studies* 65, no. 2 (Spring 1993): 153-79.

Soracco, Sabrina. "A Psychoanalytic Approach." *Scandinavian Studies* 62, no. 4 (Autumn 1990): 407–412.

Spink, Reginald. *Hans Christian Andersen and His World.* London: Thames and Hudson, 1972.

Stirling, Monica. *The Life and Times of Hans Christian Andersen.* New York: Harcourt, Brace & World, Inc., 1965.

Toksvig, Signe. *The Life of Hans Christian Andersen.* New York: Harcourt, Brace and Company, 1934; New York: Kraus Reprint Co., 1969.

Wangerin, Walter, Jr. "Hans Christian Andersen: Shaping the Child's Universe." From *Reality and the Vision.* Edited by Philip Yancey. Dallas: Word Publishing Group (1990): 1-15.

Ziolkowski, Jan M. "A Medieval 'Little Claus and Big Claus': A Fabliau from before Fabliaux?" From Karczewska, Kathryn and Tom Conley, editors. *The World and Its Rival: Essays on Literary Imagination in Honor of Per Nykrog,* Amsterdam: Rodopi, Amsterdam (1999): 1-37.

Acknowledgments

"Introduction" to *Hans Christian Andersen: Eighty Fairy Tales* by Elis Bredsdorff. From *Hans Christian Andersen: Eighty Fairy Tales* (1982): 5–9. New York: Pantheon Books. © 1982 by Elias Bredsdorff. Reprinted by permission.

"The Fairy Tale of Andersen's Life and Andersen's Literary Work" by Wolfgang Lederer. From *The Kiss of the Snow Queen: Hans Christian Andersen and Man's Redemption* (1986): 71–90. Berkeley and Los Angeles: University of California Press. © 1986 by The Regents of the University of California. Reprinted by permission.

"Andersen's Literary Work" by Wolfgang Lederer. From *The Kiss of the Snow Queen: Hans Christian Andersen and Man's Redemption* (1986): 91–96. Berkeley and Los Angeles: University of California Press. © 1986 by The Regents of the University of California. Reprinted by permission.

"Andersen's Heroes and Heroines: Relinquishing the Reward" by Celia Catlett Anderson. From *Triumphs of the Spirit in Children's Literature*. Edited by Francelia Butler and Richard Rotert. Hamden, Connecticut: Library Professional Publications (1986): 122–36. © 1986 by Francelia Butler. Reprinted by permission.

"Hans Christian Andersen's Fairy Tales and Stories: Secrets, Swans and Shadows" by Jon Cech. From *Touchstones: Reflections on the Best in*

Children's Literature, Volume Two: Fairy Tales, fables, Myths, Legends, and Poetry. West Lafayette, Indiana: Children's Literature Association (1985): 14–23. © 1985 by the Children's Literature Association. Reprinted by permission.

"Nemesis of Mimesis" by Karin Sanders. From *Scandinavian Studies*, vol. 64, no. 1 (Winter 1992): 1–25. © 1992 by the Society for the Advancement of Scandinavian Study. Reprinted by permission.

"Hans Christian Andersen—The Journey of His Life" by Hans Christian Andersen. From *Bulletin of the John Rylands University Library of Manchester*, vol. 76, no. 3 Autumn (1994): 127–43. © 1994 by the John Rylands University Library, The University of Manchester. Reprinted by permission.

"War" by Alison Prince. From *Hans Christian Andersen: The Fan Dancer*. London: Allison & Busby (1998): 261–82. © 1998 by Alison Prince. Reprinted by permission.

"Hans Christian Andersen and the European Literary Tradition" by Niels Vilhelm Kofoed. From *Hans Christian Amdersen: Danish Writer and Citizen of the World*. Amsterdam and Atlanta: Rodopi (1996): 209–56. © 1996 by Editions Rodopi B.V. Reprinted by permission.

"Heroes in Hans Christian Andersen's Writings" by Aage Jørgensen From *Hans Christian Anderson: A Poet in Time* (1999): 271–87. Odense: Odense University Press. © 1999 by Odense University Press and the authors. Reprinted by permission.

"Kiss of the Muse, 1860–1865" by Jackie Wullschlager. From *Hans Christian Andersen: The Life of a Storyteller* (2001): 373–98. New York: Alfred A. Knopf. © 2000 by Jackie Wullschlager. Reprinted by permission.

"Counteracting the Fall: "Sneedronningen" and "Iisjomfruen" The Problem of Adult Sexuality in Fairytale and Story" by Jørgen Dines Johansen. From *Scandinavian Studies*, vol. 74, no. 2 (Summer 2002): 137–48. © 2002 by the Society for the Advancement of Scandinavian Study. Reprinted by permission.

Index